Renewals

0115 ~~293388~~

01 159 293388

www.bromley.gov.uk/libraries

THE LONDON BOROUGH
www.bromley.gov.uk

Please return/renew this item
by the last date shown.
Books may also be renewed by
phone and Internet.

30128

D1330130

When Daddy Came Home

How war changed family life forever

Barry Turner and Tony Rennell

arrow books

Published by Arrow Books in 2014

1 3 5 7 9 10 8 6 4 2

Copyright © Barry Turner & Tony Rennell 1995

Barry Turner & Tony Rennell have asserted their right under the Copyright, Designs and Patents Act, 1988 to be identified as the authors of this work

Crown copyright material in the Public Record Office is reproduced by permission of the Controller of Her Majesty's Stationery Office

Extracts from *Daddy, We Hardly Knew You* by Germaine Greer (Hamish Hamilton, 1989) © Germaine Greer, 1989. Reproduced by permission of Hamish Hamilton Ltd.

First published in Great Britain in 1995 by
Hutchinson
Random House, 20 Vauxhall Bridge Road,
London SW1V 2SA

www.randomhouse.co.uk

Addresses for companies within The Random House Group Limited can be found at: www.randomhouse.co.uk/offices.htm

The Random House Group Limited Reg. No. 954009

ISBN 9780099591474

A CIP catalogue record for this book is available from the British Library

The Random House Group Limited supports the Forest Stewardship Council® (FSC®), the leading international forest-certification organisation. Our books carrying the FSC label are printed on FSC®-certified paper. FSC is the only forest-certification scheme supported by the leading environmental organisations, including Greenpeace. Our paper procurement policy can be found at www.randomhouse.co.uk/environment

Typeset in Goudy Std by Palimpsest Book Production Limited,
Falkirk, Stirlingshire

Printed and bound in Great Britain by CPI Group (UK) Ltd, Croydon CR0 4YY

'They came home in various moods. Some so weary they could hardly think straight, some so bitter and disillusioned it was almost like brain damage. Some came home cheerful, hopeful and raring to get back into civvy street. Actually they were the ones who suffered most. Civvy street, as they knew it, no longer existed. Civvy street was beaten into the ground by fear, shortages and sheer weariness.

Some had no homes to go to, no jobs, no families even. They couldn't drown their sorrows in drink because drink was in short supply. Cigarettes and sweets were hard to get too. Most of us had our little hoard where we painstakingly saved something out of our rations for when the boys came home. We put flags up for them, we had parties for them, but the boys that came back were not the boys who went away. They were men. Different men with different ideas, and they found us different too. The shy young girls they left behind became women, strong useful women with harder hearts and harder hands capable of doing jobs that men never dreamed women could do. Some of us were mothers, and the babies did not know their fathers and the fathers did not know their babies.

There was jealousy on both sides. The children who had mum to themselves had to share her with a man who was almost a stranger. There were a lot of bedroom rows, I can tell you. A man who dreamed of lying in his own bed with his wife would have to fight a furious little son or daughter who thought they had a right to be there too.'

Letter from Margaret Wadsworth, of Blackpool

Contents

Acknowledgements

A full roll call of the kind people who have helped in the writing of this book would take us into a second volume. Pride of place in the thank you list, goes to all those who responded to our appeal for reminiscences of the war end and its aftermath. That they took the trouble to write at all and in such illuminating detail is remarkable enough. But in many cases, it took great courage to say openly what had remained unsaid or confined to the immediate family circle for almost half a century. When we followed up with supplementary questions, they were answered patiently and constructively. We have tried to respond to every letter. If, inadvertently, we have missed out on any correspondents, we take this opportunity to apologise for what, at times, was a heavily over-loaded administration. Those we have quoted directly are credited within the manuscript.

Librarians and archivists were generous with their time and expert advice. We owe grateful thanks to the Royal British Legion, the Soldiers', Sailors' and Airmen's Families' Association (SSAFA), Women's Royal Voluntary Service (WRVS), the Salvation Army, St Dunstan's, the BBC

Written Archives Centre, the Royal College of Psychiatrists, the Imperial War Museum, HMSO, the Forces Help Society and Lord Roberts' Workshops, the Regular Forces Employment Association, *Soldier Magazine*, the Public Record Office, the London Library and to *The Times*, the *Sunday Times* and the *News of the World* Cuttings Libraries. Thanks too to the *Sunday Times* for its enthusiastic endorsement of this project and to Angela Connell for delving into the archive.

Errors of fact or interpretation are entirely the responsibility of the authors who have been saved from many a gaffe by their research assistant, Jill Fenner. When stray facts were to be chased up, Jill chased them with a dedication and discernment that would have done credit to Sherlock Holmes. Without her, it would not have been possible to hold to the tight deadlines we set ourselves.

When Daddy Came Home

Foreword

There are troubles so deep they never heal. They are also willed to the next generation. 'My father's war didn't just leave him deaf in one ear from a beating by a Japanese soldier,' recalls Bryher Scudamore (née Mitchell), 'it left lifelong scars on his psyche and his soul. He survived the experience physically but at enormous mental cost.' And it was not just he who paid the price. His daughter, born in 1950, four years after her father's return from slave labour on the infamous Burma Death Railway, grew up with the backwash and the backlash of all the horrors he had seen and endured – the crippling toil, the casual cruelty and humiliation, the comrades beheaded and bayoneted to death, the starvation. By some miracle, he came out alive but terribly mentally scarred.

'Daddy was an angry, volatile and troubled man, an alcoholic who lived entirely for the moment,' she says. 'I feared and despised him. He would turn up drunk at school open days. He sold my precious christening gifts – a sapphire brooch and an antique silver spoon – to buy booze. My mother and I lived every day with the fear of his presence and dreaded the sound of his key in the front door. What would it be this time? A drunken, self-pitying rage or a terrible hate-filled silence? He died in 1991 from a massive stroke. He was seventy-five. I shed no tears. I simply had no feelings left. To this day, many memories of my father still sting me.'

Forgiveness was a long time coming – the result of finally understanding a fraction of what had made Douglas Mitchell the embittered, impossible man she knew. It came in 2014 – two decades after her father's death, seven decades after the end of the war – when Bryher saw the film *The Railway Man*. This is the moving, true-life story of Eric Lomax, a British army officer who was also filled with hate after enduring the Burma railway as a prisoner-of-war. Years later he returned to the scene of his torture and also tracked down and confronted one of his tormentors face to face, fittingly on the bridge over the River Kwai. Lomax found closure of a sort – as, in her turn, did Bryher.

Lomax's deeply moving account of his 'journey' was a bestseller as a book and subsequently made into a film (starring Colin Firth). 'I entered the cinema with some considerable fear and trepidation,' Bryher recalls, 'but also with hope that it might reveal to me something of what my own father went through. I thought it might even allow me a greater understanding of the complex man he was. Daddy never talked about his experiences, never revealed the sheer brutality of what he had endured. The only time he came even close to unburdening his soul was when we watched *Bridge Over The River Kwai* on television one Christmas when I was a child. He flew into a rage and turned the TV off, shouting: "It wasn't like that! You have no idea." After that, I was too scared of his terrifying temper to ask him what his time on the Death Railway was like.

'His silence about his ordeal was not unusual. In *The Railway Man*, many PoWs are similarly taciturn about their experiences. Those who survived and came home don't talk about what happened because they thought no one would believe what they endured.' Watching the film was like replaying her own childhood. 'So many painful memories were excavated in that darkened cinema – of Daddy's unexplained rages and his inability to show any affection. But I finally had some understanding of why he was as he was and how my relationship with him had been profoundly affected by his despair. He had seen the worst of humanity, living for years on a knife edge that, at any moment, could have seen him beaten to death. And he lived the rest of his life with hatred for the people who had treated him so terribly.

'I don't think anyone could survive that experience

undamaged, and I see now why he turned to drink to dull the pain. So many men like my father became forgotten soldiers, whose experiences and memories went unrecorded. Watching *The Railway Man* opened a well of grief and emotion within me. For the first time, I wept for my father – and even found in my heart some compassion for what he went through. I came to see him as a brave man, a war hero. I can forgive him for all those years of cruelty he inflicted on me.'

The late Douglas Mitchell was an extreme example of what war can do to good men. Before the Second World War, he was by all accounts a pleasant and promising young fellow, blessed with a secure home, a sound education at Dulwich College and prospects. At the end, he came home utterly changed – as did millions of other servicemen and servicewomen. The vast majority had not come close to the suffering he endured but they were still transformed by the experience of war, of life in the military, of years away from home and loved ones. Re-entry into the atmosphere of the real world – particularly given the speed with which it often happened – was not easy. Many crashed and burned in the process. Those loved ones – wives, children, parents – had had a different experience, one of hardship too, given the bombing and rationing back in Britain, but also of greater independence in thought and deed. The 'little filly' a man had left at home while he rode off to do his duty for King and country was likely to be a horse of a different colour now.

In theory, all those reunions when Daddy came home were to be wreathed in smiles and Vera Lynn sentimentality. As it waited to be reunited, in bases overseas and in pubs at home, a still separated nation joined together in serene harmonies of 'We'll meet again . . . some sunny day'. When that day dawned, it all too often failed to live up to the hype. The war was won, Hitler dead, the Japanese atom-bombed into submission, but the homecoming in a blitzed, bedraggled, broke Britain was bitter-sweet at best. The expectation was that lives would be resumed as before. There had been a hiatus, an interlude, a six-year gap, but now real life, civilian life, would begin again as if nothing had happened – *'The shepherd will tend his sheep/ The valley will bloom again/ And Jimmy will go to sleep/ In his own little room again'*, as the divine Miss Lynn promised. *'Just you wait and see . . .'*

But it wasn't like that. Normal service was not resumed. The war had created new expectations in place of old certainties, a different social and political order was in place, the world had changed. There was no going back. Even Winston Churchill was dumped by a nonetheless still-grateful nation because he seemed to be a figure of the past rather than the future.

It is this theme that, for decades, post-war historians tended to focus on. They examined the policies of the incoming Labour government, the economics of the welfare state, the National Health Service. They mapped the re-shaping of world power blocs, the drift into Cold War diplomacy, the death throes of the British empire. The leap forward into the 'never had it so good' Fifties was proof that the war was done and dusted – a thing of the past. That Bobby Moore and the lads could thrash the Germans at Wembley in the Sixties showed that enmities could be played out on a less destructive field of combat.

In all this, however, people tended to be forgotten – particularly those still trapped in the past, those for whom the war had not ended with signatures on a peace treaty but went on in their heads, their lives, their thwarted hopes, their damaged relationships. The authors picked up a sense of this in the early 1990s from various straws in the wind. In his autobiography, politician Lord Hailsham confessed how he had been invalided out of the army in 1942 and arrived home in London from the Middle East without prior warning to find his wife with a French officer and his marriage over. 'My life was in ruins,' he wrote. Denis Thatcher's first marriage was another casualty of war. When he returned from fighting in Italy and France, it was to an empty bed. For his then wife, the years apart proved unbridgeable, and he was so devastated by their divorce that, like many of his clammed-up generation, he simply refused to make any mention of it. Countless thousands similarly came home to find the hearthside deserted or another fellow in their place. So much for family life carrying on as before.

Then there was a late-night encounter with an eminent historian of international repute who, over a bottle of whisky, broke down sobbing as he recounted how his Spitfire pilot father had been killed before he was even born. He had grown up without a father and it hurt. This was a reunion that never took place, his Daddy one of the 350,000 men in Britain who never came home. Once again, so much for family life carrying on as before.

The final straw in the wind was a colleague born in 1949 whose elderly mother had suddenly and sadly died. After the funeral he reported that his older brother had taken the death very hard, for historic reasons. As a small boy, he had been with his mother throughout the war while his father was away and there was a very special bond between them forged in that difficult time. So what had happened to that bond when Daddy returned after an absence of maybe five years? Readjustment was not easy for this family or any of the millions of others who went through a similar experience. And in the realisation that, for the nation as a whole, that time when Daddy came home was as full of turmoil as of joy, of loathing as much as of love, of distrust and distress as much as of relief, the idea of this book was born.

And perhaps, we wondered, the after-effect of all this trauma was still with us. What if the emotional hurt that had inevitably accompanied disastrous reunions did not simply melt away over time but blighted lives for not just one generation but two, and maybe more? Public records and archives yielded up the views of officials and bureaucrats but the voice of real people was missing. There was only one way to uncover this and that was to ask. It was 1994, the fiftieth anniversary of the D-Day landings in June 1944, and in the *Sunday Times* edition that marked that occasion, we appealed to readers to send us their recollections of the end of the war and demobilisation. A similar request went into dozens of local newspapers.

Replies poured in from men and women across the country. It was as if a whole generation had planted itself on the psychiatrist's couch and was taking the opportunity to open up at last on a subject – and, in many cases, a grievance – it had held at bay for far too long. Suddenly those days of demobilisation, that return to civvy street so often glossed over by historians as they homed in on policy and politics at the expense of people, came alive for the first time – the joy and sorrow, pleasure and pain, hope and despair. Sweet memories of reunited families mingled with nightmares of lives blighted for years, perhaps for ever. Here was the tangle of conflicted emotions and experiences Britain lived through *When Daddy Came Home* – the title of the book we first published in 1995 and which is reprinted here.

Since then, other social histories have caught up, adding to the evidence we amassed. Books such as Maureen Waller's *London 1945*, Alan Allport's *Demobbed* and David Kynaston's *Austerity Britain* ploughed similar furrows. The BBC and the Imperial War Museum combined to harvest individual memories of the conflict in their People's War project. But, two decades after its original publication,

When Daddy Came Home still stands its ground, not only as important testimony of those immediate post-war years but as a critique of how Britain generally was thrown off course by the high hopes and swift disappointments of that era. The speed with which the euphoria of victory in Europe and Asia turned to gloom still astonishes. Cynicism and distrust were the hallmarks of a war-weary land that was all too plainly not fit for heroes and barely fit for purpose. The undamaged United States was on a roll, the Soviets were successfully carving up huge slices of Europe, even defeated Germany west of the Oder was reconciling and rebuilding at a furious rate. But broke Britain stagnated, and, in rationing of food and, more importantly, in morale, went backwards.

Six months after Winston Churchill's Tories were ousted in the election of July 1945, a Conservative pamphlet complained of a woeful shortage of food, a disastrous lack of housing, a chronic shortage of teachers and 'queues outside the shops larger than ever'. Party *pris* it may have been, but it was demonstrably true as Clement Attlee's Labour government sought to usher in socialism. Everything was regulated. Officialdom ruled the roost. And rules were rules. It transpired that the promise a man's job would be there for him when he returned from fighting for King and country applied only to conscripts. The small print said that if you had volunteered instead of waiting to be called up, you forfeited your right to security of employment. It didn't seem fair, and it wasn't, as willing recruits were shoved to the back of the queue for work, penalised for their eagerness. Meanwhile, the agreed plan for a slow and steady demobilisation was adhered to religiously, leaving millions of men kicking their heels in khaki and waiting their turn while at home 30,000 German and Italian prisoners-of-war had to be drafted to bring in the harvest.

Actual homecomings were often deliriously happy, but just as often a let-down, as flat as a punctured tyre. Instead of the fatted calf, men walked in their own front door to a tin of pilchards on the table and a note saying everyone was at work. Children hid from the stranger who had just walked into their lives, bold as brass, as if he belonged there, as if it was his! A sergeant who bent to stroke his own dog was bitten to the bone. Many men came home with changed personalities, particularly those who had seen action, watched friends die, perhaps been wounded themselves. Once happy-go-lucky husbands and fathers were withdrawn, impatient, irascible, unkind, misunderstood. 'My father and I never got on together,' wrote one correspondent. 'He hit and punched me frequently for no good reason. I know he knew he was cruel to me because I once found him weeping by my bedside. He swore he would change but never did. His was a life wrecked by the war. As was my mother's. And mine.'

Domestic harmony proved easier when you were miles apart, infinitely harder on the doorstep, in the kitchen and the bedroom. Families had got on well enough without a man in the house. Now he was back, if he thought he could just take over where he had left off, he had another think coming . . . There were consequences, summed up by the sadness of the girl who was ten when her father came home. As a grown woman, she told us: 'Things were never the same. My parents had changed. Life had changed them. They had missed so much of each other. My father had an enemy to fight. My mother had the constant struggle to keep the home fire burning. I don't know who had suffered most, but within a couple of years my father had left, and all I had left to hold on to were my precious memories of the four contented pre-war years when we were all together.'

Even when families weathered the storm of separation and reunion, relationships were not always totally mended. 'I never really knew him' was a recurring theme from grown-up children about fathers who came home but could not fill in for lost time. And back in 1995, with the generation of men who had fought the war reaching their seventies and beginning to die in large numbers, the chance was gone for good. In poignant reminiscences, sons and daughters grieved for what might have been but never was – that crucial intimacy and ease, love and support, undermined by years apart. The smallest of grievances became mountains impossible to climb. Ten-year-old Roy went to the railway station to greet the father he had not seen since he was a toddler. An independent youngster who had learned to be the man of the house, he suddenly found his hand grabbed when he went to cross the road.

'To my horror, Dad insisted I walk with him, like a five-year-old! My first experience of having a father again! Unfortunately, this was only the start, and I don't think I ever adjusted to his (well-meaning) attempts to dominate me. Dad was always generous and kind to me, but I could not forgive his absence, and then his overpowering return into our lives, which brought so much upheaval and destruction, arguments and anger.'

When Daddy Came Home was first published in 1995, amid the celebrations to mark the fiftieth anniversary of VE-Day and the end of the Second World War in Europe. Among a library of new publications analysing the Allied victory, plotting the downfall of Hitler and re-enacting the joy of those May days when the fighting stopped, it was a sobering contribution to the canon. After every laughing girl had kissed every soldier, sailor and airman in Trafalgar Square and cheered the King, the Queen and Winnie to the echo outside Buckingham Palace, the reality of peace proved harder and more complicated than anyone ever imagined. The Joy and laughter/And peace ever after promised in song was, we demonstrated, short-lived.

As the historian Antony Beevor wrote, 'The experience of war had changed both men and women. Illusions harboured over great distances for a long time proved dangerously brittle.' In the Daily Telegraph, he praised When Daddy Came Home for the 'perceptive and sympathetic' way it revealed previously unrecognised problems of re-adapting to civilian life. Donald Trelford agreed. He wrote in The

Foreword

Times: 'Historians have tended to pass over the massive demobilisation campaign as a self-evident success, celebrated with bunting and jolly street parties. Barry Turner and Tony Rennell present a more disturbing picture. They develop a far-reaching thesis that demobilisation was not only a miserable experience for many individuals, but a root cause of Britain's post-war social malaise. At first, the book's original sub-title – 'How family life changed forever in 1945' – seems a publisher's overstatement, but the cumulative testimony is hard to deny. It does not seem fanciful to relate the bloody-mindedness of trade unions in the decades after the war, the distrust of authority and the growing acceptance of family breakdown in our society to the traumas and emotional dislocations of that time.'

Trelford added revealing personal evidence of his own. 'I was eight when my father returned from the war. Like witnesses in the book, I have a vivid memory of the rough khaki uniform and a prickly moustache. I also remember that he refused to talk about his experiences in Italy and North Africa. Anyone old enough to remember the end of the war will find much in this book that is poignant and evocative.'

That very poignancy troubled the *Independent*'s John Walsh. On reading what he rather unkindly called the 'sob'n'smile stuff' of personal reminiscences in *When Daddy Came Home*, he feared he might 'drown in gloopy sentiment', while at other times, he admitted, he could not see for the tears in his eye. Unwittingly he had hit the nail on the head. Of course sentimentality – an excess of emotion over rationality – ruled. It was inevitably the chief ingredient of family reunions after long absences. How could it be any other way with so much over-expectation on all sides? But in many cases the aftertaste of that sentimentality – when the romance of it all collided with reality – was disappointment, a massive hangover after the binge of bonhomie and best intentions, smiles then sobs. The eighteen months it took from June 1945 to January 1947 to get the boys home were, said Walsh, a 'bewildering moment of social history' in which Britain was 'a land of disorientation, a nation of jolted misfits struggling to put their lives back in order'. Here was 'the bitter shell that surrounded the fondant Daddy's-home sentimentality'.

For some – as ex-Waaf Joan Wyndham pointed out in the *Sunday Times* – homecomings were out-and-out disasters. 'Sometimes hubby would turn up smashed, with a gang of drunken pals or, after a heavy peck, throw himself down in front of the radio to listen to football. Others took one look at the careworn matriarch who had replaced their pretty little wife and wondered why on earth they had ever bothered to come home. Even worse off were those men whose bored and lonely wives had taken to drink, dancing and tracking down Yanks. One returning soldier who had heard such rumours, found his telegram unopened and the shed full of vodka bottles. "I didn't come for their bloody leavings," he screamed to his wife. "Bugger off!" Other women, not so lucky, had their throats cut.'

One element largely missing from *When Daddy Came Home* was the concept of Post-Traumatic Stress Disorder (PTSD). It was little understood in 1945 and attracted no sympathy. Those whose nerve broke under fire were not shot, as they had been in the First World War, but they were hurried away from the front line and out of sight as quickly as possible. Bomber Command crew – a full half of whom died on missions – knew how slim their chances of survival were but what they feared more was being classed as Lacking Moral Fibre (LMF) and sent into a purgatory of shame for letting down their comrades. Men in all the services sucked up the horrors of war and battled on regardless as best they could, but, with the peace, many returned home with the scars of what they had seen and done implanted in their minds, never to be erased.

They screamed in their sleep – some for the rest of their lives. A sailor we met who was trapped three decks down when the battleship *Prince of Wales* was torpedoed in 1941 was, in his ninetieth year, still racked with guilt that by some miracle he managed to survive when 327 of his shipmates died. Men who'd danced so closely with death found the normality of family life not a haven but a torture. They couldn't forget and they couldn't move on, and in a world desperate to look forward instead of backwards, many were lost souls. It didn't help that everyone had their own hardship story, including the blitzed-out wife and kids they came home to. What seems saddest now about the years when Daddy returned from war is how little empathy and sympathy there was for him. Knuckle down and get on with it, was the order of the day, and for all the foreseeable days to come. Far too many couldn't manage it, not without lasting damage to those they had spent their war years dreaming of coming home to, but, when they did, could never find peace with.

In the second decade of the 21st century we are better at recognising the psychological after-effects of war. Nonetheless, in February 2014, the Journal of The Royal Army Medical Corps reported that thousands of British servicemen and women who fought in Iraq and Afghanistan were abusing alcohol to block out the horrors of battle. Violence at home was also a problem. One in seven attacked a wife or partner in an explosive rage after returning from the front line, and fears were growing of a 'ticking time-bomb' of ex-servicemen suffering flashbacks, nightmares, depression, anxiety attacks and other life-changing mental problems.

That time-bomb was ticking furiously in the immediate post-Second World War period too, virtually unseen and unheeded. It exploded, like some slow-release device, over many years and, as with Bryher Scudamore and her father, whose story began this introduction, ricocheted down through the generations and into the present day. But we are not totally helpless when it comes to the traumas of the past. 'My biggest regret,' she says, 'is not finding out more about Daddy's life when he was alive. I believe too that if he had told his story then he might have found it therapeutic. So I now work with charities to help make this possible for people in similar circumstances to tell their story, and, at the age of sixty, I started a business helping people write their life stories – www.autodotbiography. com. From the many emails I received I know how much families come to treasure these unique books of memories. Sadly, the one book I will never read is my own father's autobiography.'

Sadly too, as you read *When Daddy Came Home*, twenty years on from its original publication in 1995, many of those we quote may well now be dead but the power of their voices and the sadness of their memories is as strong as ever.

Barry Turner and Tony Rennell
April 2014

CHAPTER ONE

'Call Me Mister'

Title of a guide to civilian life, 1946

I have been weighing up the pros and cons, and I think it will be every bit as difficult as taking my men into action for the first time I am worrying about it a lot.[1]

This was a young officer writing home from Italy in mid-August 1944. It was not the thought of another military campaign that bothered him. The war in Italy was over. His preoccupation, as far removed from the risks of fighting as it was possible to get, was the promise of peace. It would not be long before he would have to surrender his uniform and badges of rank to return to civilian life. The prospect was disturbing.

'Coming out of the Forces into civilian life is rather like plunging into a tepid bath,' 'Call Me Mister' a popular guide for the demobbed warned. 'One finds neither the icy, tingling invigoration of a cold shower enjoyed on first enlisting, nor the steamy, heart-warming glow of a hot bath enjoyed on leave.'[2]

It was a paradox that became increasingly common as the Axis powers crumbled to defeat in Europe. The exhilaration of victory and the anticipation of the pleasures of ordinary life were tempered by concerns about relationships and love affairs after years apart, making or recreating a family home, finding work, and simply coping with ordinary, everyday life.

Memories of the débâcle after the First World War were still vivid. Then it was to be jobs and homes fit for heroes. The reality was crushing: a short, sharp boom followed by the collapse of the financial system and mass unemployment. For thousands of ex-soldiers, the feeling of abandonment and hopelessness lasted for the rest of their lives. The disillusionment had set in with demobilisation itself. For complex reasons of their own, Ministry of Labour officials had given priority to those needed for key civilian jobs, but since these had generally been the last men to be called up, it looked a lot like 'last in, first out'. The resentment, coming at the end of a war that had built up social unrest, was swift. There were mutinies at several army camps and a demonstration by 3,000 soldiers who occupied Horse Guards Parade. It took Churchill, as Secretary of War, to restore order by substituting a fairer scheme.

All that was a quarter of a century ago. This time it would be different, wouldn't it?

Maurice Merritt, late of the Eighth Army, was among those who were not so sure:

> Instead of being completely thrilled with the realisation of no more parades, drills, rules, no more having to ask for a pass (we'll tell the sergeant major to stick his passes up his . . .), I experienced a strange feeling of loneliness as each turn of the ship's propellers brought me nearer to the English coast and civvy street.
>
> If it had been humanly possible, I would have had the ship turn round and go back at that moment. What would I find when I returned home?[3]

Much political effort had gone into anticipating Driver Merritt's question. As early as September 1942, the indomitable Ernest Bevin, one-time boss of the giant Transport & General Workers' Union and now Minister of Labour in Churchill's coalition government, was instrumental in setting up a committee under the Paymaster General, Sir William Jowitt, to prepare for demobilisation. The plan would have to be economically and socially viable. It was quite a challenge, given that the outcome of the war was far from certain, and that the armed forces were still actively recruiting. The peak of mobilisation, when the forces accounted for over four million men and women, was a full year away yet.

In retrospect, the timing seems odd – to be considering how to bring the boys home when the end of the fighting was such a long way off. But, of course, nobody then could know that the war still had the best part of three long years to run. On the contrary, there was every reason for optimism: if 1940 was the year of backs-to-the-wall survival and 1941 a year of defeats and setbacks, then 1942 was a visible turn for the better. By now the United States was in the war, and defeat by Hitler was therefore out of the question for the first time. As Churchill realised with relief after Pearl Harbor delivered to him his most important ally, 'We should not be wiped out . . . our history would not come to an end.'

With victory on the agenda, it was right to think ahead. Indeed, a government that wanted to steer its bombed-out, worn-out, rationed-out people away from despair *had* to ponder a post-war future. Not that the ministries in the national government – which had probably the most far-reaching and draconian powers to direct the lives of its people than any other in modern British history – were content just to ponder. The Bevins, Beveridges and Butlers of this era were planners. From them was coming the blueprint of a new and better society, once the war was over and the men were home.

Influenced by the 1918 'last in, first out' disaster, Jowitt limited his recommendation to the simple but forceful principle that the oldest and those who had served longest should be released first. There were some special-priority cases to circumvent the age and service rule – those with rare skills, returning prisoners of war, married women and personal hardship cases – but they were very few.

Bevin was not satisfied. True to his socialist principles, he wanted demobilisation to have more purpose. He saw the winding down of military power as a corresponding winding up of the domestic economy. Discharge from the services had to be linked more closely to the employment needs of critical industries and the so-far barely formulated plans for the modernisation of the British economy. The argument for close regulation was reinforced by social needs. The Minister of Labour and National Service saw a strong connection between demobilisation and housing policy. With the social blunders of post-1918 uppermost in his mind, he asserted that a mass homecoming required homes to come to. A building programme of this size (enemy action destroyed or damaged nearly four million homes) demanded government planning on a formidable scale.

> We must do it for the sake of the men who have married since the war, for 2¼ million marriages taken place since war broke out . . . Not more than 10 or 12 per cent have homes. They are living with their families or in furnished rooms . . . The one essential thing if you are going to stop moral disaster after the war is to enable these young folk to start off under reasonable conditions of home life as quickly as ever you can.[4]

This was Bevin speaking at Wigan on 17 November 1943. A few weeks earlier the Cabinet had invited Jowitt to take another look at how demobilisation might be organised. The update was justified by growing confidence that Germany would be defeated sooner rather than later. By now, Italy was out of the war; on the Eastern Front, a demoralised German Army was on the retreat and preparing to fight a rearguard action through another desperate Russian winter; in the West, the battle for the Atlantic was all but won and planning had begun for Operation Overlord which in seven months' time would land the Allies on the beaches of Normandy.

A complicating factor was Japan. The war in the Far East, it was commonly assumed by strategists and military planners, would run at least two years longer than the European conflict. This meant that demobilisation could at best be only partial as forces were diverted to the Pacific to join in what might be a bloody beach-by-beach, island-by-island slow march to Tokyo. But those two years would also allow for an orderly and phased return to civvy street, one that could be synchronised with the plans to boot the post-war economy into action and in particular to find jobs and houses for the homecoming heroes. Only a privileged few were aware of the top-secret atom bomb research in Los Alamos, New Mexico, that would spectacularly explode that theory.

Much to Bevin's irritation, the reconvening of the Jowitt Committee was approved while he was on holiday. The slight, probably real since the Ministry of Labour was not consulted, led to one of the rare clashes between Bevin and Churchill. The upshot was a fresh set of proposals hammered out within Bevin's own ministry. Aside from compassionate cases (Class C), age and length of service were still the basic criteria for deciding the order of release. Thus the oldest and the longest-serving fell into Class A. To produce a workable formula, two months' service were judged to be the equivalent of a year in age. Bevin stoutly refused to complicate the issue by bringing marriage or overseas service into the calculation – an early instance of the beauty of the plan being allowed to override human considerations. This meant that a single man who had spent the war at, say, Aldershot, would have the same entitlement as a married man who had been in India for the duration. The system was building in unfairness.

Demobilisation took on a more radical note when it came to formulating Class B, the category of releases urgently required for reconstruction work. The terms were restrictive. Nominees for Class B were to be retained on the active reserve, subject to recall if they left the jobs to which they were directed, and to receive three instead of eight weeks' paid leave as a gratuity. This was economic planning with a vengeance.

Those brought up on Thatcherite government might query why a predominantly Tory coalition was ready to go along with Bevin. Were they all socialists at heart? It is true that the exigencies of war had produced a generation of Conservatives who were quite at home with state planning, at least for the duration of the emergency. The whole of industry was subject to the war effort, which meant following the orders of the gentlemen in Whitehall. By late 1943, 22 million men and women between the ages of 14 and 64, two-thirds of the age group, were in uniform or working to support the military machine under government direction. Private consumption was tightly controlled by rationing and price control, and though the black market was always there for anyone who could afford it, cheating on the system was not so blatant as to detract from the principle of fair shares for all.

The great levelling of total war was also responsible for a succession of social welfare measures that would have caused political mayhem just ten years earlier. Supplementary pensions compensated for cost-of-living increases, milk was supplied at a low price or free to all mothers with young children, school meals were subsidised, residential and day nurseries were set up for mothers on war work and a national health service was seriously mooted. Embracing all these piecemeal reforms and more, much more besides, was the Beveridge Plan, essentially a national insurance scheme 'giving, in return for contributions, benefits up to subsistence level, as of right and without means test'. Published in 1942, Sir William Beveridge's report inspired a younger generation to believe that a welfare state free of want, disease, ignorance, squalor and idleness was a real practicality. It had a huge impact on the men and women in the armed forces who saw an ideal worth fighting for. The report sold over 600,000 copies and was known about by 19 out of 20 people polled by Gallup in 1943. As the historian Peter Hennessy reminds us, 'There has never been an official report like it.' But it went too far for Churchill. 'It is because I do not wish to deceive the people by false hopes and airy visions of Utopia and Eldorado,' he observed in Cabinet soon after the report appeared, 'that I have refrained so far from making promises about the future.'[5]

But whether he liked it or not, the armed forces saw Beveridge as just such a promise, their reward for national solidarity and sacrifice. Beveridge, in the words of a *Times* leader, 'succeeded in crystallising the vague but keenly felt aspirations of millions of people'. Bowing to the inevitable, the government pledged its acceptance of much of the Beveridge Plan, including family allowances, a health service and subsistence unemployment pay. Younger up-and-coming Tories like R. A. Butler, the architect of the 1944 Education Act which promised secondary education for all, saw a developing role for the state in raising living standards. 'This country,' Butler told Parliament, 'stands before the world as a living social experiment.'

Whether Butler's enthusiasm for state welfare would have extended to the wholesale direction of labour as part of a demobilisation package was not immediately put to the test. Discussion on the subject was limited to the Cabinet, in which Butler had still to win his place.

Bevin's demobilisation plan was approved by Cabinet in February 1944, despite Churchill's lack of enthusiasm. He thought the plan to be overcomplicated and was suspicious of the degree of state control of the economy implicit in Bevin's vision. But Churchill the warlord had other priorities; the problems of peace could wait. Meanwhile, the graft of setting up an administrative structure to handle demobilisation was well under way. The job was taken on by the War Office in the person of Brigadier J. V. Faviell, who wrote:

> There was a good team who I found had already done some useful preliminary work. But on the wider questions, it was not so easy for me to persuade other branches of the War Office to pay any attention to future problems of release when their minds were, quite rightly, focused on fighting the war. However, progress was continuous if slow and by the end of 1944 the Demobilization machinery was virtually complete with all the release centres ready to function.[6]

All this was done in secret. Frustrated by ignorance of the government's intentions, Parliament was less than charitable to Bevin, who was assumed to be waiting on events – the very reverse of the truth. Misunderstandings multiplied after one of the rare House of Commons debates on demobilisation. This was in early 1944, with the introduction of a bill confirming the right of service personnel to have their old jobs back when they returned to civilian employment. MPs were critical. Peter Thorneycroft denounced the proposal as a near swindle since employers' obligations were not clearly defined, and there was no attempt to reconcile the entitlement of former employees to a job with the claims of those who had replaced them. The Reinstatement Committees were proposed to arbitrate when two or more laid siege to the same job but these were bound to fall short of their duty. Any decision would be seen as unjust. It was no excuse for the government to argue that it was merely reinforcing the pledge made in the 1939 National Service Act, or that to have abandoned that pledge would have plunged ministers even deeper into hot water. Reinstatement was an impracticable idea – as experience was to prove. But it might have been received less cynically if it had been discussed openly as part of a general debate on demobilisation.

Bevin knew this but felt he could not speak until the outcome of the European war was beyond question. The turning point came in the days after 5 June 1944 when it became clear that after the triumphant invasion of France the Allied armies were unstoppable. There was an assumption – false as it turned out – that Germany would collapse like a pack of cards as it had in 1918. If all went well, Montgomery reckoned the war could be over by Christmas.

Urged by Bevin to come into the open, the Cabinet approved a White Paper which he presented at a press conference on 21 September. There followed a long, hard sell to the citizens' army to persuade them that all was being done in their best interests. Those like Ralph Walton who had seen lengthy service overseas were the hardest to convince. As he wrote to his fiancée just a week after the war in Europe ended in May 1945:

... Talk in the troops, nowadays, is always about demobilization – even as I write the fellows in the room are arguing about it with regard to Bevin's speech on the radio last night, did you hear it? I have just heard it second hand and nobody seems to have it completely correct, but as far as I can see I don't expect to be out till December – that's being optimistic! We all feel that overseas service should have been taken into consideration in this scheme, as, although no doubt, the fellows who stopped in England all that time had no choice in the matter, they at least had the chance to marry as and when they wanted, which was impossible for us ... But, and this has been my main grouse since joining this hateful army, we have absolutely no method of redress or making ourselves heard about these wrongs, imagined or not! Actually it is up to the people at home, the civilians, to raise an outcry against anything like this, but the Britisher as an individual just oozes complacent selfishness and probably read about the demobilisation scheme (if he read it at all) and passed it over with the remark 'Jolly good scheme for the lads, what!'

There are times when the political outlook of the troops verges very near to anarchy, but I think the majority of us will forget all these injustices and settle down to become good stolid unimaginative citizens.[7]

Overall, the reaction from the front line can best be described as neutral. Wait and see seemed to be the consensus; it is early days yet. The House of Commons debate on the white paper in November 1944, held after members had had a chance to canvas service opinion, was a mild affair with MPs generally trying to push special interests. Bevin barred the way, insisting on the plan and nothing but the plan. His bull-like personality was against compromise; any concession, he felt, would have opened the way to a multitude of exceptional cases. Anyway, for him, the crucial point was the belief that the war in the East would stretch on for at least two more years. Time was on his side. He won his vote.

Demobilisation, otherwise known as 'The reallocation of manpower between the Armed Forces and Civilian Employment in the interim period between the defeat of Germany and the defeat of Japan', was buttressed by schemes for upgrading the national labour force. Young men and women whose education or training had been interrupted by the war were entitled to resume their studies supported by state grants. The cost was to be covered by a switch of resources from munitions across to training. Businessmen who had been forced to shut up shop when they enlisted were told there would be no problem in renewing licences to trade. Under the wing of the Ministry of Labour, Resettlement Advice Offices were set up throughout the country.

Whatever your problem (no matter how unusual it may be or how doubtful you feel about getting help from an 'official' service) the Resettlement Advisory Officers will be ready to do everything in their power to help you solve your difficulties. These officers have been specially trained and many of them are ex-Servicemen and women. They have been supplied with full information and if it should happen that they cannot dispose of your problem finally at the Resettlement Advice Office they will, at least, put you on the right road for getting the help and advice you need.

So said an HMSO advice booklet called *Release and Resettlement*.

Some of you may feel doubtful about discussing your personal and domestic problems with an officer of a Government Department, but this need not worry you. At the Resettlement Advice Offices all interviews will be held in private and so you will be able to discuss your problems quite freely and in the strictest confidence with the Advisory Officers. They, for their part, will do everything possible to avoid an 'official' atmosphere and they will try to deal with your problems and worries in a friendly way. Remember, they are there to help you and are just as keen to assist you to get back into normal civilian life as you are keen to get settled.[8]

Employment exchanges, which pre-war were principally concerned with payment of the dole, were to take on a more positive role of putting job applicants in touch with potential employers, a critical feature of the government's manpower planning which rejected any possibility of a return to the mass unemployment of the 1920s and 1930s. Managerial and high-grade technical posts were to be handled by appointments offices, a tacit admission that the well qualified were no less likely than ordinary workers to experience problems of readjustment.

In all this preparation for the great shift from total war to partial peace, there was little in the way of practical experience to rely on. The First World War offered few worthwhile precedents, except in showing what to avoid. The only helpful indicator of what could be done was the provision made for the disabled. Their rights were confirmed by the Disabled Persons Employment Bill of March 1944, but government agencies in co-operation with national charities like the British Legion, Lord Roberts' Workshops, and the Soldiers', Sailors' and Airmen's Families' Association (SSAFA) had been active on behalf of war casualties since 1940. From then up to the end of the war, 426,000 victims of war or industrial injury were seen by Ministry of Labour officers, and 311,000 were placed in employment. When the 1944 bill came to be drafted by George Tomlinson, Bevin's parliamentary secretary, it was accepted without question that rehabilitation facilities were to be made freely available, that employers had to take a quota of disabled (two per cent of the labour force for employers with 20 or more workers) and that some occupations such as lift and car park attendants should be reserved for disabled people. A register for the disabled was created with an opening roll of around 150,000. That was in December 1945. Within three months the total had jumped by 75,000. But it took until 1949 for the register to total close to one million. The majority of these were employed but in low-grade jobs.[9] To supplement the efforts of Lord Roberts' Workshops, the government set up REMPLOY, and by 1947, 10 factories were in operation.

These were small fry problems compared with the task of reabsorbing a citizens' army of over four million. Bevin's biographer, Alan Bullock, gives full and justifiable credit to his subject for gathering all the components of demobilisation into a coherent pattern:

> The inspiration and driving force throughout was Bevin's: it was he who saw the problem of demobilisation and resettlement as a whole, secured the support of employers as well as trade unions, linked it with the provisions of the new Education Act and gave the nation for the first time a comprehensive service in which the State helped its citizens to train for and find employment at every level from the industrial apprentice to the university graduate.[10]

But there were two critical weaknesses – the first of them inherent. Bevin could do nothing to anticipate the vagaries of politics or war. His expectation of a steady, measured transfer of manpower from the armed forces to the front line of industry was frustrated by the early end to the Japanese war. Who, in 1944, would have dared prophesy Hiroshima as a factor in British post-war employment policy? But that was how it turned out. Japan's defeat, five months after the German surrender, led to an immediate and irresistible pressure to speed up demobilisation. Bevin's hopes for commanding the heights of the economy with his Class B releases were largely swept away in the rush. Instead of four million men and women being let loose on the job market over two years, a third were out by Christmas and the remaining two-thirds by Easter.

Equally, Bevin had to take a chance on remaining in charge of economic planning or being succeeded by someone who could match his punchy determination to get his own way. He was wrong on both counts. When the coalition broke up in May 1945, Churchill's caretaker Tory government had R. A. Butler at the Ministry of Labour. As his last act as Minister of Labour, Bevin signed a Control of Engagement Order requiring all jobs to be filled through the Ministry's employment exchanges.[11] Butler, as we have seen, was broadly in sympathy with a post-war settlement geared to full employment and extended provision for welfare and social security. But he was not on for the degree of state control envisaged by Bevin. In the event, Butler's two months in office were almost exclusively concerned with holding to the target figures for demobilisation against demands for acceleration from MPs eager to impress the service voters.

Then, after the triumphal election of a majority Labour government, Bevin advanced to the Foreign Office, where his bullish style came to epitomise what was left of Britain's role as a world power. The Ministry of Labour went to the safe if lightweight hands of George Isaacs, while economic power passed to Sir Stafford Cripps as President of the Board of Trade, and Hugh Dalton as Chancellor, none of them inspirational figures on a level with Bevin.

A second, if related weakness of the demobilisation plan was the failure to take account of the human element. The plan was all paper, paper, paper – brilliant in theory but hopelessly optimistic in assuming that individuals would surrender their interests to the collective need. Neither those gentlemen of Whitehall nor their political masters could grasp that human nature might not match their view of an ordered society or that a post-war environment was less conducive to co-operation and self-sacrifice.

Returning servicemen were impatient for change; that is why, in Clement Attlee's words, they voted for the party that was looking to the future and against the party that was looking to the past. But they were also tired of rules and regulations. Having had their fill in the military of being told what to do and where to do it, they expected a looser framework in civilian life. Instead, many found themselves bound more tightly by official dictates. Not surprisingly, there were times when they could be rebellious and bloody-minded.

Nor was there sufficient awareness of the effects on

all ranks of the trauma of war. This was obvious in the case of those who had endured hard fighting, but everyone in uniform had changed character in some way. For many, the simple experience of moving away from family and friends, of adapting to a new life, had the most profound influence. Ralph Walton was probably right when he predicted that 'the majority of us will forget all these injustices and settle down to become good stolid unimaginative citizens', but the sizeable minority, men and women, who were unable to conform had a greater impact on society than all the welfare legislation put together.

Yet it is the welfare legislation that has seduced the historians of this period away from what people of this country were really thinking and feeling. Historical accounts of 1945 leap effortlessly from the Berlin bunker and VE Day jubilation to rejection of Churchill and the Tories at the general election two months later and then on to the meaty problems of Attlee's Labour government and the birth of the welfare state. Forgotten along the way is the poor bloody infantry, making its way back home, not to a hero's welcome and long-awaited peace and prosperity but to a country that couldn't cope. That bluebird over the white cliffs of Dover that they had for so long been promised in song turned out to be a scrawny sparrow, more dead than alive.

The jobs, the houses, the support services to ease them back to civilian life – none of it was in place. The folks they came back to were a battered and blitzed lot; food shortages were acute; the switch from war production to peacetime industry was too slow as the new government focused all its efforts on building Beveridge's promised land instead of constructing the economy that could sustain it. The danger of disillusionment had always been there. As early as November 1940, with the Germans taking their revenge for losing the Battle of Britain by stepping up their night-time bombing of civilian targets, Lord Woolton, then the minister in charge of food rationing, had written in his diary:

> We are telling them now that they are heroes for the way in which they are standing up to the strain of the mighty bombardment – and it's true. But when the war is over they will demand the rewards of heroism. They will expect them very soon, and no power on earth will be able to rebuild the homes at the speed that will be necessary. I think there is going to be grave trouble, and the danger is that if the machine of government which can spend money so recklessly in engaging in war fails to be equally reckless in rebuilding, there will be both the tendency and the excuse for revolution.

He was wrong about the revolution. What set in instead was that feeling of being hard done by that has been the prevailing British disease in the half-century since the end of the war.

It has been argued that the experiences on the home front between 1939 and 1945 resulted in an unprecedented social cohesion. The Blitz was no respecter of class or wealth; the role of the state in directing people's lives was accepted in a way it had never been before. The social historian Richard Titmuss wrote in 1950 that 'the government had assumed and developed a measure of direct concern for the health and well-being of the population which was little short of remarkable'. Moreover, there was a mood of reform in the air, what today's politicians would pounce on as 'a sea change': 'for five years the pressures for a higher standard of welfare and a deeper comprehension of social justice gained in strength'.

Peter Hennessy pinpoints the opportunity that was there in 1945. 'Never,' he writes in his celebrated study of those post-war years, 'has a government inherited a more disciplined nation than did the incoming Labour ministers, nor, almost certainly, a more united one. Those ministers who were temperamentally capable of showing exuberance were exalted by real power at last. The ever-vibrant Hugh Dalton caught the mood when he introduced his first budget in November 1945 "with a song in my heart".'[12]

Outside of the House of Commons and 11 Downing Street there was precious little to sing about, except, perhaps, that it was still a long, long way to Tipperary. The story of demobilisation is one of disillusionment setting in with frightening speed. First there was the failure to get men home at the pace they expected. Then there was the grey, austere land they found on their return. What has been astonishing to the authors in the research for this book is to discover the deep well of desperation and unhappiness that marked the home-coming of so many men and women. Does it matter? some may ask. So, the men returning from war were disappointed at first. Surely they got over it? Some did, and in the chapters ahead there is plenty of testimony to the fact that some of the problems when Daddy came home were short-lived. But for many, the unhappiness and the sense of having been badly let down lingered on. And by the time the Labour government was ready, in the summer of 1948, to launch its brave new world of benefits, national insurance and a health service for all, the cynicism, self-interest and distrust of the state that was eventually to defeat it was already firmly imprinted on the national consciousness.

If the philosophy underpinning the welfare state was to help each other, the fact of life that was to undermine it was the instinct to help yourself. Beat the system before it beats you. Get what you can. Look after number one. In those attitudes, as much as in the financial and bureau-cratic problems it faced, was the brilliant vision of a caring society that would protect the needy and abolish poverty doomed. The Second World War ended with the hope that perhaps human nature could change for the better, with the help of the state. That optimism disappeared more quickly than has ever before been recognised; as we shall see, it died of neglect in the débâcle of demobilisation.

CHAPTER TWO

'Any Colour As Long As It's Black'

Choice of demob shoes – a soldier's view

Shortly after the VE Day celebrations in May 1945, Steve Roberts, a contributor to *Soldier* magazine, went through a dry run of a routine that by the end of the year would be familiar to over 1½ million servicemen and women.

'Today,' he wrote, 'I was demobbed – or to use the official term, "released". It took exactly eight minutes. Unfortunately (for me!) it was not the real thing. I was merely a guinea pig . . . at the first full-scale rehearsal at the Ashton-under-Lyne barracks' (the headquarters of the Manchester Regiment).

The first batch to move across the divide were men aged between 48 and 50, and married women. Next to qualify was age group 38 and over.

They were promised a speedy transition. Those from

overseas would go to one of three disembarkation camps – Reading, Oxford or Folkestone.

> You may have to spend the best part of two days at the camp, but that is the longest halt you have during your soldier-civilian transformation. And it is quite a comfortable halt with plenty of amenities, most important of which to the returning soldier are the postal arrangements. You can get in touch with your folk at home by phone or telegram.

Next stop was one of nine Dispersal Units – at Edinburgh, York, Northampton, London, Guildford, Taunton, Ashton-under-Lyne, Hereford and Belfast. This was where the overseas releases met troops stationed in the UK who were waiting to be sent to their local dispersal centre. Servicewomen went directly to dispersal centres. According to Steve Roberts, this was what they could then expect:

> On arrival I was shown into a waiting room with a number of other men who had just arrived from various disembarkation camps and collecting units, and we were sorted into our various regiments. Then we were handed an Army Book we had seen only once before, Army Book X801, the Soldier's Release Book, Class A. It is a small, buff-coloured book of 13 pages all perforated ready to be torn out when required. At least there had been 13 pages. Two – numbers 3 and 4 – were missing, having been removed at the disembarkation camp.
>
> These two pages notify the authorities of impending release,

and contain particulars which are filled in by your unit while overseas. One deals with character and trade qualifications and the other addressed to the Regimental Paymaster tells him to which local post office to send your pay and gratuities after release.

Names were called by an NCO:

'Just take your books round the tables next door, and in ten minutes you'll be civilians again,' he said. It did not take that long.

When my turn came, I entered a barrack room where there were two rows of tables numbered 1 to 10 lined down the middle.

'This way,' called an officer sitting at Table No. 1. 'What's your name and number, and where do you live?' This was merely a check to see if I had the correct book.

I had, so he stamped Page 2, the authority for my release, and tore the page out.

At the next table were an Army clerk and a Ministry of Labour representative. While the soldier made a note of when my 56 days leave expired – it starts the day after you pass through the dispersal unit – and stamped and detached Page 5 from my book, the Ministry of Labour man filled in the Unemployment Book, for which I signed. He told me to hand it to my employer if I started work before the end of my leave. Both books were handed to me, and I passed along to Table 3.

There another page was stamped and torn out, and at the

next table a Ministry of Health official filled in and handed me a Health Insurance Contribution card in exchange for a half-page of the book which would be sent to the Ministry notifying them that I had left the Army.

Page 7 was the next to go – a very complicated-looking page resembling a puzzle corner. This was the Release Record, headed 'Statistical Report to Under-Secretary of State'. It had all been filled in beforehand.

This was quick work. Four and a half pages of the book had gone in less than that number of minutes, and the next table was piled high with money. Here an officer paid the promised couple of weeks' allowance, for which I signed an acquittance roll.

To simplify matters fixed payments have been laid down as follows: Warrant Officers £10; Staff Serjeants and Serjeants £8; L/Serjeants and Corporals £7; L/Cpls and Privates £6.

There was a surprise at the next table. No page was torn out but instead an NCO stamped one and said, 'You'll want this page later on.' It was a certificate to be exchanged at the civilian clothing depot.

I had to keep the rest of the pages. One – a railway ticket – was filled in at the next table. Then I was given a temporary 14 days ration card and another page of the book was signed for me to take to the nearest National Registration office to secure an identity card and civilian ration book. Also left in the book was a certificate entitling me to free medical treatment.

Page 13 is a claim for disability pension. And on the inside of the back cover is the release leave certificate, which in addition to seeing you safely past any inquisitive policeman contains a record of trade qualifications and a testimonial from your Commanding Officer for use in finding a job.

Release day was over for Steve Roberts.

I realised that getting out of the Army was a much quicker and smoother process than getting in.

The Navy and the Air Force followed much the same procedure but had their own dispersal points. For the Navy these were at Chatham, Portsmouth, Devonport and Lowestoft. The take-off points for civilian life for the RAF were at Wembley in London, Cardington, Kirkham and Hednesford.

After receiving an advance of pay and travel allowance, returning soldiers had one last duty to perform under King's Regulations. It involved a visit to the quartermaster's stores, now known as the clothing depot. Servicewomen were spared this experience. They were given 56 clothing coupons and some cash, and were told they could keep their underwear. The men, however, had to go for a complete civilian fitting. Their model was a middle-class family man dressed for church:

Hat
Suit (jacket, waistcoat and trousers) in some 7 or 8 different
    styles and colours from town to sporting, in 40 sizes, or
    sports jacket and flannel trousers

Shirt with two collars
Tie (in many patterns)
Two pairs of socks
One pair of shoes (black or brown)
Raincoat (in four styles or mackintosh in two styles)
Two studs
One pair of cuff-links

Among the items they could keep as a reminder of their army days were ankle boots, cap badges, identity discs, braces. Drawers, cellular, short; gloves, knitted, drab; shirts, ample, drab, and a rich variety of brushes:

Brush button, brass
Brush, hair
Brush, shaving
Brush, shoe
Brush, tooth

Plus their 'comb, hair and razor, safety'.

There were minor variations between ranks and services. For some reason lost to military intelligence, naval officers did not receive any new socks. Presumably they kept those they had on at the time.

The utilitarian civilian outfit was designed for a fit and complete body. Those with injuries were assumed to have been discharged earlier, and though in most cases this was self-evidently true, the rigidly defined clothing allocation created difficulties for the inevitable exceptions to the rules. This was where the forces charities came into play.

Disabled ex-servicemen who find it absolutely necessary to use Zip Fasteners in connection with their personal clothing can obtain them free of charge upon application to the British Legion. A limited stock of Zip Fasteners is being held by the Legion by arrangement with the Board of Trade.

Millions of information booklets were distributed by the government and by each of the services. They made a huge effort to avoid the gobbledygook of the half-literate bureau-crat. The chummy tone was set by the publication *Release and Resettlement* from HMSO, which appeared just before VE Day.

When Germany is defeated many men and women will be released from the Forces and in this booklet you can read how these releases are to be made in what is called the interim period from then until the final Cease Fire. There can be no general demobilisation until Japan also has been beaten. There must be no break in our efforts until then.

Whether or not you are due for early release, the Government wants you to know what your rights are and what is being done to help you in getting back into civilian life. You will find it all in the chapters of this booklet. They have been written as clearly and simply as possible but some chapters may be more difficult to read than others. That is because some matters must be stated precisely and fully – you must be in no doubt about your position.

One thing more – if you are not due for early release you can be sure that your rights will be safeguarded. All the help and advice described here will be waiting for you when you return.

The gently, gently approach was most apparent in the literature designed for the women's services. Those about to be discharged from the ATS, for example, were assured that 'the ATS is still interested in your welfare and is anxious that your return to civilian life should be as smooth as possible'. Helpful hints extended to ways of ensuring a comfortable journey home.

Your railway warrant entitles you to be taken, by the most direct route, to the railway station nearest your home. It should be exchanged for a ticket at the booking office at least half-an-hour before the train is due to start. This will avoid congestion and improve your chances of obtaining a seat. See that you apply for a haversack ration before you start.

Advice to those returning from the Continent was left to the forces magazine.

Don't try Belgian francs in the phone kiosk – they tangle up the works and you don't get through anyway.

Small items of booty were allowed through customs without much trouble. 'But then,' said the commander of a disembarkation camp, 'we suffer from people who try to bring home more kit than they are entitled to. One chap brought back a baby grand piano in two packing cases.'[1]

The inevitable fine-tuning of the demobilisation plan caused some discord between the services. The main issue turned on the interpretation of the age and service rule. Both the Air Force and the Navy argued that a general release of the most experienced personnel would create a serious imbalance in the forces remaining. As an Air Ministry spokesman declared to *The Times*, 'If the whole of the theoretical surplus were released according to age and service we would finish up with a completely disorganised force in which a large proportion of the men would be in the wrong ranks and trades or not available for overseas service'.[2]

The stress on overseas service was understandable. The continuing war with Japan demanded an increase in RAF and naval manpower in the Mediterranean, Middle East, India and the Far East. But those who were likely to be held back could not be expected to sympathise with their commanders' military needs. The worry was of finding themselves last in line for any civilian jobs that matched their age and skills. Sir James Grigg, Secretary of State for War, wrote of their concern to Ernest Bevin.

I had not realised . . . that the Royal Navy and Royal Air Force propose to effect release be different groups in different trades.

As you know, the Army intends to release everyone in the same group or groups, applying the military necessity clause, where it is necessary to retain an individual but then only under the authority of a Brigadier or above. I think, therefore, that there is bound to be considerable trouble later when the application of the Navy and Royal Air Force scheme becomes known.

In view of the government policy to maintain as far as possible a common scheme, do you consider that it is possible to maintain this differentiation between the Services? Surely the Royal Navy and Royal Air Force plan opens the door to all the rackets you are seeking to make impossible?[3]

Bevin was sanguine. He accepted that

. . . age and service groups being demobilised at any one time will vary according to the different branches and trades in which the men are serving.

But then went on to produce a convoluted justification which missed the point entirely.

In as much as substantial numbers of men in these Services are not interchangeable I think you will find that this variation is merely another way of applying the military necessity clause and that the age and service rule will be applied strictly within the various categories. For example, although the Submarine Branch of the Navy may not necessarily be capable of reduction at the same rate as the Minesweeper Branch, releases from the respective branches will be in accordance with the age and service rule. I do not think you need to be apprehensive that the Royal Navy and the Royal Air Force plans will be open to abuse because, as I understand the procedure, the men in a given age and service group who have to be retained beyond the date of release of others in the same group, will be selected 'en bloc' and not as individuals, and that this will be done at the Admiralty or the Air Ministry.[4]

The Times took a more robust view of the problem, identifying the RAF as the chief culprit.

There is much questioning whether the RAF organization in this country is not retaining a war-time rigidity that is an impediment to demobilisation. Standards and requirements that were well approved in war may be unsuited to the transitional period when much of the strength of the RAF can expect no further employment in the duties for which its men were trained . . . Whatever can be done to ease and accelerate procedure must be done, but without infringement of the principles on which the demobilisation scheme is based. Anything which might even be suspected of undermining the balanced calculation of age and length of service in the order of demobilisation would do immeasurable harm to the discipline of the services and the contentment of the civilian population as well . . . There should be no departure from the accepted plan and no loophole for the suspicion of privilege or favouritism . . .[5]

Complaints from the doctors in RAMC uniform were particularly forceful after it was announced that the service proposed the same medical establishment – 2.3 doctors to every 1,000 other ranks – in peace as in war. The *Lancet* pointed out the disparity with civvy street – 0.7 doctors per 1,000 citizens – and censured the RAF and the Navy for releasing medical officers at later dates than other groups.

There followed a determined effort by the Navy to put itself in a better light by emphasising its commitment to flexibility and efficiency.

Sailors are becoming civilians at the rate of one a minute under the carefully organized demobilization scheme which was put into operation at Portsmouth to-day . . . The plan . . . is devised to make the sailors' return to civil life as smooth as possible. Everything that can be done is being done to achieve this end. Going first to a demobilisation centre at Stamshaw officers and men receive their railway warrants, health insurance cards, and other necessary documents together with 28 days' pay and 28 days' leave allowance . . .

From Stamshaw they go to Cosham, where a large garage has been converted into what appears to be a big departmental store. It is staffed by civilian clothing experts whose duty it is to make sure that a man leaves the store equipped with a civilian outfit, well fitting and satisfactory in all respects. As the man passes from one department to another he makes his own choice of hats, ties, suits, and boots and in each department there is an expert to advise him. All the articles issued, be they hats, boots, or suits, are of the best quality. There are cubicles in which men may change from uniform into civilian clothes before leaving the store. Every man is finally 'vetted' by a clothing expert who, if not satisfied, sends him back to be refitted.[6]

Another bone of contention was the Right to Reinstatement. Who was it precisely who qualified for this privilege of getting their old jobs back? Sir Ronald Adam, Adjutant General, was not alone in seeking the widest possible interpretation.

> . . . we welcome most warmly the proposal to extend the right [of reinstatement] to *volunteers* and I can go so far as to say that if we did not know that the Ministry of Labour were already dealing with the matter, we would ourselves be compelled to raise the question . . .[7]

It was a false hope. The Ministry of Labour was not keen to open out a potential source of conflict in the labour market. This time Bevin was unequivocal in his response.

> [The] only persons entitled [to reinstatement] are those compulsorily 'called up or called out'. Those who volunteered are not entitled to reinstatement rights.[8]

There may have been bureaucratic logic in such a sweeping judgement, but to the men who had volunteered it hardly seemed fair. They could well argue that they had gone to war of their own free will, only to come back to a free-for-all; whereas the ones who had joined up only because they had to were given the protection of the law. It was fertile ground for barrack-room lawyers and pub politicians. In making different rules for different groups, those in charge of the demobilisation opened the way for resentment in the ranks. And this was only the start. There was plenty more to moan about as the returning 'heroes' started to move through the system.

Release began on 18 June 1945. By the end of the month, 44,500 men and women were out of uniform. In July, well over twice that number were sent home. The pace of demobilisation then increased month on month to a peak in November, when 391,080 releases were administered.

With numbers like these it was hardly surprising that the system had its failings.

It was early evening when I reached the army centre and I was offered two alternatives. The first was to have a meal (the last supper), stay the night in barracks and the next morning collect a 'demob' suit, a free issue of cigarettes and a free travel warrant to any town in Britain, single of course. The other course of action was to accept the free issues and go home.

I chose the latter, but was sadly disappointed when I arrived at the stores to collect my gent's natty suiting.

Earlier that day the demobilisation centre had disposed of five hundred soldiers and five hundred suits, leaving the clothing racks on a par, or nearly, with Old Mother Hubbard's cupboard, bare. Only three suits remained – take your pick.

One suit was big, the next was bigger and could have fitted a hulking giant perfectly. The third bundle of drab-looking apparel was designed for a drainpipe.

This last I took reluctantly, silently and sullenly, giving the NCO who threw it at me a look in which I tried hard to convey anger, contempt, indifference and hatred, all at the same time. Still, it wasn't his fault, he had been dishing out clothing all day, and it seemed that all he was interested in was to get rid of me, lock up and make for the nearest NAAFI to meet his ATS girlfriend.[9]

The quality and style of demob clothing excited much comment – nearly all unfavourable.

The munificence of the army included one pair of shoes, you could pick any colour as long as it was black. Also on offer was the choice of a cap, a wide-brimmed gangster type, trilby, or the more popular model, the 'porkpie'. I didn't see any bowler hats, these were probably reserved for the Officers.

The caps were mostly in a black and white check pattern and absolutely huge, guaranteed to cover the complete head, ears included, a real 'handicap'. To complete this stunning outfit was a pair of woollen gloves, one pair of socks, and a garment laughingly called a raincoat.

Why on earth did the army authorities always issue

clothing that would fit a dwarf or giant perfectly, yet never catered for an average-sized, normal (?) member of the services? . . .

It hurt my pride to accept this itchy, drab-coloured clothing, but it hurt more physically the following day when I tried it on for the first time. Talk about private troubles, even the trousers were unfriendly, they kept their distance from my feet, in mourning at half mast.

When I reflected on my lovely fifty-shilling chalk-grey striped suit, which I had left with my landlady six years ago, I momentarily felt a bit better, then wondered if it had shrunk. Perhaps she had lent it to one of her American friends who had tried to bring a little southern comfort to her home during the war.[10]

When it came to a fitting, there were occasions when it seemed an advantage not to be of normal proportions.

I was demobbed from a unit near Tenby in S. Wales, and sent to York to be kitted out with my demob suit etc. Being slim and 'lanky' in those days, I was informed that I was not a standard size so when I arrived home I had my army uniform, a trilby hat, a fawn 'riding mac', and civvy shoes, and received my 'bespoke' demob suit about a fortnight later. Double-breasted, charcoal grey with a broad white stripe, I looked quite presentable, more so than some of the 'normally' shaped chaps whose suits 'nearly' fitted them.[11]

There was some regret among wives that the selection of civilian clothes had been left entirely to the men. Denise Mason recalls her father turning up

> . . . in a navy blue suit and a brown trilby hat. My mother moaned because they didn't match nor did his black shoes! But we laughed about it afterwards.[12]

The pleasure of getting out of uniform was reduced somewhat by the limited choice of civilian wear. Others did not need to be told that their headgear was eye-catching in quite the wrong way.

> I gave the hat to my 90-year-old grandfather. It was too big so we folded up some newspaper and placed it behind the leather band.[13]

> When on the first morning back home I walked proudly into town wearing my light grey pin-striped demob suit, looking around, I recognised all the ex-servicemen – they were all back in uniform – light grey pin-striped suits![14]

Formal and unimaginative as the standard clothing issue undoubtedly was, it had its admirers.

> We had Billy christened in a local church, and when signing afterwards, the Rector turned to Len, feeling the lapel of

his suit, and in a very loud voice for all to hear said, 'So this is one of your demob suits?'[15]

And new clothes of whatever style or quality had a ready sale on the black market, as George Betts quickly discovered as he emerged from his demob centre.

When I tucked my parcel of clothes under my arm, and set off to the station to get a train home, I was accosted by several [spivs] who were offering £10 per outfit. Although I declined all offers I actually saw several parcels exchange hands between these 'praying mantis' spivs, and demobbed servicemen.

Apparently, in these hard days of clothes rationing, these 'spivs', who dodged all hard work, were making quite a handsome profit selling these clothes.[16]

Spivvery at demob centres was so common that there were demands in Parliament for tougher policing. The response from the ministerial benches was muted.

The men are warned at the dispersal centres not to part with their clothing rashly, said a junior minister. Military police are on duty at the centres, but these transactions take place after the men have left when the clothes are their own property. I should be reluctant to surround release centres with military police.[17]

Encountering his first spiv, Sergeant Shaw was curious to discover how far he could push this 'scruffy little fellow'.

'Ten quid for yer box, sarge.' I stared – what was he on about? Inside [the release centre] the place resembled a huge Quartermaster's store but despite all the tons of stuff they couldn't find a trilby to fit my average-sized head and finally fobbed me off with a cloth cap and with a button on top of it. Never having possessed a pinstripe suit, I chose one. All my new belongings were stuffed into a big carton . . . Again I was intercepted by the little man. 'Ten quid for yer box,' he repeated and as a tenner was a tidy sum in 1945, I hesitated before refusing. 'Coupons too,' he wheedled, clawing sheets of them from a pocket. There must have been hundreds.

'D'yer print those yourself?' I asked interestedly. 'Don't be funny. I'm a registered dealer. If I sold what is in that box . . .' 'For twenty quid?' I hazarded. 'Twenty? You're barmy,' he replied pityingly. 'I was sayin' – if I sold it I'd get my coupons back.' 'I tell yer what, mate, I'll sell yer a cloth cap cheap – no coupons.' 'Yer bloody won't!' 'It's better'n yours. Got a button on top.' 'Sergeant, yer can take it away and stuff it!'

I grinned bravely down on his five-feet-nothing, saw that the redcap was getting interested, and departed. Obviously spivvery was with us until rationing ended. Later, finding that pre-war togs still fitted tolerably, I put the pinstripe into mothballs against the uncertain future.[18]

Checking out the wardrobe was an example followed by many. As a tongue-in-cheek *Guide to Civilian Life for the Newly Demobilised* urged its readers,

> On reaching home it is a sound plan, after shaking hands with your wife, to go upstairs without delay and see what you have in the way of pre-war clothes. It will at least be apparent that they have all shrunk – so much so that it will be impossible to button any of the jackets in such a way as to permit breathing. Do not throw them away on that account, however. In three months they will fit perfectly.[19]

The spivs did not have it all their own way. Private Heaton and his mate were two who triumphed by sleight of hand.

> We decided to go for a last drink together before we were civvies again. On the way back to the barracks, it's 12.45hrs now, we see these two spivs with about a dozen squaddies round them. They were buying the demob suits. Well I guess they got *some* because some of the lads were coming a double shuffle. So me and my mate tried it. The outfits were put in a flat cardboard box. My mate changed into civvies and put his battle dress in the box, which he then gave to me. He took my box of civvies. So there I was in battle dress with another BD in my box. Guess which one we sold to the spivs? Anyway, it got us a fiver, and better still, clued us up what we may be in for in civvy street, after six and a half years in the late army.[20]

Ex-Private Heaton adds a postscript.

> I still haven't got used to civvy street yet, but don't let on to the wife!

Spivvery was widespread and widely tolerated, if court records are anything to go by. Prosecutions against black marketeers were few, and when they were brought, the penalties were relatively light.

> In October 1946 a multiple grocer who had deliberately overdrawn coupons to receive extra supplies (equal to a month's food for over 8,000 people) was fined £60. The surplus was sold on the black market while checking the points in the pre-calculator age meant that some official had had to count nearly 200,000 of them.
>
> A Spitalfields fruit wholesaler with a turnover of £150,000 a year was fined £20 for systematically overcharging in 1947. Geoffrey Raphael, a magistrate at Thames court, confronted by three 'spivs' who had carried out a 'black market transaction, and a very serious matter too', fined those involved £50 and £25. The same magistrate, seeking to make 'an example' of a wholesaler who had falsified documents, fined him £200. He appealed and London Sessions reduced the fine to £75.[21]

A popular fiddle, so common as to be barely counted as law-breaking, was to beat the petrol allocation. The government came up with an easy-to-operate scheme to catch the perpetrators. According to the minutes of the Petrol Black Market Committee:

> The idea is that all petrol issued for commercial purposes should be coloured red so as to distinguish it from other petrol. The police would be given power to take samples of petrol from any motor vehicle of the private car class on the roads or in garages and car parks. For this purpose they would require to carry two tubes to extract the petrol from the tank of the vehicle and bottles into which the samples taken would be poured. In one of these bottles there would be a chemical reagent which, on being shaken, would turn the commercial petrol a deep blue.[22]

But appropriate training could help to circumvent the tightest rules. John Kitch's father reckoned that quicklime would remove the telltale dye from the petrol.

> Imagine his absolute delight when it actually worked. I remember he had a forty-gallon drum in the garden in which he used to distil illegitimate, legitimate petrol, and when the life of the lime was spent he used to bury it in the garden. It's a good job my mother never disappeared because the neighbours may have had good cause to think that he'd murdered her and was trying to dispose of the body. Integrity of actions were never questioned by anyone, and he must have distilled more petrol during and post-war than BP. There were always people calling at our house with five-gallon drums. There was the owner of the laundry, who used to roll up in a very impressive SS Jaguar, and a vicar

with an Austin Ruby who needed to administer an extensive rural parish.[23]

So that's what life had been like at home while they had been away at war. Would England ever be the same again?

One of the first out of the Army was RSM Stilwell, late of the Hampshires. A reporter from *Soldier* magazine followed him from the release centre.

Farnham lies in a valley and his home lay at the top of a green hill overlooking the town. He wanted to walk because it gave him time to think, so he did not wait for a bus but made his way between twin poplars, past the bowling green where a man with a lawn mower was busy.

'I don't think I'll take up bowls,' he thought, 'it's too quiet. I might play tennis again.' He remembered the silver cup he had won in Shanghai in 1935 and in thinking of Shanghai he contrasted the neat little shops of England and the people shopping, and the quiet streets, with the noise, babel of tongues . . . And he thought of Palestine and the feeling he had there that someone was always ready to loose off a bullet behind his back. And he thought: 'This England is good – it was worth waiting for.'

Up the hill he went until he came to Tor Road where grass grows unchecked in the centre with wild flowers. He walked along Tor Road until he came to 'Charmar'. Char, the beginning of his name Charles, and Mar, the first half of Martha, his wife's name.

She heard his footsteps coming up the path and she was there at the door to greet him. She didn't say much. They kissed and he walked in: 'Is the kettle boiling?' – she laughed and brought him tea and biscuits.

He settled in an armchair in the drawing room.

'You'll miss the Army,' she said.

'Of course I won't,' he replied, 'when we've had a holiday I'm going to work on my acre of land. Fruit, vegetables and flowers: there's a good local market for them. When I collect my gratuity it'll be about £150 I reckon. I'm going to buy a glasshouse.'[24]

The idyll was not widely anticipated or realised. For many, the journey home was an endurance test of controlled nerves.

As the train puffed away from the demob centre at Northampton and on towards London, where my sister Jean lived, I mused on the sayings of my army pals when they had discussed their pending army release. One of our unit had asked another what he would do on arrival at his house. The reply was that the *second* thing he would do would be to take off his pack. He was one of the married men.

No banners were waving in the cold London air as I made my way to Camden Town and my sister's flat. She was then a telephonist and on that particular evening absent on night duty. She had thoughtfully left me a key under the mat.

On entering her apartment, two little paper flags confronted me. One was the Stars and Stripes, as her fiancé was American, and the Union Jack in my honour.

Over six years of longing for this moment, yet now it had arrived, it was a little devoid of happiness and welcome. There was no one even to say hello – the cat couldn't wait to get outside for a wee.

There was a short note on the kitchen table. 'Make a cup of cocoa if you like . . .' – bloody cocoa, after all that time in the desert – '. . . and there's a tin of pilchards in the larder if you feel peckish . . .' Pilchards! Ask any man who has been in the army what he thinks of pilchards and see what reply you get.[25]

Having served on the Normandy beaches, John Jones was away from his family for 15 months. When he arrived back, 'the only person at home was my father-in-law who was fast asleep. He woke about half an hour after my arrival and said that he'd *almost* dozed off. I asked him where everyone was and his answer was, "One's in hospital and one's gone to Blackpool for the day." When I asked which was which, he said Joan's in hospital, that was my wife, and mother has gone to Blackpool. What a homecoming.'[26]

Fortunately, John's wife was not badly ill. In a few days, she was home again.

George Betts was fearful but philosophical.

When I eventually found a seat on the train to travel home for the last time, a feeling of utter despair and despondency prevailed upon me . . .

During this sad journey home, my stomach turned over, and I wondered how my health would affect my private life, until I consoled myself that I would soon be meeting my little family, and considered myself extremely lucky, and should be counting my blessings. After all there were thousands of families who were destined never to see their loved ones again, and also many limbless and sightless men who were determined to face a new life and adapt themselves to it.

And so, instead of moping about myself, I counted my blessings and resolved to devote myself to my family and my home that I had been privileged to live through the war for, and it was a happy occasion to be greeted by my wife and boys at the station, as they had received notification in advance, and we got a taxi for home and happiness.[27]

For Archie Clarke, the interval between release and arrival at his front door was packed with incident, not all of it welcome.

The small railway platform swarmed with khaki-clad figures and there was an ironic cheer as the local train rounded a bend and halted at the station, 20 minutes late. A few minutes' activity followed, and the 150 men, each carrying a kit bag, loaded themselves into the train. The last few to board were still wedging themselves into odd corners when with a sudden jerk the train started.

At Glasgow the unit dispersed to different platforms; I moved with the largest contingent to catch the Crewe train. The Solo

Whist school met here, formed up and boarded the train when it arrived, rather like a Rugby first row. Securing four seats together we settled down to continue the game which had started five weeks before, when the green coast of Ceylon had sunk below the horizon.

Some hours later, after steaming through a grey winter landscape, we reached Carlisle. Here we joined the throng of servicemen that surged around the Forces' refreshment room. The lady volunteers who manned it were very well organised, and in the 10 minutes the train stopped there everyone was able to secure a mug of tea and a packet of sandwiches. We munched contentedly for some miles before dealing the cards again for the final session which lasted until the train arrived at Crewe. A two-hour wait, but the bar was open and I drank beer with Norman, who was waiting for the same train. We again obtained seats on the blacked-out train. Only a dim blue bulb in each compartment, barely enough light to see the features of the other occupants. I closed my eyes and enjoyed the rhythm of the wheels chattering over the rails as the train steamed slowly South . . .

The train crawled along, sometimes stopping, and with the bored patience of wartime travellers we accepted it without comment. At about 11.30, one hour late, we arrived at Wolverhampton, and with four other people I left the train. I was now only five miles from home, but there were no taxis at this time . . . A porter told me I might find a bed at the YMCA in Stafford Street. Leaving my kit bag in the Left Luggage Department I walked there.

A man reading a book at the desk smiled grimly when I asked for a bed. 'Bursting at the seams,' he said. 'You might find room on the floor of the Reading Room.' He then pulled a sheet of paper towards him and glanced at it. 'Just a minute, there is one bed that hasn't been claimed, but it has been paid for. You can use it if you like, but if he turns up he will have to have it.' Five minutes later I was in bed and asleep.

I woke suddenly: someone was shaking my shoulder. As I sat up, fully conscious, a voice said: 'Say, Buster, you're in my bed!' It was an American sergeant and I could cheerfully have strangled him. I looked at my watch: it was 2.30. As he undressed I dressed, then I pulled the top grey blanket from the bed. 'If I'm on the floor, I need this,' I said, and he grunted as I walked out. The dimly lit Reading Room was strewn with sleeping bodies; I found a space under a table, spread my greatcoat on the lino and wrapping myself in the blanket was soon asleep again.

The next morning I walked back through cold rain to the station, collected my kit bag and caught the bus. In spite of the rain which was falling steadily I enjoyed the ride. The familiar landmarks and buildings were just as I remembered them: no bomb damage here, just lack of paint which made them dull and drab. Alighting at the village church, I walked the last lap of the journey, through the village and down the lane. I walked up the drive and the dog barked loudly; he had only been half grown when we last met. As I approached the door, he rushed from the back of the house. I stretched out a hand to pat him and he promptly bit it. Welcome home![28]

When the demob ship carrying Bert Spencer docked at Southampton it was raining and biting cold. Quite a contrast to Burma.

We had been ordered to pack ready to leave the ship early morning but did not get off until evening. I was still considered an Artillery man so had to go to Woolwich, arriving about 22.00hrs. I managed to send a telegram to say I was on my way. They quickly gave me a pass and railway warrant but with two kit bags to carry I missed the midnight train at Paddington and had to wait until morning. It stopped at every station but finally arrived at Bristol about ten. Should mention here that in the first big raid on Bristol we had been bombed out and were living in two rooms when called up. While in Burma the council had given the wife a council house, which of course I had never seen . . . Having been held up so long on the ship and all packed, I was badly in need of a shave etc. I couldn't face public transport, kit bags and all, so went for a taxi. An army captain wanted the same one and he said let's share and insisted it would be my home first. I was waiting for a dressing down because of my state but I think he understood – I did have my Bush Hat on and that may have helped. He wanted to know how long I'd been away. I told him all I could in the time, including my new address. When we arrived outside home he wouldn't let me pay, and when I got out the driver started to pull away but he stopped him. He wanted to see our meeting after nearly four years.

Not knowing exactly what time I was coming, when the wife opened the door she was wearing an apron and the speed with which she tore it off had to be seen to be believed. Why I was not to see her in one I never did find out. After the obvious embracement I looked back and the officer had the window down and as the taxi moved off HE saluted ME.[29]

After the surrender of Japan in August 1945, there was pressure on all sides to speed up demobilisation. Within the services, even those who were nervous of resuming civvy life clamoured for action. There were obvious advantages in being first out, there were none at all in being last.

On the home front the lobby for speedier releases embraced impatient families, employers in need of skilled labour and Conservative politicians trying to score off what were seen to be the Labour government's plans for 'ushering in stream-lined Socialism'. In December 1945, with the numbers demobbed climbing towards two million, from Tory Central Office came this partisan, though not inaccurate, summary of the way things were.

The nation is still suffering from a woeful shortage of food; the people of Britain are among the most badly clothed in Europe; no evidence exists of any serious attempt to put in hand a concerted drive to solve the immediate urgency of the disastrous lack of housing; the shortage of qualified teachers in the schools is chronic; a great variety of consumer goods are in shorter supply to-day than they were during the war while the queues outside the shops are larger than ever. [Yet the Government] has neglected the very issue which affects the revival of trade and industry as well as the happiness of millions of homes in the land.[30]

The Conservative opposition was not alone in believing that the Government was reluctant to change the Bevin plan because it was *the* plan. As a contributor to a House of Lords debate put it, 'the rate of release seems to be determined not by the consideration that men and women should not waste their time in idleness, but by the fear that more speed would interfere with the orderliness of the process of release'.[31]

In the end, it was the demands of industry that forced a change of policy. It became clear, even to those suffering from extreme ideological myopia, that Bevin's plan had totally misjudged the nature and strength of the post-war recovery.

Industrial readjustment to peace-time conditions was in itself a massive logistical challenge that depended on a ready supply of labour. Yet the move out of industry threatened to exceed the intake. Now that the emergency was over, the men and women who had stayed on in their jobs well beyond retirement age were ready to go. There were over a million of these. Then there were the two million or so women who would not have been in paid employment but for the war. Their exit rate was predictably high. On the other hand, the counterbalance of new workers coming into industry was weakened by the declining birth rates of the 1930s, and by conscription, which was still taking large numbers of 18- to 30-year-olds. Everywhere there was a shortage of skilled labour which Bevin's Class B release scheme for workers essential to aid economic recovery (20,000–30,000 a month) did little to mitigate.

The first reaction of the Ministry of Labour to the impending crisis was to speed up the transfer of essential workers from munitions to priority industries and services – housing, food, clothing, energy and transport. That more were needed became clear when the harvest in autumn 1945 was threatened by a labour shortage. Disaster was averted by allowing servicemen 28 days' 'agricultural leave' and by enlisting the services of 30,000 German and Italian prisoners of war.

Even now, a government promise to 'study the possibility of increasing the rate of release from the services' was heavily qualified. On 11 August, the day Japan surrendered and barely two weeks after Labour had taken office, the Ministry of Labour warned against optimistic 'speculation regarding the rate of demobilization. Until the war in the Far East is definitely over, and until the Government have had an opportunity of reviewing the whole manpower situation and the requirements of the fighting services, it is impossible to announce whether any changes can be made. In the meantime it should be recognized by everyone that unauthorised forecasts of sweeping changes in the rate of demobilisation may cause unnecessary disappointment among men and women in the services, their relatives, and friends by raising hopes which may not be realised.'[32]

This was endorsed by Clement Attlee who, in one of his early speeches as Prime Minister, emphasised 'the heaviness of the commitments still facing this country after victory'. Alistair Horne, the historian, recalls, as a 20-year-old subaltern stationed in the Middle East, hearing Montgomery use that same word – 'commitments' – when explaining to the troops there why it would be some time before they were allowed home. He was baffled by it at the time; later he was to understand that Monty was referring to India. If that was the field marshal's view, other military leaders and politicians – notably Churchill, now in opposition, and Bevin, now Foreign Secretary – had different commitments in mind: what to do about the Soviet Union. Stalin was insatiable in the post-war carve-up of Europe; there was no question of his troops and tanks going home. Just three days after the end of the war, Churchill had observed: 'Great pressure will soon be put upon us at home to demobilise partially. In a very short time our armies will have melted, but the Russians may remain with hundreds of divisions in possession of Europe, from Lubeck to Trieste and to the Greek frontier on the Adriatic.' With Britain continuing to play the world power, the armed forces had to be kept up at least to pre-war strength. Against some expectations, the King's Speech offered no relaxation of the call-up of men up to the age of 30.

Within a week the government was shifting its ground on demobilisation. By then, the Ministry of Labour was awash with complaints from employers that the production targets they were being set went far beyond realistic expectations. Moreover, it was now clear that the Class B releases were not about to perform the economic miracle Bevin had hoped for. There were too few of them, for one thing – a mere 9,650 in September against 117,450 in Class A. But there was the additional problem of persuading the Class B releases to do what they were supposed to do: to fill what the government deemed to be the critical jobs in essential industries. On paper, ministry officials had full power to direct labour where it was most needed. One of the first acts of the newly elected Parliament was to extend the life of employment controls for another five years. But no one really believed that coercion would be pushed to the limit or, for that matter, that Class B releases who failed to obey the rules would be ordered back into the military. Even to have thought this was a possibility was a crucial misreading of the state of mind of those coming back from war. They had had enough of rules and regulations; the citizens' army, having done its job, was not about to be a nationalised workforce. *The Times* acknowledged as much:

Mr Isaacs [Bevin's successor as Minister of Labour], for instance, proposes to release more women from the forces under the Class B scheme provided they return to the textile, clothing, laundry, and similar trades. But if considerable numbers of women so released refuse to honour their commitments when they return, how far will Mr Isaacs venture to apply the Class

B sanction – effective while the Japanese war continues – of recalling them to the colours? The Government, as Sir Stafford Cripps recently foreshadowed, will have to rely increasingly on attraction rather than direction, and this implies, as he made clear, that wage increases and other improvements in many of the trades now to be expanded are probably unavoidable.[33]

Also unavoidable was faster demobilisation. The new figures announced by George Isaacs added 250,000 Class A releases to the original target for the year of 750,000. The likely impact was enhanced by the decision to transfer over a million civilian workers from war production within two months.

The future of Class B was left to the Prime Minister to tackle in his broadcast on 3 September.

We have made arrangements to speed up the releases in Class B by offering release immediately to all those selected for this category. We have decided also to improve the conditions of release in Class B by granting them payment of their war gratuities, post-war credits, and leave payment in respect of overseas service as soon as possible after release instead of waiting until the end of the emergency.

These payments will be made retrospectively to all those already released in Class B. I would ask all those men and women in the forces who may have to stay and do routine duty for some time yet to be patient. We will release you as soon as possible; do not be apprehensive that you will be kept longer than is absolutely necessary.

We are desperately short of man-power. We want you out just as much as you want to come, and we want you back as quickly as possible. To meet the continuing needs of the services men between the ages of 18 and 30 are being called up to the forces unless they are urgently needed as key men in vital work of reconstruction.[34]

To go beyond these guidelines said Attlee, would be to create chaos.

It was not enough to satisfy the critics. Why was it not possible to match the ambitions of the US military to reduce manpower from over 8 million to 2½ million in a single year? *The Times* commented:

It may well be that there are serious practical obstacles to a substantial increase of releases . . . But unless they are fully explained and fully understood by the men in the forces, nothing can prevent the chaos which Mr Attlee rightly fears. It is already being widely reported, on the one hand, that the Ministry of Labour does not want men to be released 'too quickly', and on the other hand, that many military commanders are resisting the concentration of units and commands which demobilization makes inevitable, thus clogging the flow of releases. If these dangerous and contradictory reports are not to gain wider credence there must be no further delay in publishing the precise numbers of men and women in each release group in the different services and their distribution in the various theatres of war.[35]

But open government was not on the agenda. After five years of largely covert activity, secrecy was endemic to the service departments and the civilian ministries. It therefore came as a shock when, at the end of September, Field Marshal Montgomery spoke out in favour of slowing down the pace of demobilisation for officers 'in practically all areas of the services'. One of his concerns was for the British presence in Germany, where 'many units would not be able to fulfil their tasks' unless officers were held back. At the same time it was accepted that 'officers who have qualified for nothing but war are likely to be the hardest to place satisfactorily in professions, and a delayed start can only increase that difficulty'.[36]

Meanwhile, the pressure from industry continued to build, finding dissatisfaction within the forces and criticism from the press and Opposition. On 2 October, a further concession was announced: half a million more than planned would be released by the end of the year. In the event, it was not as easy as that; Bevin's plan still had a sting. Logic, and distance, dictated that the additional releases should come from home-based forces rather than overseas, even if this upset the age and service rules. From the opposition benches, Churchill made the point:

Let us take an extreme example. If, for instance, 100 men have to be kept idle in England, because 10 men higher up on the list cannot yet be brought home from Hong Kong, or Rangoon, or Calcutta ... everyone would admit that that would be pushing a good principle to absurdity.

I would rather address myself to the 10 men and, by substantial additions to their pay or bonus or leave on release, and by special care for their future employment or otherwise, make up to them any disappointments which they may feel because others lower down on the list have got out before them.[37]

But the government was not ready to take the bait. It was best to proceed steadily. The dread of stirring up trouble among troops in India and the Far East by blatantly flouting the sacred age and service rule far outweighed any credit that might be gained from beating the critics at their own game.

CHAPTER THREE

'Depression, Jealousy and Resentment'

Army psychologist's warning note

We see them here and there already in our streets, those straight, bronzed figures, moving with a precision that no civilian suit can disguise, although the outward bonds of discipline have been escaped and we wonder what they are taking back home in their minds.

We shall not easily discover it. Their stories, their service slang, their new habits, preferences and prejudices, will be more easily understood than the inner man.[1]

Some will come home riding on the crest of a wave of jubilations, fit and brown, and bursting with tales and ideas, having made new friends, and finding the old job kept warm for them. Some will come home maimed in body, facing a prospect over-shadowed by a sense of frustration; others will return to realise acutely for the first time the poignancy of war-time losses – home, effects, relatives gone in the great catastrophes.[2]

The *War Cry* had a way of cutting through the bureaucratic guff. Its evangelical style and tendency to sentimentalise was not to everyone's taste. But the Salvation Army was one of the few bodies with an interest in demobilisation to realise that the civic challenge of accommodating over four million service personnel could not be met by a simple application of a rule book.

Yes, there had to be jobs to go to, houses to live in, a welfare system to take away fear – and an army of officials to administer these noble objectives. But there was a vital element missing.

There is little public feeling now for the man leaving the Services. He may once have been treated by the public with propitiatory fêtes and rites, like a sacred sacrificial animal, but naturally, now that the war is over, he is an anachronism, and any difficulties he may have in becoming a civilian he must handle as best he can, with few social agencies to help him.

It would be easy to exaggerate the extent and the depth of these disturbances, and it would be tempting to shut our eyes and to argue the problem in terms of intrapsychic conflict, but it would be folly to assume that it is a problem too small for consideration, easy to understand, one to be dismissed as a natural consequence of demobilisation which time will heal.[3]

This was said on 10 October 1946. The speaker was Lieutenant Colonel T. F. Main, one-time psychiatric adviser to the Director of Military Training, an unsung hero of his profession who dared to articulate what his masters preferred not to know.

As early as March 1944, Main had warned

The demobilisation period is likely to present many problems of behaviour in our army. Many of these will be considerably influenced by the degree of efficiency with which the demobilisation mechanism works, but others will be the inevitable result of the fact that some men will be demobilised a long time before others and the justice of the selectivity of the process will not prevent unrest and discontent. It will not be a sufficient solution to these problems to give continual reminders to soldiers of the necessity for patience.

As he saw it, and how right he was, the very prospect of demobilisation

. . . is likely to lead to a loosening of the bonds of mutual effort and of the larger group loyalties which sprang up in the period of national danger. The social conscience of the individual . . . will be weakened and there will be a return of personal ambition and self-centredness which will express itself in the desire for privilege and requests for 'special consideration'. Appeals to the army to continue to carry a burden for the sake of the nation will meet with little response now, and it will be difficult to convince our armies as a whole that the national welfare warrants further voluntary acceptance of minimal individual satisfactions and rewards, of separation from home, and of military discipline and service. The return of personal interest will thus be coupled with . . . complaints of unfairness; . . . indiscipline; depression; and epidemics of jealousy and resentment against different sections of the nation.

Bearing this in mind, the authorities should not have been surprised when in late January 1946, 2,000 RAF personnel in India, Ceylon and Singapore went on strike in protest at the slow rate of demobilisation or when three months later, 258 men of the 13th Battalion of the Parachute Regiment refused orders at Muar Camp near Kuala Lumpur.[4] But the heavy-handed response – five years' hard labour for eight of the Para 'mutineers', for example, and two years' hard for another 247 (later quashed on grounds of trial irregularities) – suggested that Colonel Main's appeal for understanding had not reached overseas.

In a War Office paper intended for broadcasters transmitting to British forces, Main identified what he believed would be the salient features of demobilisation.

Grumbles about the 'unfairness' of any demobilisation scheme and about those responsible for it.

Eagerness to take part in the scramble for jobs and

unwillingness to participate in a co-ordinated demobilisation; increase of demands for privilege for certain groups and individuals; 'hard luck' stories and grouses; increase of malingering and petty crime; desertion and absence without leave.

Seriously increased discontent at the difference of financial reward between soldiers and civilians, and at the money 'lost' by remaining in the army.

Loss of loyalty to the army as a whole and certain of its leaders.

Unpopularity of politicians, and loss of faith in certain national figures; a search for the causes of war and an inability to believe that the whole blame for the war rests on any one people; search for personal scapegoats among our own and other nations.

Growth of belief in certain quarters that the war was hardly worthwhile; and the scrutinising of every national proposal for evidence of partisanship and self-seeking.

Resentment about inequality of sacrifice during the war and the demobilisation period towards civilians, munition workers, women-workers, our allies, the War Office, etc. A general desire for scapegoats on which soldiers can fix their bitterness and resentment descending also on certain early-demobilised groups especially those from the Home Forces.

A wide belief in men abroad that nobody cares about them and their fate. A feeling of hopelessness, impotent anger, and despair. Depression sometimes to the extent of suicide.

An increase of anxiety about wives' infidelity and an

increased tendency to exaggerate the incidence of this, which may be fairly high anyhow.

A widespread desire for pleasure-seeking holidays, parties, dancing, drinking and general social enjoyment. These desires will arise and be spontaneously catered for in the population at home, but the soldier abroad, having less opportunity for satisfaction of this sort, will resent it in others and suggest that those at home are not interested in the nation, and only in having a good time.[5]

The symptoms began to show as soon as the laughter died on the last victory celebration. In a sample survey, Main estimated that a quarter of non-prisoner repatriates were as unsettled as the most unsettled former prisoners of war.

The feeling of post-war anti-climax building to resentment against civilians, and vice versa, was analysed with grand self-perception by Maurice Merritt:

Demobbed and totally free of the army and its jurisdiction, the longed-for occasion had arrived. It was as if you were waiting for something to happen which did not. Somehow, something seemed to be missing.

In 1939 no one knew how long the war would last, but when the Armistice did arrive, lots of thoughts and secret hopes and fears that had been subdued by the exigencies of war started to ferment in one's mind.

No soldier in the battle zone at the height of action would

ever have considered that he might at a later date wish to be back in uniform, yet it was hard to settle down to a way of life which, although longed for a short while ago, now seemed alien and difficult to accept . . .

Perhaps egoism or conceit on my part prompted me to imagine that on my return to England to be demobbed after six years spent abroad, a tumultuous welcome would be waiting, and many civilians would be eager to hear stories, true or false, about the various campaigns, or how many Jerries you actually shot!

It did not happen that way at all, actually the reverse was often more apparent, for a soldier wearing his medals and a glorious tan invariably seemed to annoy civilians. This was apparent if he entered a pub. Hostile faces would turn to him, and a bystander was once heard to say, 'Lucky b . . ., look how brown he is, he's had a bloody good time.'

This kind of aloof treatment which seemed to be meted out to ex-servicemen was not a figment of the imagination and not easily dispelled during the first few weeks after arrival back home.

Many could not settle down, for the continuous activities that had encompassed different countries in his travels abroad had instilled a very restless feeling in some men. Army life, though often sworn about and maligned by a serving soldier, had taken care of many aspects that he was now responsible for, and did not always welcome.

His civilian life confined him in a much smaller orbit which proved a source of partial frustration, and sometimes had a bad influence on domestic life . . .

A serviceman on his return home often felt like a prisoner in his own environment. Often there was a wife or mother to please, a boss at work to satisfy, possibly a child or two to placate, a mortgage and insurance to attend to, home decoration to do after all the years away, and a garden to maintain.

There was no friendly chat or little exchanges of 'bull' with army pals. Some of those pals were going through the same phase of adjustment to people, conditions and routines that were entirely opposite to a life led for six years in a wartime army.[6]

It was true, as Main had said, that what in normal times would be counted as minor irritations swelled now into major injustices.

My experience of being demobbed and coming home was mixed. A warm welcome from wife and family, relations and near neighbours, but not from my church who had for some time been collecting for a party to welcome returning servicemen home. After being home for three or four weeks, during which I attended church two or three times, but wondered why neither the minister nor church officials ever spoke to me . . . I met one of them in town one day and asked him what was wrong. The answer I got was that the church had held the party three weeks before I or a few others got home, and that they felt ashamed. As far as I know they never said sorry to any of us.[7]

For some, the sense of let-down started with the journey home.

We arrived in Toulon on Christmas Day 1945 and it was, of course, snowing. We were then held up because there was no officer to sign for the two railway wagons that made up my part of the train. As an NCO I then approached the railway authority and I was allowed to do the signing. We left Toulon about four hours late. Our journey took nearly two days and I remember seeing the river Seine as we went over the military bridge around Paris.

Some time after, we arrived in Dieppe and were put into accommodation that to say the least was disgusting. From where we were we could see our boats in the Channel. Their movement on the tide was about 12 to 14 feet up and down. We were told that there was absolutely no chance of our boarding until the sea subsided, so in horrible accommodation we went to bed! Lo and behold, we had only been asleep about four hours (on and off) when we were shouted into wakefulness and told we would board immediately.

We were loaded on to trucks and taken to the docks. The boats were still going up and down on the tide by some 15 feet, and we had a hard job to get aboard. We finally boarded and were kept waiting about another two hours. By this time most of the RAF blokes were seasick and unfit to travel. Nevertheless, we were eventually forced to sail under threat of being returned to our units. We eventually came into Newhaven and were installed in railway carriages that had been in a siding for some time and were coated in a deep film of hoar frost. Of course, in true RAF tradition, there was no heat and we travelled to London Paddington without any. On arrival we were loaded on to open trucks and conveyed across London in the sleet and snow to St Pancras and installed in coaches at about 85–90 degrees of heat. We were now on our way up the country via Leamington etc. to Cosford where we were detrained on to the wooden platform there. We were now in somewhat of a state and starting to come down with severe colds and other complaints. It wasn't over yet, and after about 1½ hours our truck transport arrived to convey us, not to Cosford *half a mile away*, but to Hednesford 19 miles away, and it was still sleeting.

We arrived at Hednesford into an unoccupied demob wing and were then detrucked and left to ourselves after about 45 minutes. A corporal arrived with billet keys and we were left to make our own arrangements for beds. It transpired the following day that two miles away, on another wing, the duty staff had lit the fires and the dining rooms were all in action awaiting us. Out of about 110 of us, 18 were in sick quarters for two weeks, myself included, with pneumonia and the rest escaped with minor troubles.

I was eventually demobbed on Jan. 6th, 1946, and arrived home on Jan. 7th, 1946. My sister who had been waiting for four or five days was shopping in Coventry when I arrived at the front door.[8]

For others, the welcome home was not exactly joyous.

I think it odd that nobody came to Southampton or the demob centre, Hednesford (30 miles from home), to welcome me. Although my parents had a car, I was turned out to catch a bus. The wife was out when I returned to the house.

With hindsight, I don't think anybody wished for me to reappear to upset their life and I certainly did not want to come back to civvy street. I was too organised in the RAF.[9]

Running through so many reminiscences is the conviction that the war had weakened the moral backbone of the country. Thomas Hanley was 28 when he left the Navy. Newly married, he decided to move from Lancashire to Devon where he imagined the environment would be conducive to a 'settled existence'. After fifty years he says it is hard to forget the impact of disillusionment.

I found business, even in a small seaside resort, was run on chicanery and spivvery. I found that men, some not much older than myself, who had managed either by reason of age or health to miss a call-up controlled all aspects of public life. In an atmosphere of rationing and shortages, interlopers like myself had a hard time. Helping hands were weighted by self-interest. Even persons of the utmost integrity, after six years of war, were motivated by self-preservation. It wasn't so much of 'dog eat dog', rather to make sure that no opportunity of easing one's existence was missed. I doubt if a single Englishman did not avail himself of the help of the 'black market'. Expedience was the name of the game. A returned serviceman, generally tired, used to depending on his 'mates' and with a reasonable sense of values, could find the going tough. His main attribute was the stoic acceptance of the inevitable, so much a part of his service life. His formative years had been taken from him. At least he was alive![10]

The shortages of ordinary household comforts were so bad as to become a joke.

In another village some children called the local coalman 'uncle'. It took me a little while to realise why, even then it was only when one of the local lads with a grin all over his face said that some folks would go to any length to get an extra bag of nutty slack.[11]

The pain of realising that a new life had to be made was all the greater for the disabled.

When my brother eventually arrived home, complete with an artificial leg, the whole household revolved around him. He had difficulty sleeping because of nightmares and we all took it in turns to keep him amused by playing cards, darts, and things like that. My main job was to go out walking with him – and to get help when he fell over. It sounds terrible – but I remember it with great affection.

One thing that always stuck in my brother's memory was that the only officials to meet him off the train in Shrewsbury were ones from the Salvation Army armed with dressing gowns, blankets and other useful things. When my brother died, three years ago, he still remembered their goodness and left them money in his will.

One other thing that I remember well is this. When my family arrived at the hospital in St Helens my brother's words were, 'What the Hell are you doing here?' My mother's answer was, 'We've come to see you,' at which my brother said, 'I don't know why. No one's come to see these other poor buggers.' I remember the ward was full of wounded men and it is true that I never saw any visitors bar us. This is not to say that there were no other visitors – I just never saw any.

There was one radio in the centre of the ward and it was continually being turned on and off as the men argued with each other. They were all in such a desperate state – the ones with arms missing hated the ones who had two arms and the ones with legs missing hated the ones with two legs and so on. It really was most sad – they were all 'bomb happy', as the saying was then.[12]

The government was not entirely unaware of servicemen's misgivings and grievances, real or imagined. And it had an answer, of sorts: the Resettlement Advice Service. The first priority was to help repatriated prisoners of war. In mid-1944, a residential centre was made ready at Derby where vocational guidance, psychiatric and welfare workers co-operated on developing four- to six-week residential courses to help POWs ease their way back into the community.

> Men who have lived abroad for a number of years are apt to find difficulty in settling and readjusting themselves to life in this country. Experience has shown that these difficulties are present in a fairly specific form and often to greater extent in the ex-prisoner of war, whose separation from home has been wider and whose knowledge of his own country and people, and of war-time conditions, is apt to be confused and inadequate. The Civil Resettlement Units will, in fact, be re-orientation and recovery units. While the intention is that they shall be run in close co-operation with the Ministry of Labour, they will in no way be job-finding agencies. Their main function will be to help repatriates to re-orientate themselves to life as civilians.[13]

Twenty centres were planned, each capable of handling up to 250 ex-prisoners. With an average course of five weeks, the centres would cater for a total of 20,000 men over six months, a modest ambition given that the number of British prisoners held behind enemy lines was 172,592.

Equally modest, at least on paper, were the proposals for occupying the time spent at the resettlement centres.

1. Discussions on current affairs and problems.
2. Elementary training under highly qualified instructors in

such crafts as woodworking, metal work and building. This training will not be vocational, but will have for its objective the stimulation of interest and the recapturing of the enjoyment of the use of old skills as well as providing amenable recreation.

3. Visits to Government Training Centres.
4. Visits to Employment Exchanges.
5. Visits to industrial undertakings, businesses and other organisations.
6. Physical rehabilitation, games and PT.

It is hard to avoid the impression that the officer class were not expected to be part of this exercise.

On the credit side was the allocation at each unit of a resident psychiatrist,

... to give practical help to the repatriates with regard to their domestic and social affairs – particularly with regard to adjusting themselves to changed conditions at home and in understanding and accepting, as far as possible, the difficulties which both they and their families may be having in settling down in harmony with each other.

Such counselling did not extend to the general run of servicemen. Their resettlement advice offices, 367 of them by 1947, spread across the country on the same pattern as employment exchanges, were concerned entirely with practical matters. As envisaged by Ernest Bevin they were there to warn against the horrors that he had seen as a trade unionist after the First World War. He recalled how, in 1918,

> no explanation was given to the country about the transition from war to peace. For example, in the London Docks, although the normal number of men employed was 30,000, we found 100,000 applying for jobs. On demobilisation men received their gratuities and were induced to part with them on all kinds of wildcat schemes. Advice was given to them by alleged voluntary societies who disappeared after taking money from the men. Over 100,000 lorries were sold by the Government to ex-servicemen to enable them to set up in business, but most of the men lost their money in three months. Men were thoroughly disillusioned to find, on coming back to civil life, that their jobs had been given to other people. They felt they were 'nobody's children' and could turn to nobody for help and advice.[14]

Bevin was the first to admit that those who gave advice needed to do so with tact and sensitivity.

> There must be no attempt to regiment the Resettlement Advice Service. We must have a human outlook and be patient in dealing with the men who come to us. They have good reason to be unsettled and disturbed in their minds and we must, therefore, be sympathetic. There must be no 'official' outlook or coldness of manner. Cases will vary greatly but we

must not hesitate to give help or advice even if a case is not covered by instructions. Every man must be dealt with as an individual in need of help and advice.

At the same time there was a tendency to equate resettlement advice with the nuts and bolts of starting up again – employment, training, finding one's way through the official rule book of do's and don'ts. The intimacies of family life were barely referred to and there was no attempt to guide young men and women through crises that were part and parcel of T. F. Main's clinical experience. Writing in the *Journal of Mental Science*, Main detailed four case studies which he believed were symptomatic of inadequate care. His first concerned a young man seen by him earlier in the year.

In 1939 at the age of 18½ he joined the Army, and in 1940 went to the Middle East with an armoured unit. Three times in the next three years his unit got to the salt flats of El Ageila, and twice it was driven back. During this time his home and his father and mother were destroyed by bombs. He lived, mainly in the sand and sun, a life full of thrills but little day-to-day interest with the compensations of tight comradeship and freedom from responsibility for the major decisions of the day. During these three years he had two leaves in Cairo and spent £200 in two weeks in hotels, cabarets and brothels. He returned to his own land last year and immediately fell into difficulties. Though a young man of 25 he had never been in an English pub, and panicked on the two occasions when he tried to ask for a drink. He felt awkward because he did not know what behaviour was normal in any social situation and felt that he was a foreigner, liable to be looked and laughed at. Any public places – a café, a railway station, a dance hall, a bus – brought up problems of behaviour and common convention which made him feel inferior and ignorant. How to behave as a visitor in somebody else's home puzzled and worried him, and he was afraid of young women, diffident and uncertain how to address them, unsure of the proper approach, and unable to decide whether women were Madonnas or harlots. It was difficult for him to think that they might just be human beings like himself. So, unsure of himself, somewhat lost and bewildered, and unable to feel settled at a home in his own city, his sleep was disturbed and he became morose, angry with civilisation, bitter about the lack of comradeship in civilian life, quiet, asocial and depressed. He wanted to rejoin the Army or join the Palestine Police Force or to emigrate, but felt too ill because of recurrent nightmares even to take up simple work. When he was seen he had spent all his gratuity in a vain search for enjoyment, and had come to the end of his tether.

The sad inadequacy felt by this veteran of the desert campaign was demonstrated yet more poignantly in the case of a former prisoner of war and regular soldier.

Now 26 years old, he had been brought up in a slum home, from which he escaped into the Army in an endeavour to lead a decent, clean, orderly life. He enjoyed the discipline, the regularity of pay and food, and began to respect himself. He seriously hoped to reform his widowed mother, who disgraced him even before his slum neighbours by drinking too much. The war broke out when he was abroad. His great pride in his unit for its subsequent fighting record suffered a terrible blow when he and it were captured at Tobruk. He was then subjected to the dirt and disorganisation of Italian prison camps and had to fight for his food with other men who, too, had once known civilised manners. When placed with Indians in Salonika he endeavoured to uphold his own high standards of behaviour and refused to take part in the scramble for garbage, feeling contaminated by and guilty about the primitive savagery of the struggle for existence. When he was transferred to Germany he joined in the ordered, intensely democratic life of a German prison camp and settled usefully, but lived for the day when he would be released – Britain would be fine; the people there were decent and homely and clean; there was freedom in Britain, and comradeship and honesty. In his need for affection he often dreamed of his mother, whom he saw as a clean, thrifty Scotswoman, and made all kinds of excuses to himself about why she had never written to him. He had fantasies about his home-coming, felt sure it would resolve all his hopings, and planned to attend night school and become a wireless engineer.

On repatriation he went back to his home street and found

a stranger in his home. His mother had moved, and he found her living in one dirty slum room. He was shortly the centre of a drunken civilian cheering party that he tried vainly to enjoy. He had to sleep on a mattress on the floor for a week or two and began to get angry at life; his fantasies had been destroyed and life faced him as it was – difficult, dirty and ill-organised, demanding further efforts of him. It was easy to exchange trivial commonplaces with people, but nobody understood how he felt. He resented sympathy, and felt fury at the bomb stories that defensive civilians thrust upon him. He could not understand how people could hold such empty values and knew that they could never understand his own. In despair he picked up several street women, and there, too, found disgust and despair at the emptiness of the relationship. He spent his gratuity on drink, went to London and slept in air-raid shelters, had violent feelings of destructiveness and murderous wishes towards policemen – 'Smug and happy as if nothing had happened.' He was admitted to hospital, violent, suspicious, bitter about Britain, and scornful about any offers of help – 'I've seen your sort before; you're trying to get my story so that you can laugh at me.' He said he was a slum rat – 'Let's have no pretending – send me back to the filth where I belong.' He ground his teeth and clenched his fists constantly and hit viciously at doors and walls. A week later he was classified as schizophrenic.

Main was dealing here with extremes. The circumstances were tragic and demanded attention but they were not typical, as he readily acknowledged. His other two case studies were illustrative of more violent and widespread sickness. One story was anecdotal but easily recognised by many families, as letters to the authors confirm.

I heard a woman behind me in the crowd gossiping about a more recently demobilised commando – 'Two and a half years! Back only a fortnight and she doesn't know what to do with him. He sits in the back room by himself. Won't speak to anybody, won't go out, won't read. Won't do nothing. She doesn't know what to do. There'll be trouble there.

And then there was the modest, gentle character who felt as if he was being swept along by barely understood events that were, in any case, beyond his control.

He was a labourer before the war, was placed in the Pioneer Corps during the war years, and although he missed his wife at first, settled down to good work of a routine nature. He had comradeship and had no worries about money, food or a job. He got on well with his officers and his fellows and felt proud of his uniform. When he returned to civilian life he felt himself a stranger and was badly puzzled by regulations about food and clothing and shortages, and felt inferior in the presence of people who understood these things and handled them casually. Things were too much for him to understand and he felt foolish and shy before the complexity of life. He kept to the house, could no longer take his wife to the cinema, and resented the fact that his wife was now managing his affairs, and was trying to get him a job, although he recognised that it was necessary for somebody to do this in the face of his own incapacity and lack of initiative. He developed headaches and indigestion and went to his doctor, but was too ashamed to confess his own puzzlement at the civilian world and quietly accepted the medicine which was given him, although he felt it would do him no good. 'If only he had asked me what the real trouble was I might have told him, so I just told him about my stomach.'

The resettlement advice offices failed to help these casualties; failed even to recognise them. Why? A large part of the blame rests with the Ministry of Labour where, despite Bevin's injunction about flexibility, politicians and senior officials alike imposed a narrow definition on the functions of the service.

In compiling the *Resettlement Advice Handbook*, Miss E. M. Batten, a principal in the Military Recruiting and Demobilisation Department, set the tone when she stressed that in deciding how far staff responsibilities should go, 'the operative word should be resettlement'.

The difficulty has been to plan that the Handbook should contain all that it ought to contain and yet not become unwieldy. I have tried to suggest all the more immediate problems of resettlement. We shall probably have to add more as time goes on and we discover the sort of questions which are asked. In view of the experience reported to you that the Repatriated Prisoners were more concerned with domestic and personal matters than with employment, I have endeavoured to be comprehensive without being too detailed with regard to such matters, at the same time covering all questions of employment, training, etc.[15]

In other words, notwithstanding evidence to suggest that finding jobs was not the very first priority of returning servicemen, Miss Batten stuck doggedly to the idea that that was what the resettlement office should be all about. Other than routine cases

. . . should be referred to a Government Department or local Authority for the help he needs, if that is possible, and should only be referred to a voluntary organisation if and when no statutory provision exists to meet that need.

Her senior W. J. Neden, Principal Assistant Secretary at the Department, began by taking a more liberal stance.

If we are to live up to the implication of the title 'Resettlement Advice Service' we must be prepared to advise on problems which are *not* related solely to employment and this means breaking new ground. There are many indications that men now in the Forces will, on release, be primarily interested in personal and domestic problems of immediate concern to themselves and their families and that getting back to work will be a secondary though important consideration.[16]

The brave words fell victim to a staff recruitment policy which relied chiefly on attracting applicants from within the Ministry of Labour, those preferably 'with social service experience' whose knowledge of the wider world would be topped up by a 'three month course for personnel managers but adapted to our purpose'.

However well intentioned, this little band of aid workers was not best suited to cope with the revelations of T. F. Main's consulting room. As the service got under way (the first resettlement advice office was ready for business in early June 1945), W. J. Neden confessed that there were 'personal and domestic problems with which officials as such are not in the best position to deal with'.[17] His solution was to refer cases to appropriate voluntary bodies. It was a neat example of passing the buck, all the cheekier for having followed on from a clutch of inter-ministry exchanges on the inadequacy of the voluntary sector.

Throughout its four-year life, the Resettlement Service was essentially a stopgap for 'general advice and assistance' on a fairly mundane level, which was what Ernest Bevin had intended in the first place. Time and again, he referred back to men 'who, after the last war, put all their resources into a chicken farm or similar precarious venture'.[18] These were the victims Bevin wanted to help; perhaps their problems – jobs, work, money – were the only ones a man with his experience could comprehend.

Within this narrow context, the resettlement advice offices may have achieved their purpose. At the peak of their activity, they coped with nearly 50,000 enquiries a week. To take a month at random, in March 1946, there were close on 191,000 enquiries across the country. Of these, 10,000 were sufficiently routine to be dealt with by reception clerks. Another 67,000 enquiries were cleared by qualified staff. But then, yet another 60,000 enquiries were referred to other government departments or to local authorities. This left just 4,000 cases which were thought to be quite beyond the abilities of the civil service. These were handed on to the voluntary organisations.[19]

Notwithstanding the number of zeros on every figure, the impression remains that resettlement officers were paper-pushers whose chief function was to act as ciphers for other welfare workers. Certainly they were not overwhelmed with work. After April 1947 they took on responsibility for issuing passports without disturbing the even tenor of their days. Maybe it was not altogether surprising that when the service closed in 1949 all records were treated as 'confidential waste' and destroyed.[20]

The question remains, could the government have done more to help in the mass transition from military to civilian life? The conventional denial assumes a lack of resources, not least an army of social workers. But it is one of the great illusions that high-level professional qualifications are a prerequisite for giving sympathetic common sense advice. It is accepted that T. F. Main's first two case studies were for the skilled psychiatrist, as too were the 'severe disturbances . . . revealed in the public courts, in the separation orders, in the charges of attempted suicide or murder or child neglect, and in the Juvenile Courts, where children from a disturbed domestic scene show the social forms of their distress.'

This was only part of the story, however.

The mildest forms of industrial unsettlement may be present on our own doorsteps, in those employees who have returned from the Services and cannot settle easily into their once familiar regime, who want to apply for other jobs, who are restless and dissatisfied with their careers, who drink more than they did, or who are quieter and less at ease than they were.[21]

What these people needed above all was a friendly and sensitive listener who could explain the commonality of war weariness and its symptoms. With adequate training, resettlement officers might have performed this role. But they were better at filling in forms for others down the bureaucratic line, or compiling their statistics. It was an awful warning of what would happen when the welfare state was launched; here was the first example of the caring society losing its way in bureaucratic shortcomings.

A second line of defence is to claim that there was insufficient knowledge of the trauma experienced by those who had to adjust to domesticity after four, five or six years in the military. In fact, there was plenty of evidence to show what an abrupt switch of environment could lead to. As early as 1940, psychiatrists were observing 'evacuation psychosis' in older men and women evacuated from their homes to bomb-free areas in the countryside. The psychosis showed itself in depression, apathy and confusion. It was the same with children, except in their case there was less public sympathy. Letters to newspapers aired complaints against billeted youngsters who were said to be rebellious, rude and delinquent. Middle-class families assumed that this was how their social inferiors behaved all the time. An old joke was revived. The only effect of compulsory education, it was said, was to reduce the height of the writing on lavatory walls. But the more perceptive commentators pointed out that disruptive behaviour was characteristic of all young people who had been uprooted from their families and dumped down in unfamiliar surroundings.

It should not have taken great imagination to extend these behavioural patterns to the armed forces or to anticipate widespread problems of emotional adjustment. Two factors weighed against an enlightened policy.

The first had to do with the nature of the war and the way in which it had been conducted. In contrast to 1914–18, when all the action was 'over there', the civilians of 1939–45 felt themselves to be in the front line. The German bombing offensive made sure of that.

Thousands of men overseas had a hard life, but when compared with the everyday routine of civilians back home, some soldiers had been infinitely better off than their folk at home.

Some wives in Blighty thought that the men overseas had had a good time whilst they had endured incessant bombing.[22]

For John Peacock, returning to Liverpool, the evidence of hardship was only too apparent.

As I made my way home all I could see was devastation, buildings and houses, you name it, bombed to the ground. Then I noticed queues of people outside the butcher's shop, bakery shop, grocery shop, greengrocery and fish shop. All clutching their ration books. They had to go from shop to shop queuing for hours. Homes still bombed-out shells. Huge air-raid shelters still in what were beautiful parts. Ships burned out in Seaforth Docks. Large concrete blocks along the shore. Having to go to large stores to have your name put on a list for a pram. Yes, if you had the money, you could buy anything. Yes, black market went on. The furniture one could buy had to have coupons. It was called 'utility furniture', made out of box wood. Walking miles looking for a house to rent. Still on rations.

A devastated city to live in. After five years away trying to come back to normal life, I said to myself, is this the land fit for heroes to live in? One had to be a hero to exist in it.[23]

But throughout the country, 'the population had had to undergo the endless and enervating routines of war, the long working hours, broken nights in damp air-raid shelters, food rationing, endless other restrictions and always the interminable queuing. The required dress of female munitions workers, with their turbaned hair, long smocks and clogs, hardly compared favourably with their sisters in smart military uniforms. There could be no swaggering for them. Some of the soldiers' letters home (determinedly cheerful as they were) painted a picture of adventure and excitement calculated to raise the envy of anyone in blacked out, austerity Britain.'[24]

Civilians were not easily persuaded that soldiers who had come through without visible injuries deserved any special privileges, or special treatment. After the euphoria of the welcome home there was little sympathy for ex-servicemen who did not immediately knuckle down to the practicalities of life.

Commonwealth and American civilians who had not seen or felt anything of the war at first hand were inclined to be more understanding. This was particularly true of the United States where the urgency of demobilisation was matched by a readiness to devote to the task all necessary medical and social resources. In an effort to inspire a complementary movement in Britain, T. F. Main circulated War Office colleagues with a paper by a senior consultant in neuro-psychiatry to the American army. The writer identified a deep-rooted malaise in many of his patients.

Examination usually shows little more than is apparent on the surface. The emotional tone is consistently one of sadness. Often these patients have some insight into their condition. They say they are 'down and out', have 'lost their nerve' or that they are 'no good to themselves or anybody else'. Sometimes they insist that nothing is the matter and are resentful because their officers or comrades have thought that anything was wrong with them. Those with insight say that absence from home, delay in receiving mail, anxiety over the welfare of their families or discouragement over the prospect of soon returning is responsible for their down-heartedness. They agree that their attitude is not their usual one nor that of the good soldier but say that they cannot help it, they reproach themselves for it or they take refuge in a sullen attitude and say that they 'have done their bit'. Not infrequently it is discovered that such patients are ruminating over the death of comrades or some particularly distressing experience in action that, although it made little impression at the time, now fills their thoughts and dreams. Sometimes they reproach themselves for infidelity, neglect of duty or some slight and perfectly unintentional injury they may have done to others. Lapses into alcoholism or apparently unexplainable acts of delinquency are not infrequent.

Treatment began with an early consultation with a psychiatrist, a recommendation that had already proved effective for 'not less than ten thousand [army] patients with mental and nervous disorders'. The figure was made doubly impressive by the date on the article – 21 December 1918. It was a sobering thought that the standards of treatment achieved by the Americans after the First World War were still beyond the British after the Second.

If civilian resentment was a strong counter to any proposal for returning servicemen and women to be made a special case, it was reinforced by an equally strong British reserve, a reluctance to bring into the public domain matters that, well, were better left to the intimacy of the home. The inhibition factor was illustrated at the 1945 conference of the Soldiers', Sailors' and Airmen's Families' Association, that same conference at which W. J. Neden admitted that his resettlement officers at the Ministry of Labour were not up to dealing with certain 'personal and domestic problems'. Delegates spent much of the first session listening to Mr Neden and to a spokesman from the Ministry of Pensions. At the conclusion, the chairman, Air Vice-Marshal Sir Norman MacEwen, broke across questions and answers on the thorny question of the repayment of loans for buying prams.

I have a question raised by Berkshire. Matrimonial problems, co-operation with Marriage Guidance Council, Moral Welfare Associations, and other local bodies. My answer to that is, this matrimonial question is so very serious that the more we co-operate with all associations dealing with it and get their advice and help and give our advice and help, the better. I think it is the only thing to do. We cannot take it all on our own shoulders; we must ask other people to help us with these very difficult problems. At the present moment we cannot give the answer, and I do not think anybody in the world could. We are trying our best to get over it.[25]

And with that, they broke for lunch.

The conference did not return to the subject. Yet SSAFA was one of the leading agencies advising servicemen and women on domestic issues, a task supported by government funding. Some discussion on the wider issues – as requested by the Berkshire delegation – would seem to have been in order. Unfortunately, it was just not done to introduce certain matters into open forum.

Recognising the many limitations of the voluntary sector (the most obvious being its reliance on unpaid workers who were not necessarily best suited to their responsibilities), it was still the last hope of servicemen and women trying to cope with personal crises. It was safe to assume, with T. F. Main, that many would not consult their doctor 'because of fear of impending insanity' and that 'some of the men in great but secret distress would be furious if their problems were openly broached'. And psychiatrists were thin on the ground. But mixing in with others of like background and experience – old comrades – as in the British Legion, could help to put individual worries and grievances into broader perspective. It was one – often the only – way towards self-knowledge and self-help.

The *British Legion Journal* of the 1940s was a rich source

of advice to and grouses from ex-servicemen. The advice could be pretty anodyne.

> Successful resettlement will not be achieved until the ex-Serviceman feels himself a real civilian again and a full member of the civilian community, and he will not obtain that feeling until he has successfully mixed in again with the non-service employees in his firm. This mixing-in is, therefore, a very important part of resettlement which everyone should do their utmost to further. It will depend largely on mutual understanding and goodwill.[26]

The grouses less so:

> Eighth Army Man Speaks Up: Sir – we are very very dissatisfied with conditions in this country. Between us we have been in N. Africa, Italy, Burma, Normandy, Holland, Belgium, France and Germany; some of us have lost limbs, children, wives and homes in the blitzes – we are the people who have fought for Britain and we are getting a very shabby deal – until this is remedied there will be great unrest and labour troubles.
>
> No: 1: Our food is appalling – one day's honest food a week, and with our miserable pensions and poor jobs now some of us are maimed – we cannot afford to buy profiteering meals for ourselves and families outside our homes.
>
> No. 2: Our wives are exhausted, some neurotic and ill through war work, lack of essential food and then queuing for hours.

No. 3: We cannot even keep warm through lack of fuel.

No. 4: We are living in squalor almost through housing shortage. We who have been recently in Europe know Holland and Belgium are recovering faster than any other countries and already have more and better essential foods generally. We were there and know it.

We are not interested in Germany now we are back – we are, for a change, interested in ourselves. USA, that has suffered little, could easily feed Europe and leave us to recover.

We ask you to let every branch know how the ex-Serviceman feels and help us before we start demonstrating. This, the most heavily taxed and victimised (bureaucratically) country in the world, should have at least some 'fruits of *our* Victory'. To commence with, we need considerable increases of essential rationed foods quickly.

Tell the Ministries for a body of Alamein and Normandy fighting Eighth Army – Leslie Smith, L/Cpl Portsmouth.[27]

And there was always a correspondent who could be relied upon to regain a sense of balance. Here is Squadron Leader Vernon Noble with his assessment of debits and credits from wartime service.

I HAVE LOST –
Five years of married life; the interest and pleasure of watching and guiding my boy between the ages of five and ten. Two pounds in weight. A weakness for grumbling at little things – 'fussing' as my wife used to call it. My desire to fly any

more. A conviction that I didn't know what fear was. An urge to visit foreign lands. Forty-seven friends (killed on operations). My youthful laughter.

I HAVE GAINED –
A firm belief in human nature – brotherhood, camaraderie. Deep furrows in my cheeks, lines under my eyes. An ability to walk upright and talk straight. Appreciation of the beauty of clouds when you look down on them. A more satisfactory sense of values which doesn't include a former urge to make a fortune. A knowledge that the Dutch have a mixture of the plainest and yet the loveliest and bravest girls I've ever met. A never-dying memory of the thrill, sickness and beauty of dusk take-offs and dawn returns.

I SHALL ALWAYS RETAIN –
A dislike of saluting and being saluted. A feeling that girls were never meant to wear uniform. On the whole, I think I'm up on the credit side, except for the loss of friends.[28]

The running theme of the *British Legion Journal* was the need to recreate the spirit of companionship.

On demob, few of us found things to be quite as we expected them. The single fellows noticed particularly that the old friendships were hard to rekindle, while new ones, though easy to make, were hard to keep.

There are many reasons for this. Some of the dearest of

our pals were left out there; some have settled down elsewhere; and many are far too busy with their own particular post-war problems to be able to give us much of their time. We soon find, perhaps, that our own thoughts and plans begin to turn inwards in an unhealthy manner. This can lead to all sorts of pitfalls, not the least of which is self-pity, and should be shunned like early-morning PT.

Whatever you do, when you become a civvy again, don't give up hope of finding the companionship which made Service life so satisfying at times. There are many thousands of other young men and women of your own age who are experiencing exactly the same feelings . . .

If you find yourself sinking back into 'It doesn't matter' . . . don't! Keep your precious individuality; keep the muckin' in, chins-up attitude . . . The world needs just precisely that indomitable spirit. If you find that the people at home haven't got it to the same degree, give it to them. Don't change and become like them: raise them up to your level. Whatever you do, don't get browned-off.[29]

Those with time on their hands were urged to find kindred spirits in the Scouts or Boys' Brigade or in youth hostelling.

This is perhaps the hobby which has most to offer to the war-weary ex-Serviceman or woman. There is nothing so healing to tired nerves and minds as a walk along the quieter roads and lanes of Britain. You miss so many delightful things

when travelling in a vehicle, which are readily available to
the pedestrian. The walker can become one with the countryside in a way in which the driver or passenger never can.
It is so restful to escape from the hustle of modern life into
the refreshing tranquillity of nature.[30]

This may sound perilously close to the old admonition
handed out to public schoolboys to take regular cold
showers. But affirmation of the joy of the open road was
not inspired by fears of Legionnaires getting up to no good.
Rather, it was one way of breaking out of the lethargy of
disenchantment.

The British Legion was, and remains, a campaigning
organisation, a powerful lobby working for the interests of
former servicemen and women. Housing and employment
were dominant concerns but it also made an impact on
issues where civilian and service opinion was liable to clash
– to mutual disadvantage. A notable success was the
Legion's opposition to functionless war memorials. Statues
and monuments, declared the 1945 Conference, should be
rejected in favour of 'a communal hall, hospital, convalescent home or similar useful building'.

That same conference viewed 'with alarm the increase
in the number of organisations which deal ostensibly in
servicemen, ex-servicemen, their wives, families and other
dependants, thus cutting across the main function of the
Legion'. The overlapping of effort was a matter of genuine
concern. By early 1945 there were over 10,000 charities

linked in one way or another to the war effort. Widespread fraud was suspected but remained unproved since the majority were not even registered under the War Charities Act and were thus immune from publishing a balance sheet or opening their accounts to inspection.[31]

Of those of any significance, SSAFA was closely associated with domestic issues, though, as we have seen, the emotional strain of readjustment was given less attention than financial practicalities. Nonetheless, as beneficiaries would testify, SSAFA deserves great credit for what it did achieve.

Baby, aged 2, father serving, home hit by flying bomb. Mother, grandparents, aunt, and two elder children killed. Baby, sole survivor, dug out of debris several hours later. Taken into a SSAFA Home and finally found a suitable foster-mother.

Twin boys, aged 10, father killed in action. Placed in good Military School within two months.

Wife of serving soldier went into hospital for a serious operation. Her three children placed in SSAFA Home for one month at a moment's notice.

Two children, father serving, placed in SSAFA Home during mother's confinement. Complications set in and baby was stillborn. Stay of children extended in order to enable mother to make good recovery.

Child, aged 4, son of Sgt in RAF. Mother deserted. Child taken into SSAFA Home immediately and then found permanent home.

Boy, aged 6, father Royal Marines killed in action, mother in WRNS. Boy placed in good school.[32]

Women's groups, notably the Women's Voluntary Service (WVS), tried to make demob less of an impersonal formality. The WVS was a spin-off from the Women's Institute and Townswomen's Guilds, then very much the refuge of middle-class ladies with time on their hands and an inexhaustible capacity for bottling fruit and making jam. By early 1940, two years after its foundation, primarily to help with air-raid warnings, the WVS was a volunteer force of some 600,000 who set about 'boosting food production by gardening and poultry-keeping, organising collections of scrap metal, coping with evacuees and receiving servicemen who were often billeted with them at short notice.'[33] Such women were essentially playing their conventional domestic role on a grander scale. Or, as Herbert Morrison as Home Secretary put it, 'These magnificent women are applying the principles of good housekeeping to the job of helping to run the country in its hour of need.'

The women of one provincial centre had already mended 50,000 army socks before wholesale darning was taken on officially, when WVS adopted the feet of the army. Practically all centres did their quota in making 129,588 camouflage nets working masked, gloved and overalled – amid dust and fluff, the one thing essential being a good pair of knees, as the greater part had to be done on the floor. A nonchalant account of the patching of 200,000 green drill jungle jerseys reveals a miracle of perseverance against time; after their completion by army contractors the garments had been found to need reinforcing at shoulders and elbows for men crawling about in dense tropical undergrowth. If the Burma men could see their women-folk intent on this tedious job, we are sure they would no longer think of themselves as the 'Forgotten Army'.[34]

Earlier, at the receiving end of the Dunkirk evacuations, the WVS 'helped the men at ports and railway stations, provided tea and food, washed weary feet, wrote and telephoned messages to anxious relatives' and subsequently 'went to camps and sewed thousands of flashes and ribbons on new uniforms.'[35] Thereafter, the WVS was on hand whenever soldiers in transit needed feeding at short notice. In 1943, the service was extended to combat zones.

All this was valuable preparation for helping servicemen make the faltering move back into civilian life. The WVS was ever popping up with good ideas – organising a nursery in Northolt, for example, where children could be left while former servicemen and their wives spent a few hours in each other's company, or setting up an All Ranks Social Club as an adjunct to the RAF Rehabilitation Centre in Scarborough.[36] But their best work was with former prisoners of war. Here are the WVS ladies at Rangoon welcoming prisoners at the beginning of their homeward journey.

At the RAF station there is a large reception room set with long tables and comfy canvas chairs. The place looked rather bare at first, just red brick walls, shuttered windows, wooden tables and a stone floor. But some white sheets were soon produced to serve as tablecloths and we went out to collect bunches of lovely flowering shrubs which grow here for decoration. The next problem was vases. Someone had the bright idea of using small lacquered milk tins, and these we filled with flowers for each table. The RAF made curtains of mosquito netting, and draped muslin, coloured red, white and blue, round the top of the walls. The soft furnishings were completed by spreading a parachute, dyed a lovely golden colour, fanwise on the end of the wall.

The condition of the men seemed to vary. Many were suffering from malaria – they had had as many as sixty attacks in some cases – and some were suffering from deficiency diseases due to bad diet. It was not unusual to see a man with several days' growth of beard and a pinched white face with very little flesh on his limbs. They were touchingly careful for each other and their pets and precious belongings. Yes, they brought their pets – a duck in a basket lined with green cloth, a parrot and some kittens. The greatest treasures were some things that had been ingeniously constructed out of scraps of material: a white ensign, the standard of the Cambridgeshire Regiment, musical instruments and so on. One of the most impressive sights was to see men of the Gordons and Argyll and Sutherland Highlanders walk in their dress kilts. They had been carefully guarded and pressed all through captivity, much to the amusement of the Japs.

We saw some most peculiar clothes being worn, including some home-made hats. The shoes were made of bits of canvas, wood or any stuff that could be picked up. Quite a number had no footwear of any description. Their normal dress had consisted of a couple of squares of material caught together with string.

We talked of home and the places we all came from. They wanted to know so much about everything. We had to answer numerous questions on industrial and domestic details. Then came the fun of finding people from our own counties and towns. This was the most thrilling part of all, as we could sometimes give the men first-hand information about their families and homes. We heard of the gallant work done by doctors in the camps, stories of amputations with fret saws, of operations for appendicitis and mastoid, the latter done with an ordinary hammer and chisel, sometimes with no anaesthetic. We heard stories of men taking the rap for others, of beatings and killings, of the Salvation Army colonel who worked among the men to alleviate their sufferings, until six weeks before his release, when his mind began to go.[37]

The services had their own charities, of course. But the chief purpose of the Royal Naval Benevolent Trust, the Royal Air Force Benevolent Fund and the Army's regimental associations was to provide comfort and financial help to bereaved families and to the disabled. There was little enough in the way of support for those who had handed in their uniforms as part of the general demobilisation and there were frequent complaints from ex-servicemen that from the moment of discharge the military lost interest in them.

It was modest consolation to read in service journals the cheerful encouragement of those who had gone before. One ex-soldier wrote in the *Manchester Regiment Gazette* in April 1946:

Civvy Street is one long queue – for food, buses, pictures, shoes, and even to buy a paper! But the civilian seems to suffer more than the ex-soldier; they chafe terribly in queues, while you can stand at ease and employ the same technique as when on parade waiting for the General to arrive. This makes the tardiest bus into an express.

After the thrill of the first few days wears off, you will probably begin to feel rather flat. The sudden changes in habits, lack of real exercise (round the houses instead of a jolly 24-hour scheme), and the loss of all your old pals all combine to produce this. Fear not – it will pass. During this stage you will probably derive the keenest pleasure from an unexpected meeting with someone from Battalion – it's surprising how heart-warming it is.

By this time you will be fully launched on picking up your pre-war threads, and if you go back to your old job, will probably be surprised to find how much you have forgotten – to say nothing of how much you have never known, for there have been many changes during the war years which those on the spot have assimilated bit by bit, while to you they represent a mountain of unknown facts.

Be polite. Most civilians are so rude to each other to-day, so discourteous and unhelpful, that they seem to get a positive shock if anyone is polite to them. Often the results are astounding, especially with shopkeepers and in cafés.

But then came the word of warning that must have sounded odd to fighting men who thought they were returning as heroes to a grateful nation.

One final word – don't try and tell civilians about your experiences, even if they ask you. The two of you are talking and thinking a different language, metaphorically, and never the twain shall meet. They are as convinced as you are that they have had a hard war, and you've got to live with them from now on, so why argue?

Don't believe people who tell you nothing can be done. Discouragement and apathy are rife in Civvy Street – use your Army initiative and drive and it's surprising what can be done after all. There is still plenty of scope for the man who wants to get on; employers are desperate for men with 'go' about them. If you can't get the salary you hoped to start with take what's offered and show them what *you* have to offer. You didn't start at the top when you were called up, did you?[38]

Helpful hints came from all directions. The Salvation Army produced a weighty brochure of advice that amounted to an appeal to both sides to work it out together.

All our longings and prayers and pride of the war years will be summed up in the various expressions of greeting which will be ready for you. Perhaps there will even be a little feasting; and I know there will be much thanksgiving. Take it all! It will be your right! If they want to carry you round the hall shoulder high, give them the pleasure, no matter how uncomfortable you feel inside. If they appear to exaggerate your deeds, don't be too hard on them! Let them say it with a flourish!

Then remember that welcomes come to an end and that there may be something of a reaction. The people at home are a little war-weary. They have carried heavy burdens without complaint, and are liable to exhaust themselves rather more quickly than is normal.

If, after the welcome, there is a flatness, this will not mean that they have lost interest. You may notice some becoming a little 'touchy'. Don't let that hurt you. They haven't had the same training in adaptation as you have; and they are home without the thrill of a return to sustain them.[39]

How difficult this was to achieve in practice was revealed by reports from the Salvation Army's own training college.

The close proximity of military service made discipline irksome, especially among the men, and the staff had to apply themselves with considerable tact and wisdom, otherwise there might easily have been trouble. Service life, with the great social renaissance, tended to create a critical attitude to all leadership. A serious breakdown in regard to a member of the staff, who was rather admired, became the subject of a continuing crop of rumours, creating considerable anxiety.[40]

The BBC put out a series of broadcasts on release and resettlement at what was then radio prime time, seven p.m., on Wednesday evenings on the Home Service. The style was chatty and comforting.

We've got to remember that civilians have been shifted about a bit as well – that the war's made a mess of some of their lives, too. First of all about home. That's the place that every single member of the forces is looking forward to – home – but home isn't just a place – it's people – it's you and me, and you and I are not the same individuals we were two, three, four or more years ago – and we mustn't expect men who've been fighting over half the world to be the same either. But I do think we shall have to meet them more than halfway. It's much more difficult for them to realise that we've grown a bit older, a bit wiser, perhaps a bit tougher and almost certainly a bit shabbier. So it seems to me that somehow we've got to scrap the idea that any of us is 'Coming back' to something we left, or that there's any real difference between the serviceman and the civilian, and try a new idea – we're going to start something together – on pretty well equal terms. Then there's the children. It's been grand to have photographs and to hear all about them in letters – but it's quite a different thing to live with them after living for years with other men, in ditches, in barracks, in jungles or in ships. How much do the children really know about Daddy? Is he just a strange man who comes home on leave sometimes – if he's lucky? Mind you, I don't believe in being all solemn and high-hat about all this – I'm just saying – really – it's worth planning for – *this* is resettlement just as much as jobs or training – and it's the part of resettlement which no one can do for us – we've got to do it for ourselves.[41]

Once or twice an idea was mooted that today would leave listeners gasping at the crass insensitivity of the perpetrators.

The Government of Southern Rhodesia has offered to back a scheme called the Fairbridge Memorial College, out in Rhodesia, where children who need homes and a new start in life can go and live. They'll grow up as citizens of Rhodesia with all the benefits of free education up to fifteen, with the possibility of scholarships to the universities in South Africa. Children who go out under the scheme will get free medical attention too. In fact, they'll have a chance to play an important part in the development of Rhodesia. This part of the Empire is growing up now, and very soon will need professional and technical experts in business and industry, so there should be good openings for the children from the Fairbridge

Memorial College when they grow up. The people who're backing this scheme are raising the funds now and they've got the approval of the British Government. That's just one scheme which I've heard about which struck me as being very much well worthwhile.[42]

So that was all right, then. The chance of a new life but at a stunning price. A correspondent recalls an aunt who took advantage of this scheme on behalf of her two sons, aged ten and eleven. She never saw them again.

For a somewhat harsher and more realistic view of demobilisation and what it meant to a typical family, the listener had to turn to the BBC Overseas Service, to *Civvy Street*, a programme broadcast, most improbably, under the generic heading *Calling the West Indies*.

Back in 'Civvy Street', the demobbed soldier stares unbelievingly at the beflagged house, at the motto picked out in coloured beer tops over the fanlight, 'WELCOME HOME GEORGE', and suddenly he is on the other side of his dream!

The door is opened by the wife he hasn't seen for years. After the fervour of the first embrace he is introduced to his family; I say introduced advisedly, for the children have grown almost out of recognition. The fatted calf (perhaps in the shape of a hoarded tin of Spam) is killed for him, and a party or two is thrown; every time he goes down the street he is clapped on the back, and for a while life seems very good indeed. Then his leave is up, and the question of a job arises.

He may be given to understand that his old job is waiting for him, but he does not greet this offer of security with the enthusiasm expected. After all, perhaps he was a Sergeant, Pilot, a Lieutenant-Commander, or a Squadron Leader, and now he has different ideas of living. And so one sees the 'Situations Wanted' column of the Newspaper crowded with this sort of thing: 'Ex. Squadron Leader requires administrative post with scope for energy, initiative and personality. Qualifications: Youth, health, intelligence, ability to work hard.'

Unfortunately, he discovers that his list of qualifications is not enough. They are looking for skilled men – Chartered Accountants, Engineers, Salesmen – and so our disillusioned hero finds himself exchanging the bravery of uniform for a bowler hat and pin-striped trousers, and catching the 8.15 to town with monotonous regularity. He is once more that nonentity, a civilian, and profoundly bored.

Instead of wings and a wide sky, he has to travel in trains crowded to bursting point – recently one young woman fell on to the railway line when a carriage door burst open!

At the office he hasn't a typist, and the mid-morning cup of tea is without sugar. Sausage meat comes up in various disguises at his midday lunches, for which he has to queue. At the end of the day he returns to a tired, harassed wife, who hasn't put his slippers to warm because there's no coal for a fire! He wonders how to while away the evening; he can't go out with his wife, for there's no one to mind the children, so he sets off disconsolately to the 'local' where he and other ex-servicemen solemnly agree that life is not what once it was.

That is a very large part of his trouble – expecting life to be as it was. During the war gallant womenfolk, not wishing to undermine his morale, wrote cheerful letters, suppressing the more tedious details of life, and although he gathered there were trials and shortages, in his heart he treasured a romantic picture of his wife with the firelight on her hair, and a laughing chubby baby in her arms.

Of course, some men have returned to real trouble – an unfaithful wife, a family of deserted children – but for the majority it is the difference between reality and their dreams that is so hard to reconcile. The girl-wife has grown up, and perhaps become 'tough' from factory life, while the husband may have acquired more refinement in the Officers' Mess. The houswife and mother, becoming a huntress for food, has given up glamour for a time-saving turban and stout-soled shoes.

Family relationships are made doubly difficult by the housing shortage, many couples being forced to live with relations and in some cases having to separate, the husband staying with his people and the wife with hers. Of course, there are harmonious households which take overcrowding in their stride. I called to see a friend, who said: 'I'm sorry I cannot ask you to stay, but I'm going to tea with Margaret.' Margaret and her husband have two rooms in her mother's house!

When there are children the situation is often aggravated.

I overheard a young couple on a 'bus: she said, 'It's no good, if I scold Johnnie, Grandma just turns and gives him a sweet. Gosh, if only we had two rooms where we could be on our own.'

Some organisations are trying to do something to help the settling-down problems. The WVS is seeking to provide responsible people who will mind the children for an evening and give the husband and wife a chance of finding each other in companionship once again. They are assisting, too, with gifts of furniture for families who lost their homes through the bombing.

Civilian rations do not help the cheerfulness of the demobbed soldier, who finds himself rapidly losing weight. The husband of a friend of mine came home 'full of beans' and said, 'I'll do your shopping, old girl.' He brightened as he passed a shop where sausages were displayed. Knowing them to be off the ration he queued for twenty minutes, only to be told, 'Sorry, sir, only for our Registered Customers.' A trifle dashed, he went to the fishmonger's where a notice read, 'Fish at 11 o'clock.' He joined the queue, although it was only 10.30, and at 11.30 the last of the fish was sold, to the woman in front of him! He returned home convinced at last of the difficulties under which his wife had laboured for years.

Another barrier to companionship is the divergent personality which each has developed during the years of separation. I saw a letter from a girl whose husband had been perfectly satisfied with her before he went abroad. She wrote to her friend: 'For goodness' sake tell me how to become intellectual quickly! Before he went away, John was quite content to potter about the garden, and go to the pictures occasionally, but since he's been in Italy he's crazy about opera and art. I have to listen for hours to music I find faintly comic, and stand raptly before pictures I don't understand. The only thing of which I am conscious is my poor tired feet!'

I feel that a woman with the sense of humour and co-operation that *she* manifests won't let her marriage come to grief, but it will take years to get many couples attuned again.[43]

CHAPTER FOUR

'Mummy, Tell This Man To Put Me Down'

One child's reaction to Daddy's homecoming hug

Those who knew least suffered most. For many a young child Daddy was a shadowy figure, a dimly remembered bringer of presents on his last leave or a recreation from a family photograph. The reality of homecoming rarely measured up to the fantasy.

I was five and I had never seen him before. I was born while he was in Kenya with his regiment. My older brother, my mother and I were living with my grandmother in Tipperary with my mother's younger brothers. We got along very well with our young uncles: one in particular indulged us both thoroughly.

Excitement built to a pitch when the day drew near for 'Daddy' to come home. I knew he would be better than all three uncles rolled into one. For him, with my fair curly hair, I was 'Judy' (Garland) – the apple of his eye.

But when he appeared he was 'old'! His hair receded. I didn't like him! He took me to the shops to buy me a present, anything I wanted. I didn't want anything from him. Finally I let him buy me a comic.

We never really got on. We were a disappointment to each other. I'm not sure it would have been any different without the war's intervention. Two brothers and three sisters followed in quick succession. It's difficult to discuss these things with my sisters. We probably all saw him differently.[1]

Gwen Price was born on 3 June 1940. Her father went away when she was ten months old. She did not see him again for over four years.

No one prepared me for our meeting. I remember it so well. We were at Reading railway station on this cold December day and all of a sudden this great big man picked me up and cuddled me! I screamed the place down and nothing my mother could say or do would allow me to go near him for quite a while. It was a very difficult time. I had mostly slept with my mother or grandmother during the war, and for this man to want to sleep with my mother really made me very fed up and lost! It took years before I actually stayed in my own bed all night but I still think there was an underlying resentment.

My father had returned from the War a different man from

the happy-go-lucky husband and new father. He was withdrawn, unwell and I can never remember he and I being close, although we muddled through.[2]

Fortune was doubly unfair to George Bennett and his brother. Their mother died in 1933 when George was three and his brother two. Four years later they were put in an orphanage while their father, a merchant navy officer, went off to the Far East. Having just managed to stay ahead of the Japanese advance he had two more narrow escapes when ships on which he was serving were sunk by German bombers.

Our orphanage was evacuated to a country estate on the Wirral peninsula at the outbreak of war and in 1944 I was playing with other boys among pine trees when I saw a wizened elderly man with a stoop coming towards me along the drive. His hair was white, he had a waxed moustache and he was wearing a French-type beret. Altogether an odd-ball, I thought. He asked me the way to the headmaster's office and after directing him I continued playing. Some time later a young boy ran up to me to say that the headmaster wanted me in his office right away. God, I thought. What have I done now? When I reached the office the headmaster was chatting with the strange man.

'Ah, Bennett,' said the headmaster, turning to me, 'this is your father!' Neither of us had recognised the other. And my younger brother was equally nonplussed when confronted by this weird character. After a seven-year separation we were complete strangers; and though I saw my father numerous times after that meeting I always felt awkward, shy and ill-at-ease in his presence – even after I'd left the orphanage and was living in digs. We were never able to bridge the chasm those seven years had formed. I recall he chastised me for concluding a letter to him 'Yours sincerely' instead of a more affectionate term of endearment. Had we not been so closely related I think it would have been easier to surmount the barrier that seemed to separate us.[3]

The arrival of the 'stranger' is a recurring theme in the memories of children of the forties. Who was this man? Why had he come? Why was Mummy so preoccupied with him? What was he doing in Mummy's bed?

Patricia Testrow was ten months old when her dad went to war. Early on he was reported 'missing believed killed', but reappeared five years later, having trekked across country from a POW camp in Poland into France. When he came home, Patricia was nearly seven and not at all clear how she should relate to this man.

I called my dad mister for a long time and then Uncle Frank because my cousin called him that.[4]

Matching the image of Dad with the real thing led to some wonderful misunderstandings and embarrassments.

In the back lane where we children all played, I was the only child who had never seen her father. This particular morning I woke in the dark next to my mother and was aware of another person sharing our bed.

I whispered to my mother, 'Is Grandma sleeping with us?' 'No,' replied my mother. 'Your Daddy has come home.'

My father slept late. He'd arrived home earlier than expected, after a tedious journey. As he stirred and finally awoke it was to see a circle of children's faces staring at him.

'That's *my* Daddy!' I cried.[5]

The public announcement of a Dad back in residence was handled a little more tactfully by Sandy Gardner.

My earliest clear memory is of berating some council workmen who were taking a tea-break from some clearing-up in our back green.

'C'mon youse,' I said. 'Mah daddy's comin' hame fae the war next week and Ah want this place lookin' nice fur him.'

The first thing that was special about the Big Day was that I got to ride in a car for the first time – an unheard-of luxury in those days! There was no way that our returning hero was going to travel the final leg of this journey home on a bus or train – so my grandpa hired a taxi to take me and my mum the twenty-mile round trip into Glasgow to meet my dad.

Queen Street Station was packed with people. I have a very clear picture of the engine of the troop train when it arrived. It was steam-driven, of course, and had an enclosed boiler. The engine and carriages were very dirty on the outside. As the train drew into the station, the driver gave a long blast on his hooter and everyone – the soldiers in the train and the families on the platform – all started cheering.

Me – I nearly jumped out of my skin. And then he was there.

We were soon back in the taxi being driven home to Bellshill in great style. As soon as we arrived I went out the back – the common space around which the tenement flats were grouped – and rounded up all of the children I could find. They were then ushered into my grandma's kitchen, where my dad was sitting by the fire – still wearing his uniform.

When all my pals were duly assembled, I pointed at my father and announced as loudly as I could – 'That's mah Daddy!'

Most of the other kids' fathers worked in the steelworks and had not been called up for military service. I was one of the few who had grown up without a father in the house. Now I had a dad just like them—

And I was awful proud of him.[6]

For the three-year-old Margaret Macleod, Daddy was a photograph on the sideboard to which she said 'Hello' each morning and 'Good night and God bless' each evening.

I can remember the excitement during the days leading up to his homecoming. My mother had told me that an aeroplane would bring him to England. We listened for every aeroplane passing overhead and wondered whether Daddy was in that one. When THE day arrived the excitement and preparations were intense. No one had been able to give a time for his arrival and in the event it wasn't until the evening, long after I had fallen into an exhausted sleep on the settee and been carried off to bed.

My first sight of him was the following morning when I woke and went into my mother's room. I remember the fear I felt when I saw a man with her. My first words were, 'Tell that man to get out of your bed.' When she held out her arms, calling me to her, saying 'This is Daddy,' I just stood and stared. Eventually I said, 'I want that other Daddy' – words which could have ended a marriage! Mother asked me to show her which Daddy and we all went downstairs where I pointed to the photograph. 'That Daddy – the one coming in an aeroplane.'

In my child's mind I had expected My Daddy to arrive at the door in an aeroplane and I wasn't prepared to accept any other. Nothing could persuade me that this man was the one in the photograph.[7]

Another case of mistaken identity compromised a most unlikely suitor for Mum's affections.

During the years that he [Dad] was away, my mother and I lived with my grandmother in Sonning, about five miles from Reading. Our elderly neighbour, who I called 'Uncle Bill', was very kind to me and used to make me toys. Uncle Bill had a wooden leg.

I shared a bedroom with Mum. One morning, very early when it was not quite light, I woke to see two people in Mum's bed. I ran across the room to wake Mum. 'Who's that?' 'Who do you think it is?' says Mum. 'Uncle Bill,' I shouted.[8]

After a long build-up of excitement, the young Ludkin brothers could be forgiven their little misunderstanding.

It was 1944 before we were to see him again. I was ten years old, my brother twelve and sister eleven. A telegram arrived saying he would be arriving home on a certain date. The excitement was beyond description. Mum rushed around borrowing clothing coupons and ration books, for a new dress and clothes for us kids. She cleaned and cooked and on the day we were 'paraded', everything and everybody were shining like new pins! We waited all day. At four p.m. another telegram arrived! Disaster. He wouldn't now be coming until the following day! We all had a sleepless night and were up at dawn to face another day of uncontrollable excitement and apprehension. Just after midday there was a knock at the door, we all rushed into the hall. Through the frosted glass in the front door we could see the figure of this big man. Mum opened the door and there stood the tanned smiling man, our dad. He dropped his two kit bags, gathered Mum into his arms and then one by one, amid all the laughter and tears, he hugged each one of us. He then turned to Mum and said, 'You have done a wonderful job of bringing them up.'

The kit bags were opened and presents passed around. Fez

hats from Cairo, wood carvings from Africa, so much excitement. We had our lunch and listened in awe as Dad related stories of the war and his travels.

It was at this point that Mum left the table and called my brother and me to the kitchen. She took my brother's hand and pressed a half-crown piece into it and said, 'I want you two boys to go off to the pictures!' We were stunned, we just could not believe that after waiting nearly five years to see our dad we were being sent out after just a couple of hours together!

The motive became so obvious in later years but at the time it was incomprehensible to us two young lads.[9]

Jane Gladstone was taken to Cambridge rail station to meet the father she could not remember,

My mother kept reminding me that he would have 'legs' as apparently a friend of mine who, like me, had only seen photos of her father until his arrival home, had exclaimed on seeing him, 'But he's got legs!' Apparently all the photos she had seen of him only showed him from the waist up!

My father shook hands with me and promptly left me in charge of his luggage while he and my mother went off for what seemed ages. I was terrified of losing it as he had impressed on me how important it was that I did not let it out of my sight. The only problem was when he returned, I would not let him have it as I did not recognise him!'[10]

Recognition held no dread for May Griffiths, who was eleven at the time of her father's demob.

But my then baby sister, at just under two years old, had never seen her daddy. His picture on the wall was her daddy and she insisted on kissing his picture good night for some considerable time rather than him. Of course then we did not fully appreciate how hard this was on my father. He had been saving his chocolate ration. Starved of such luxuries my sister would normally go to anyone for a square of chocolate but my father had no luck even with a whole block. There was a look of complete amazement on her face when she first saw him lather his face to shave.[11]

The odds against reconciliation were lengthened when, for psychological or physical reasons, Dad could not measure up to the expectations of an ordinary father.

Muriel Woodhead was eleven when the war ended.

My twin sister and I looked forward to our father's return from India where he had served as a captain in REME. As the day approached I was filled with a sickening dread. I remember sitting on my bed and praying the incongruous prayer, 'O God, if there is a God, let me recognise my father.' The fear of not recognising him and worse still, knowing that I had not recognised him dominated my waking moments. The scene remains vivid. Above all I remember the hot embarrassment and shame. Surely no good child could fail to recognise her own father?

He would cross the threshold and be a stranger and my non-recognition would reveal the unpardonable sin. I didn't love my father.

This sense of my father being a stranger persisted through the rest of my childhood and adolescence. After he died and I heard people talking about him, I realised that I had never really known him. The long absence during the war and the strains the war had put on those left behind took such a toll that the threads of a happy family relationship were never fully recovered. I am sure it was so for others.

The most cheerful recollections are of the exotic presents and souvenirs he brought back from India – the perfumed wonder of real Turkish delight, a whole glutinous box full, lengths of sari silk, and leather-thonged sandals and satchels embossed with elephants and smelling mysteriously of dusty bazaars and ships' holds. The contrast with the grim realities of wartime austerity was exquisitely potent.

But such pleasures faded as he became ill. A rash covered his skin, the result we were told of some tropical disease. We were 'shushed' if we made a noise and crept around on tiptoe. The doctor came and went. The house was filled with antiseptic smells and steaming bowls of potassium permanganate were carried to his room. When he did appear his skin was dyed indigo. Looking back I wonder if the rash was in part psychosomatic, caused by the stress of trying to adjust to family life.

So much was hoped for. Just old enough to remember the pre-war days, Muriel was desperate to recover the secure routines of the old life. But there could be no putting the clock back.

The most bizarre attempt my parents made to recover 'normality' was to spend most of my father's demobilisation gratuity on a holiday. That would be the panacea, it was felt, for all emotional and physical ills and would bring us together again as a family. It was a disaster. A trip to London coincided with an electric storm of such alarming ferocity as to leave me numb with fear. The crashing of thunder directly overhead and bolts of lightning hitting rooftops nearby was so reminiscent of the bombing that I lost my power of speech for a while and became catatonic with shock. This was followed by a wretched fortnight in Yorkshire. It rained the entire time. Ghastly boarding houses and awful landladies quibbling over rations. We returned sick and exhausted with the money gone and nothing to show for it. The fragile relationships within the family could not withstand even trivial anxieties like the non-arrival of a train, which meant waiting for hours without food on a cold platform. The 'bonding' which was meant to occur, the coming together of one happy family on holiday, with Daddy safely back in charge, did not happen. Nor could it ever happen.

Muriel adds:

We honour our war dead. But there were other 'deaths' which have not been written about or commemorated. Recollections of victory are often rose-coloured high with the excitement of street parties and bunting and ribbons of welcome for returning heroes. But for some families the experience was far more complex than that.[12]

There are many examples where childhood memories of happy families before the fighting started brought disenchantment when the fighting ended. Kay Chorley is one who might feel that she would have been better off without pre-war reminiscences to sharpen the disappointment of realising that nothing could ever be the same again.

On my 4th birthday in September 1939 I woke to find half a crown under my pillow. My father had 'joined up' as a volunteer. Apart from a few days' leave after training and before being sent overseas, this was the last I saw of him for five years which he spent in the Middle East.

We lived in a remote part of Hertfordshire away from my mother's family in Ireland and my father's in Suffolk. I was an only child. A school from London took over the Big House where my father had worked as a butler.

The postman on his cycle was always very welcome. There was always a cup of tea for him before he set off again on his bicycle to complete his round, which was a total of about 20 miles. He brought letters from the two families and an occasional parcel from my uncle in America. Most important of all were letters from Daddy. These were read and re-read. They were a very precious link. Then began the next long wait and worry.

Gradually his face began to fade from my memory and the

signature 'Daddy' took over. It seemed the closest I could get to him and it was just for me. It was something to hold on to along with my memories of planting the garden, feeding the hens, walking in the lanes beside my tall strong daddy who would always be there for me. I had been his shadow. Now my sun was missing.

I started school in the village, learnt to read, write, sew, play the piano and ride a bike. He learnt of these achievements through letters and it was all so second-hand. I missed his cuddles and words of praise which had shown his approval. These I remembered from when I had first reached the pump handle which was our source of drinking water, the hole I made properly to take the seed potato or on giving him the right tool when 'helping' with a job.

I could not understand why some children had their fathers around. Why didn't I? Never mind, the war would soon be over and he would be back with us. One particular thrill was to hear my father's voice on the radio one Christmas in a services broadcast to their families. Oh but how short it was! I can remember saying his words over and over in my head and trying to remember the sound of his voice.

Every Christmas and birthday we hoped he would be with us for the next one. We knelt every night and prayed for his safety and the end of the war.

At last, after five years he returned with a small pair of clogs and a china doll from Belgium which was his last posting after his return from the Middle East. Everything would be great again. My daddy was home. The demob suit was worn to visit both families. Everyone was happy again. But things were never the same for us. My parents had changed. Life had changed them. They had missed so much of each other. I don't know who had suffered most. My father had an enemy to fight. My mother had the constant struggle to keep the home fire burning.

Within a couple of years my mother and I were on our own again as my father had left. I never heard them argue but shortly before my father's death at the age of 80, on the only occasion he really spoke of my mother, he gave me the photo of her which he had carried throughout the war. He said the war years had changed them both too much to pick up the threads again.

After my long wait for things to return to former happy days I knew they never would. I had to hold on to my precious memories of the four contented pre-war years.[13]

The war years were not necessarily dismal for children. Enterprising mums made sure they were well fed and clothed. Bombs might threaten but they won't touch us, will they? Of course, the answer was no. One correspondent recalls his delight when a bomb dropped on the church hall. No more Sunday School. What bliss. It never occurred to him that his own house had escaped by a mere nudge of a joystick. If life was good, Dad had a hard time in making it even better.

It was one of those long summer evenings. My brother and I were already in bed – we shared a bedroom in those days – when we heard the front gate opening and footsteps coming up the path. Then the front door opened.

After some time, during which we could hear muffled voices from the sitting room, there were footsteps on the stairs. Into the bedroom came our mother, aglow with emotion. And with her was this strange man. I knew he must be our father. I knew I was expected to be thrilled at his return. And, anxious to please, as well as being a rather dramatic child, I jumped up, stood on the bed and flung myself at him.

I went through the motions in fact. But inside, I was feeling shocked and dismayed. The immediate aftermath of his return is blurred in my mind. I can recall few precise details of how we all set about learning to live together again. Instead I have a rather vague impression of a not particularly welcome change to the family structure. I think in some ways I resented my father's presence. Having been the main focus of our mother's attention my brother and I had to accommodate his need to have time with her. We had to learn that she belonged to him as well as us, that she wasn't just our mother but his wife as well. My father gradually became part of the family again, tolerated, rather than fully accepted on my part.

To say that I did not grow to love my father would be untrue. He was a lovable person, but always somehow slightly remote. And our relationship was never entirely easy. Over the years, we did manage to get to know each other and do some things together. In fact, it seemed to me that this was the best way to make things work – to actually get together on some project. He went fishing occasionally and would sometimes take me with him. I used to enjoy sitting with him on a river bank, for he was a keen naturalist and would teach me the names of wild birds and identify their calls for me. And I would take home caterpillars from my rambles over the fields and marshes for him to identify.

But I don't think I ever shared much of my emotional life with him. I never felt as close to him as I believe I would have been had he been there during those early years. He had a much easier relationship with my younger brother.

Ann Farrant goes on to speculate on the long-term effect of an unsatisfying father-daughter relationship.

Certainly I believe the absence of my father in my early years coloured my own behaviour when I married and had children of my own. I was very much the 'Queen Bee' of the household and subconsciously, perhaps, did not include my husband in the children's upbringing as much as I might have done had I had the role model of a 'hands-on' father.

And when my own marriage was breaking up I had feelings of enormous panic about the loss of my husband – quite irrational and out of all proportion to the reality of the situation, which was that I could survive without him. It somehow triggered off some very deep fears about the man in the family going away.

Most of all, I feel great sorrow for my father (now dead) for the loss of those years with his young family. He missed out on so much of what should have been a rewarding and enriching experience and, despite the best of intentions on both his and my mother's part, nothing could ever make up for that. We, as children, were deprived of his presence but we were blithely unaware of what was missing. He, on the other hand, had all those years away, knowing full well that he was not part of the family he so wanted and which was learning to do without him.[14]

The causes of childhood disillusionment were as many and varied as the children themselves. Expectations built on an idealised image – often nurtured by a mother with her own deep longings – were bound to be disappointed and could easily lead to estrangement. If it was hard for a prematurely aged father lately home from a Japanese POW camp to hear his daughter scream, 'Who is that horrid man?',[15] it was just as hard for the child to accept that the photographs on the mantelpiece told a terrible lie.

I was seven years old when Dad came home, having been four when I last saw him. My younger sister, not having seen him since babyhood, was now four years of age. I remember coming down the stairs the morning he came home and finding him asleep on the couch. He seemed thin and his face yellow from the after-effects of a bad bout of malaria. My mother told me later that he arrived home at 2 a.m. and threw stones at the window to waken her. My little sister and I looked at this strange man. We must have felt apprehensive having been alone with our mother for over three years. He had brought us presents, dolls and ivory necklaces from India. I remember even now the smell of the sandalwood boxes and the heavily embroidered silk cloths. We ran into the street to show the other children our presents and to tell them our daddy was home from the war at last. That evening he took me to the funfair at the local park. I still felt shy with him and wanted to bring a friend along but my father just wanted to take me. He just seemed to want to be with his family without any outsiders.

The euphoria of having him home soon wore off as our father was to suffer further bouts of malaria, added to which his nerves were very bad. He did not like any noise and we had to try and keep very quiet. He seemed to be anti-social and did not like any visitors to the house, even close family. My mother told me that he had nightmares and would suddenly wake up during the night and run towards the wardrobe thinking Japanese snipers were firing at him. Being small children we slept soundly and knew nothing of the traumas of the night. It was terrible for our mother to see him like this, not the happy homecoming she must have envisaged.

I can remember the tensions around me and my sister took some time accepting him as her father. He must have been hurt when she pointed to a photograph of him (in uniform), saying, 'That's my daddy not you.' I was very close to him when I was small and it was no time at all that we had a strong father/daughter relationship. It took longer for my sister to become attached to him, but in time she too had a very loving relationship with him.[16]

A few glorious homecomings went off without a hitch.

It was during 1946, I was playing in the street of the village, when a taxi drew up, out stepped a gentleman in army uniform. Of course, a taxi was a very unusual thing and we children had all crowded around it. The gentleman came up to me and said, 'Is your mum in?' He took my hand and we walked to the front door, that was locked, round to the back door and in we went. It wasn't until our old dog flew at us barking with delight that I realised this was someone special to greet. I knew my dad was coming home, but not when. Until then he had been a photo on the shelf and letters.

We soon made up for lost time, I can remember riding on his shoulders around the garden the next day.

I cannot say I ever felt deprived but now that I am a mum and grandma I realise how much he missed by being away during those first years of my life. I don't think those missed years have affected us in any way. He has always been a smashing dad. He is now 82 years old, but we can still have a good old laugh about the day I took a strange man into our house.[17]

Much depended on the personality and circumstances of the individual soldier. Had he managed to keep his family in mind during his time away or had memories of wife and children receded in the excitement of a man's war? Where there was a strong bond between parents which included the children the shock of encountering a man about the house was liable to wear off – with time.

My father came back two days before VJ Day. I was seven. I can remember my mother polishing the house number on the post by the front door and wondered why she was doing that, because surely he must know where he lives and had not forgotten. I was too shy to greet my father when he arrived, and ran up the garden and hid. When he came up the garden to find me, he had to coax me out by suggesting I come to look at the things he had in his kit bag. I was very impressed by small round tins packed tight with cigarettes.[18]

When Judy Vaughan's father reappeared in June 1946, after an absence of four years, his seven-year-old daughter was overcome with shyness.

Although Mum had constantly talked about Dad to me, and I kissed his photograph every night so that I would not forget him, when he finally came home I felt rather shy of him. So much so that I didn't want him to be anywhere in the house when I was having my night-time bath! I don't remember saying it, but Mum and Dad have told me since, I would say to Mum – 'I don't want him here while I am washing. Send him out!' Poor Dad had to go down to his local every night during that time. I think this went on for about six months or so until I got used to having him around. It must have been very difficult for him because he had to adjust too. As I got older I realised a little more and felt very guilty about making things even more difficult for him than they already were. Poor Dad![19]

'Mummy, Tell This Man To Put Me Down'

Mothers were urged to prepare their children for the great event by involving them in the preparation and by giving them a central role in the welcome home. The magazine *Woman's Own* had this advice in August 1945:

> Children appreciate it if we take them into our confidence and bitterly resent being told to do something which seems to them to be unreasonable for no better reason than because you tell them to. Talk to your son as man to man; explain that war has been pretty hard upon you all and you know that it has brought certain hardships to him, but point out how much more it has meant to Father to be far away from his family for so long.
>
> Show him he can make Father's homecoming happy by doing his share of the daily tasks. If you take it all with a light hand, work together and share and share alike, he won't resent it, and will develop a sense of responsibility.[20]

Major Cohen of the Royal Artillery actually took the trouble to write to his two-year-old daughter Suzette. Who knows how much of the letter came across when it was read to her by her mother? But the excitement of the event was everlasting.

> My most Darling Suzette, This is to wish you many many happy returns of your birthday. Mummy has written that you will have no party to celebrate it because I am still away but I promise to make it up when I come home which will not be long now.
>
> Thanks to Mummy I now have a complete picture of your

first 2 years of life. You have been an adorable child and apart from when you had some new teeth and when you have your hair washed, you have given no trouble or anxiety to Mummy or me but only continual happiness. (Even in the manner of your arrival in October 1943, long, long ago, you caused little trouble.)

Suzette, my Darling, do you think you will love your Daddy whom you have never seen? I hope and think you will, because our whole life is going to be devoted to your happiness. I will throw you into the air, carry you on my shoulders, allow you to cover me with sand, take you into the countryside where Mummy will explain to you and me which are the sheep and which the cows and the geese and the ducks and the birds and the hens and the pigs. We may even if we are lucky (and good) be shown a squirrel or a deer. You have no idea what happiness is in store for you if Mummy and I have our way and what happiness you will create for us too.

You have no choice as to who shall be your Daddy, my Darling Sue, because your Mummy has already made the choice but I hope that you will like the choice. But I am sure you will – especially when you come into our bed on my first morning back in Southport. That will be an occasion which I will never ever forget. We shall have fun and games and that will mark the first day when you start life not only with a mummy but also with me – real live, genuine Daddy.

For a few months you will only have us and your grandma and pa to play with but if you are a very good child we hope to present you with a baby brother whom if you look after carefully for about 12 months will then be ripe to offer you adulation and admiration.

You see, my Darling Sue, you are 'one of the family' – just 3 of us – and as such you are entitled to know all the family secrets.

My whole life is wrapped round you and that is why I wish you a very happy birthday. With all my love and xxxxs for Mummy. Your own Daddy.

The eventual meeting of father and daughter was marred, temporarily, by a prickly moustache.

I screamed, in fact I screamed all day and night. Soon, however, I began to realise what fun he was when he threw me up in the air and caught me, played all sorts of games with me, and taught me to ride my tricycle. Then when we went for a holiday to the Lake District and he ran with me in my buggy singing 'Up the hills and over the bumps and all the way home', I realised how wonderful it was to have a real live daddy. He became my life-long friend and mentor.[21]

The ubiquitous moustache was a turn-off for many youngsters. 'I want my other daddy,' screamed Celia Butler's three-year-old son when he failed to recognise the man in the photograph.[22] Diana Bites went with her mother and brother to a welcome home at Nottingham's Midland Station. They waited on platform 5.

The train arrived and hundreds of men in uniform alighted. My father picked me up and kissed me – I didn't recognise him and hated his moustache and cried.[23]

Bonus points went to fathers who loaded themselves down with goodies.

He brought me a present from the Far East, a small wooden train with carriages which were painted with black doors and windows. I can still picture the train to this day.

Another thing I remember was his RAF topcoat. This was used at night, as a quilt for our bed. I remember the great weight and terrific warmth of this coat.[24]

Mavis Taylor had to wait for her appetising bounty.

The day that Dad was demobbed I had arranged to go to a Sunday school concert. I wanted to stay at home to be there when he arrived, but my mother said he will still be here when you get home. All through the concert I was very excited, I couldn't wait to see him. He was all tanned, not a bit like I remembered him. He had brought me a lot of chocolate, Mars and Cadbury's Dairy Milk. He didn't smoke, so he used to swap his cigs ration for chocolate. It was lovely because you couldn't get hold of any sweets then.[25]

For present-giving to have the desired effect, it needed to be done with sensitivity.

I can still remember that small crowded living room in my aunt's house, too full of furniture, people and effusive welcomes, while I looked on nervously from the background. And then I suddenly became the centre of unwanted attention when this stranger who was my dad came forward to give me a present – my first-ever watch.

Somewhat embarrassed by all the attention, I fumbled with the watch strap, trying to put it on. Dad offered to help, but for some reason I refused, perhaps not wanting to seem ignorant of how to do it. (I've often wondered since how *he* must have felt at my strange reaction.)

I didn't like having all eyes on me so I escaped by 'hiding' behind the settee until I could get the watch fastened to my wrist. Imagine my mortification then, when I emerged triumphantly from my refuge only to be told I had the watch on the *wrong* wrist.[26]

Even without a disguise – moustache, sun tan, hair receding more rapidly than anyone had expected, weight loss or, rarely, weight increase – Dad was seldom an immediately familiar character.

My mother and I had been doing the housework and I had just come down the stairs when there was a ring at the door bell. Since I was closest I opened it. I shrieked 'Dad' and my mother came running. The following Sunday, the whole family – an extended Welsh one – went to chapel, as usual. After the service my mother and father were talking with other relatives in the entrance and my mother suggested that my cousin and I might like to go and play – which we did. Suddenly I saw a man walking away from chapel. I ran, calling out, 'Dad, Dad!' The man turned round and apologised for not being my father.[27]

Injuries were hard to cope with. The imagination of children rarely extended to how the effects of bombs and bullets could impinge on their own lives. Catherine Sedgebear remembers

. . . as a girl seeing POWs coming home, seeing their children for the first time, the men looking like skeletons and could hardly stand as they were so thin, they were so changed in appearance their wives didn't recognise them.[28]

For Mrs Orton's young son it was his father's war play rather than war work that marred the homecoming.

My husband was working in the London docks on the big ships that came in for repairs. In 1942 it was decided to transfer the work to Nairobi and Bersetu as was then. There was hardly time to say goodbye to me and our son of 18 months, he just about knew him then. It was arranged that the men had some exercise which was football but unfortunately mine got kicked in the head – a smashed jaw broken in several places He had to wait for transport back to England. Meanwhile, no surgeon wanted to touch him. When he was sent back to Chatham his mouth only opened enough to swallow liquid. However he was able to come to see us on the Saturday afternoon for two hours. Our son, who was then about three years old, wouldn't look at his father and when it was time to go back to Chatham the boy was so pleased to get rid of him he got out of a chair to open the front door then ran to open the gate rubbing his hands together after pushing him off. His father went back crying of course, so the next day I had to get to the barracks to try to explain. Luckily we were able to be near my husband when he was sent to East Grinstead hospital. He had three operations with the famous plastic surgeon Archie McIndoe. After a long while our son came round to the idea of having a father. Today we are the best of pals.[29]

Children are by nature self-centred creatures. In the struggle to form their own identity they draw strength from whoever is closest. In the war, in most young families, the mother was the prime mover, at once the object of affection and the standard-bearer for core values. When Dad came home, he cut right across established routines and disrupted intimate relationships. How could it have been otherwise?

I was 2½ years old at the start of the war so I couldn't remember Father until, at the age of five, I was taken to meet him at the railway station when he came home on leave. If I close my eyes I can still feel the rough khaki uniform and the strange new sensation of being kissed by a man.

Poor Dad, his war experiences had left him in a very excitable and nervous state, so two young children soon had him worn out. As for us, we had been with Mother and Granny and we tried his patience sorely. What did we know about living with a daddy? His views on parenting emerged on a very different plane from Mother's, and there were lots of rows about who was right. I can recall the confusing arrangement of Mother now going to sleep with Dad. All of the war she slept with me, and as a little girl I rebelled strongly.

The war years of separation for families were cruel and extremely damaging psychologically for many people. I confess although I'm happily married, I am often shy and awkward with men. I find myself wishing they would leave the room. I'm sure this dates back to spending near six years of my childhood mostly with women.[30]

There is a thick volume of similar stories of relationships that took years to reconstruct.

My father was in Egypt but to me he was just a man on a photograph, who sent me presents occasionally, someone my mother talked about, but who to me had as much substance or reality as Father Christmas.

I remember one day she got a letter to say Daddy was coming home. She was so excited but I think I felt just curiosity. The day he came home was a grey miserable day. I was dressed up in my best clothes and we waited. I remember now so vividly I was standing in the front room looking up the road and I saw a soldier standing talking to my grandmother who lived opposite. I called to my mother, 'There's a soldier coming down the road, is it my Daddy?' (When I recall that scene now I realise how sad that was.)

The soldier came in through the back door into the kitchen and my mother flung her arms round him. I stood in the doorway watching, feeling nothing. I was seven years old and this man was a total stranger.

My father was demobbed and went back to work in the Post Office as a driver. My two brothers were born within twelve months of each other in the next two years.

Life for me changed totally. From being the cherished only child of my mother who had all her attention, I was now part of a growing family with a stranger for a father and two baby brothers who took all my mother's time. I was part of that other life 'before the war'. With hindsight, I realise that it must have been very hard for both my mother and father having to get to know each other again and cope with a young family whilst they made their own adjustments to what was a very different life for both of them.

I tried very hard to have a normal father/daughter relation-ship with my father and I'm sure he did too in his own way, but we never achieved it. We never spoke to each other – never greeted each other on coming home or said goodbye if we went out. Any communication was done through my mother. I feel she never understood just how difficult for me all this was, I think she thought I was being awkward.

This state of affairs continued through my teens until I got married. Things seemed to improve then, possibly because I'd left home. I had three sons quite close together and my father had a different attitude to them. He loved them dearly, would play with them and chat about all kinds of things with them. Because of them we moved closer; we had a common bond.

Monica Maher adds:

As I have written this the tears have flowed.[31]

Where there were two or more children, there was a strong tendency for Daddy to favour the youngest, at the expense of a child who had matured in his absence, in other words to take up family life where he had left off.

My mother had my sister then and I suppose she took my place. My father and I only could speak through my mother for some years. We are friends now but it has taken its time. I was married before I could hold a decent conversation with him.[32]

For Mary Rutter, the few years' difference in age between her and her sister led to permanent estrangement from her father, to a degree that is chilling.

I was a little girl of six years when my father came back from the war. I was in hospital the day my dad came home but was coming home the day after. My mum came for me in a taxi with this man. I did not know him and always thought of my dad as a soldier, so I would not have anything to do with him.

I had a sister later and then things really got much worse.

If we went out as a family my dad would pay for meals, bus fares, pictures, or whatever for mum and sister and himself, but mum had to pay for me. If they went on holiday he never wanted me with them. I grew up, started work, but things never got better. Everything I did was wrong.

Friday nights he would come home from work with sweets for mum, sister and himself and I was left out. Can you imagine the hurt I felt?

I got older and met my husband. When we wanted to get married John, my future husband, asked my dad if we could do so but he said ask her mother, it's nothing to do with me. He told my mother he would not give me away.

I never gave my mum and dad any trouble. I worked as a weaver and had six looms so earned a lot of money which I gave all to my mum and only had a small amount back.

I am 56 years old and still get upset when I think back. I never hated my dad but never loved him. This still carried on till he died. It was everything for my sister, nothing for me.[33]

There were occasions when Dad had to compete for a child's affection against the rival claims of a surrogate father, a kindly relative, perhaps, who with the best possible motives had tried to fill the void. Restoring the balance was all the more problematical when living conditions were hard.

I was born 14.10.42. My father was at war in the army. We lived with my uncle who had an off-licence shop with plenty of spare accommodation. I thought the world of my uncle. My father to me was a stranger in the distance. When he came home in 1945 he was still a stranger.

In 1950 my parents got a council house on a new estate, and we moved away. The move for me was a nightmare. The three years in that council house were the worst three years of my life. I hated my father and never forgave my mother for not letting me stop with my uncle. That three-year gap was never bridged.

Whether my father didn't know how, or couldn't or didn't want to, is hard to say. I had no love for him whatsoever. Not once did he show me love or give me any encouragement at all. He was just a stranger in the background.[34]

The relative who stood in for a parent in time of need was not always a willing helper – or particularly kind. Mike Ward was a year old when his father joined up.

Early in 1941 my mother decided I should live with my father's aunt Annie. As a result, my mother would be able to earn money as a shop assistant at the local Co-op. Years later, by which time I had become aware of my mother's need for male company, it struck me that my incarceration elsewhere also provided her with the opportunity for evening entertainment.

My earliest memory takes the form of an awareness of doom as I trundled along Tillotson Avenue towards the home of my great-aunt, holding tight to my mother's right hand whilst, in her left, she carried a small brown suitcase.

For the next four long years I lived with Annie, then a severe woman in her mid-fifties, a devout Roman Catholic who was long past the age when she wanted to be bothered with a toddler. Years later I learned that she only agreed to look after me because it provided her with the opportunity to bring me up as a Catholic.

Every Friday evening my mother stopped by the house, obviously to pay my board though I didn't realise it at the time, and I would scream and plead to be taken home. I had literally to be dragged from her skirts when she left.

Throughout those unhappy years, every night through my tears, I told myself that my misery would be put right 'when my daddy came home'.

I was finally allowed to return home in late 1945.

In January 1946 there was a knock at the door. Then silence. This was unusual as we lived in a small village and, except during the night, all the street doors were left open. Visitors simply tapped lightly on the door and then came inside calling out, 'It's only me.'

On this occasion, however, no one entered, and then there was a second knock; then a third. I opened the door and there stood a tall man with a moustache. I was immediately suspicious. I only knew of two men who had a moustache, Hitler, and Charlie Chaplin. I had been told that Hitler was dead, and I knew the man in front of me wasn't Charlie Chaplin.

The tall man said nothing. He just looked down at me and smiled. I looked up at him, unsure of how to deal with strangers. I didn't much care for the look of him; his skin looked somehow darker than anyone else I had ever seen.

We remained motionless staring at each other. Seconds went by. Finally my mother called out, 'Oo is it?' I called back, 'I don't know.'

Clearly exasperated, the man suddenly pushed past me, brushed aside the draught curtain and moved into the room. Startled, I closed the door and followed him. In quick succession he kissed and hugged my mother and then took my baby brother in his arms. I didn't understand what was happening.

My mother suddenly turned from him and looked at me. I could see how happy she was. She looked at my astonishment and said, 'Don't y'know 'oo it is?'

'No,' I replied. She looked at him again and said, 'It's y'daddy.'

I looked at him again; he looked at me. He asked me when I'd last cleaned my teeth. I knew I'd been wrong. My misery was not about to end when my daddy came home.[35]

The war gave grandparents a new lease of life, whether at work, where they were encouraged to stay on beyond retirement age, or in the home, where they could do much to compensate for an absent father. But having moved in, who could blame them if they found it hard to move out?

I think it was very difficult for us to get to know Dad again. He had seen many things which obviously altered his outlook on life, though of course we were unable to appreciate that then. Also during the five and a half years he had been away, my maternal grandfather had died and my grandmother had come to live with us where she remained until her death in

1953. We lived in a small house and my grandmother suffered ill health, therefore it was not possible for my parents to resume a 'normal' family life at first.[36]

The infant Julie Burville lived with two generations of her mother's family while her father was away in the Army,

Grandad a naval pensioner and Customs' coastal patrol man, and Gran with Croydon ballroom experience slightly dissatisfied with her Cornish 'backwoods' life. Their only son to survive childhood had drowned whilst serving with the Royal Navy in the Southern Oceans. It was not a household to which soldiers were welcomed, particularly when this one had stolen my mother away from a matelot.

Julie's parents married in 1941, a year before her birth and her father's posting to North Africa. When he returned in 1945, it was to a home ruled by tiny jealousies.

I had always shared a bed with my mother, and one of my earliest memories is of the night my father was demobilised. My mother's excitement was tangible, even to a three-year-old. She kept telling of the wonderful event that was to happen, trying to share her expectations with a child who felt discomfited at the prospect of an unknown daddy, superfluous in a home already amply supplied with loving and overindulgent mother, gran and grandad.

We went to bed together as usual and I slept. It seemed the

middle of the night when I was lifted from the eiderdown's warmth to be sat on the bottom stair whilst my mother, in best flowing nightgown, hurried to answer the knocking at the back door.

They embraced; he seemed utterly foreign, no part of me or her. When he gathered me up his face was rough and his khaki was harsh with an alien smell. I wriggled to escape, not wanting to be held. What followed was worse: I didn't sleep with Mummy any more.

Poor Dad, 27 years old, impatiently returned to a beautiful young wife but now the package included a spoilt daughter and less than enthusiastic in-laws, and there was little prospect of making a home of his own.

Gran's favourite game was to ask me whom I loved best and I obliged, listing in order of preference the loves of my life, 'Mummy most, Gran next, then Grandad and Daddy last.' It must have hurt him.

With a family to support, the ex-soldier became a policeman but his posting was to the other side of the county and, as this was before the days of police houses, it meant another separation. Mum and I stayed put and visiting was infrequent, involving tedious journeys by bus.

In the Army my father had risen to the rank of Regimental Sergeant Major, he was accustomed to be in command. Now he was a constable obliged to take orders from Police Sergeants who had not seen overseas service. It couldn't work and it didn't.

My Grandfather's retirement [from the Customs] provided

an opportunity and my father sucessfully applied for his vacant post despite it being normally reserved for naval pensioners. So we were together again in an extended, but not so happy, family and this time with an addition on the way.

In 1947, thanks to my father's persistent harassment of the local authority, we were given a newly built council house. This independence eased tensions but did not improve his relationship with his first-born. This continued to be uneasy: we had been too much apart, were too much alike, too jealous of each other in my mother's affections.

With age, my father mellowed; with maturity, I softened, and we rubbed along though it was only in his final year of life, whilst he was so bravely fighting cancer, that we came to love each other.[37]

Life with Mum, her parents and her brother was, for Wendy Reeves, wonderful consolation for not having her father with her throughout the war. She knew he had been taken prisoner and looked forward to his return with all the enthusiasm of a five-year-old brought up to expect love in return for love. Instead,

I did not like this tall, weird, cold man. After such a close relationship with my lovely warm, kindly grandad and uncle Colin, whom I worshipped, as they adored me. Of course, I did not understand at the time – but it became clearer as I became older – that Dad had become quite mentally unbalanced by his incarceration. He used to sleep in a separate room from Mum, was unkind to me – I received the first smack I had ever known, from him – and I became frightened of him.[38]

Re-establishing the traditional family hierarchy with Father as the head of the household took some getting used to. There was a new code of discipline to learn, one based on a paternal assumption that orders would be obeyed – just as they had been in the forces.

I remember I was just learning how to tie my shoelaces. He tied them up for me once and I promptly untied them as a game. He did them up again and I undid them again. He threatened that if I did it a third time I would get smacked. Not believing this, I undid them a third time and promptly got walloped. I ran bawling up the garden where my mother was hanging out washing and complained, 'That man hit me!' I felt he had no jurisdiction over me and was only there on sufferance. It must have been very difficult for him as he had been used to soldiers leaping to attention at his slightest command and he could not cope with a small child defying him.

We had many a scene at meal times where I inevitably ended up facing a corner in our hall if I had not finished my meal. I got tired of hearing that the starving children in Russia would be grateful for what I spurned. How I wished they would eat it for me. I remember on one occasion refusing blackcurrant tart. I hated the flavour and refused to eat it all and was sent into the hall for what seemed like hours. I was told I would stay there until I ate it all up. Eventually I was allowed out but the by now congealed tart was re-presented at the next meal so I decided I might as well eat it as I was told it would keep coming back until I did![39]

In this family there was a great love between father (an RAMC major general) and infant daughter which quickly overcame all misunderstandings. But the military experience often changed men in ways that made it hard for them to show love.

I was 7½ before I truly 'met' my father. I found a great deal of difficulty in accepting him as a member of the family, particularly because he was never demonstratively affectionate. He brought an old wooden ammunition box with him, which he fixed to a tree in the back garden by way of a swing, and I think he believed he had done his bit for me.

There were German prisoners of war in a camp opposite our house occupying the space left by four houses that had been destroyed by their Luftwaffe colleagues. My father obtained three or four ducks from some friend or other. The German POWs helped him to construct a cement-sided pond in the back garden but Dad succeeded in falling into it on his own. It was a comic moment which I'm afraid was rarely repeated. I think his war experiences tainted his entire outlook on life. I was 42 before he and I sat down for a drink together in a pub.[40]

Where there was a strong-willed wife and independently minded children the military disciplinarian was likely to meet his match. Jill Tyler was 13 when Brigadier Tyler returned from the Middle East.

He was very protective to us children and as we had considerable freedom we found it difficult to have our hands clutched as we crossed the road. Mum also found that after managing all our affairs it was difficult to hand over. And, indeed, in what was a very happy marriage Dad never did take back the running of the house. He took us sailing on the Broads in 1947 and learnt there that we were capable of responsibility and much more grown up than when he had last known us.[41]

But the inability to adapt to the needs of a growing family was commonplace.

Eileen Dibben's husband was in North Africa and Italy for two and a half years. He returned in September 1945, just in time for their son's second birthday.

I eagerly awaited my husband's return and could not wait to show him the beautiful boy I had produced alone. My husband had had a difficult war in North Africa and Italy but became Town Major near Rome where he had a great deal of authority and realised also that he was attractive to and attracted by women. So in place of the fun-loving affectionate boy I had married I found this military martinet with a large ego. He considered our boy spoilt and undisciplined and proceeded to rectify this while the baby asked me in a loud voice, 'When is that man going away?'[42]

Mrs Dibben had another baby, a girl but 'there was always friction between my son and husband'. Eventually, the marriage broke up.

Mike Hughes remembers what should have been one of the happiest days of his life as one of the saddest.

It is as though it were yesterday – my mom telling me to get dressed in my best clothes as we were going on the bus for a special day. We got off the bus and walked to High Level Station in Wolverhampton. At that moment I was simply enjoying a bus ride and a walk with Mom.

I recall Mom saying, as all moms would, 'Don't go near the edge of the platform, stay by me and be patient.' I remember a train arriving and hordes of men getting off in all colours of suits – some Army, some Navy, some RAF, some best suits (demob suits probably). I recall standing back shy and quiet when Mom suddenly rushed up to a strange man, hugging and kissing him! She turned to me and said, amongst her tears, 'This is your dad, Michael.' What does a small 7- to 8-year-old child do or say? I copied the big boys and extended my hand to shake hands with my own father! He held my hand and then swept me up into his arms amongst many tears and embracing Mom at the same time.

It was a long time later that Mike Hughes learned

> . . . how the bitter experience of war had changed Dad from a caring man, keen on his garden, to becoming an introvert and indeed jealous man![43]

The feeling of paternal rejection experienced by many war babies could be accentuated by the post-war arrival of a brother or sister. There were some happy times for young John Taylor, whose father found work as a truck driver working out of Billingsgate Market. Among the good things he recalls were 'visits to the pub, meeting my uncles, having a lemonade or two dressed up in my Sunday best'. His brother was born in 1950.

> Dad could see him growing up and took more interest and even now my brother is his favourite. After my mother died three years ago, the relationship between us cooled and then he met a companion and has not kept in touch with me or my family, including his grandchildren.
>
> He stays in contact with my brother though, and I get the news from him on how he is getting on.[44]

An articulate mother, used to talking with rather than down to children, could prepare the ground for Dad's return, gambling on the assumption that he would return. 'Like all service wives,' writes Rea Lowe, 'I had brought up our son to look at photographs of his father and to talk about him constantly.' A colonel with the RAMC Field Ambulance Service, he was demobbed in October 1945.

> It was the happiest moment in my life when he rushed into the house and saw his three-year-old son for the first time and we were blissfully reunited.

This did not remove all anxieties.

> There is no denying that an element of jealousy crept in at first, as I tried to combine the role of wife and mother. Also, it was not long before I detected the effects of the horror of the war, particularly in the frightful campaign against the Japanese in Burma, when so many of his men and fellow officers died, sometimes in his arms. Truly, this was to haunt him for the rest of his days. Today, we recognise these effects but it was not so in 1945.[45]

With no prospect at all of families talking over a long-distance telephone, it was the letter-writers in the forces who had the best chance of creating an identity that children could recognise.

> My father went away in 1942, the same year that I started school, but I have no memories now of my father before that time, and only a couple of family snaps to show me what he looked like pre-war. However, a steady stream of letters and aerogrammes from him, plus photos and special

Xmas parcels with Turkish Delight (the real thing) and sugared almonds, all kept his 'presence' very much before us at home, and, as I grew older and more able to write, I was increasingly encouraged to contribute to the family's replies to his correspondence.[46]

Contrast the experience of Brenda Bajak who was told nothing – until it was almost too late.

My father was in the Irish Guards and went right through the war with General Alexander. My mother had to work in a factory, but my father insisted she try to get out of London. So, my mother and eldest sister went to a large house in Hertfordshire, where my mother cooked for and cared for a number of evacuees. She was only allowed to keep one of her own children with her, so I had to be evacuated with her brother and his wife. I was a baby at the time. I knew nothing of my life before my aunt and uncle. My mother managed to visit twice a month, but I only saw my father twice before I was seven years old.

Children were told nothing in those days and I totally accepted the situation but always wondered why I didn't live with the lovely woman I called 'Mummy'. I adored my uncle, but wondered what a 'Daddy' meant! I used to run up to men in the street and ask them if they were my daddy. Then, suddenly, one day, my mother and sister arrived and I was told I was going to live with them now. Much as I wanted to live with my mother, it was all *very* confusing.

My father joined us some weeks later. He was a total stranger to me and I didn't like him! My uncle had been interested in books, and my father was not. He was moody and very demanding. He ordered us about as though he was still in the Army. He and my mother argued a lot and I wasn't used to grown-ups arguing. We moved back to London where my father had various jobs and then settled at the BBC as a commissionaire. He had *no* idea how to behave with daughters. He shouted a lot and insisted things were done immediately. He told us little of his war. His moods were dreadful – he was great when out at work or with other people, but dreadful at home. He never participated in a 'family' life. He just worked and slept. My mother did everything for him and was the 'peacemaker'.

I left home and travelled as soon as I could, living abroad for over 14 years. *But*, now that I'm in my 50s, and with my mother dying three years ago, I have been caring for my father who is now 92.

I realise now that at the end of the war, he wanted to stay in the Army – that's the only profession he'd ever had. He was a regimental sergeant major, was respected by his men and appreciated by his officers. He must have been totally lost in civilian life – that's why he became a commissionaire! He'd had no family life for *years* so I'm sure my parents had a lot to overcome when they eventually started living together after the war. He'd had to take all sorts of menial jobs and had to live with his 'female' family, who were strangers to him.

He *still* acts like a sergeant major, but I'm so glad to have had these three years with him. I *finally* see him in a different light and I really do understand what he must have gone through when he came home at the end of the war.[47]

Well before the war ended, Ian Jackson and his sister Molly were able to hear their father, though he was thousands of miles away. It was the same message played over and over again on a gramophone record. No matter. This War Office idea for keeping the troops in contact with home was one of its best.

We sat at the dining table which was covered with a blanket and several tablecloths to protect the varnish. I was six and my sister Molly was three and a half years old. It was the same table that Mum and Granny sat us under to protect us from German bombs. There wasn't always time to get to the shelter at the bottom of the garden.

Dad was the reason why we were there. He'd sent us all a food parcel from Africa and a little gramophone recording with his voice on, to let us know he was safe. A wind-up gramophone was borrowed from a neighbour to allow us to listen to the recording.

Mum and Granny carefully spooned on to saucers our share of a gooey brown mess from the parcel, while my sister and I listened to our father's voice. The parcel had started its long journey from Africa many months earlier. The brown mess had been green bananas. I can't recall what our father said but I can still hear his distant voice on that scratchy old gramophone. Ever since then I've always loved the taste of overripe bananas.

But for the younger members of the Jackson family, identifying with a voice was a long way from readjusting to ordinary life. The testing time came in 1946.

Dad was a difficult man to get to know. This wasn't his fault. He went to work as a postman in the early morning, before we got up for school, and didn't come home until after we'd gone to bed. He did this seven days a week with very few days off. When he did have a day off he'd dig the garden with Granny, as it was her house and we couldn't get one of our own.

They produced delicious fruit and vegetables. When the peas were ripe, Molly and I sat on the back step shelling them into a saucepan ready to cook for dinner. Often the peas from a whole pod would slip into my mouth by mistake and I'd crunch them like sweets.

Sweets were still on ration. We didn't see any unless Granny and Mum made toffee from a tin of treacle. Molly and I sat and watched them stirring the mixture in a large cast-iron saucepan until it was ready to pour on to a greased tray for cooling. Granny dropped some of the mixture into a basin of water to test it. If we were good, we got the bits from the basin as a treat. I was always good when Mum and Granny were making toffee.

The following year was fun, especially in the winter. Granny had left some washing out overnight to dry. It froze instead. Molly and I fought each other for the right to carry the frozen clothes, as stiff as boards, into the warm kitchen to thaw. Dad had fixed up a drying rack on the ceiling which pulled up and came down on a rope. I spent a long time learning how a pulley worked until Dad suggested my discoveries might bring the kitchen ceiling down.

Late one night, I woke suddenly, as someone had put something under my pillow. It was dark so I turned on the bedroom light. My dad had left a whole pile of comics. I was very naughty, as I sat in bed reading them as late as 10 p.m. We had to be in bed by six. Dad taught Molly and I how to do things for ourselves which Mum and Granny had always done for us. I was beginning to like having a dad.[48]

Patience was a quality that John Marvelley needed in full measure in coming to terms with his young daughter. Margaret writes:

I refused to acknowledge his existence. I would not be alone with him. I ignored him totally, even when he spoke to me. I replied through my mother or anyone else present, prefacing everything with 'Tell that man . . .' I would not allow him to touch me. He was very patient and understanding, never pressuring me, but there were occasions when it was necessary for me to be helped. If he tried I would struggle to release myself, screaming, 'Mummy, Mummy, tell this man to put me down.'

All this was very painful to him, he could never bear to talk about it, not even many years later. It was my mother who filled in the details for me.

Fortunately, there was a happy ending. One morning, when

I had slept late and my parents were at breakfast, I woke up and called out, 'Daddy.' Hearing me call, Mother had stood up automatically but she was almost knocked over as my father bounded up, pushing her aside, saying joyfully, 'She called for me! She called for me!!' He was accepted. From that day we never looked back.[49]

There were, of course, many reunions achieved without undue anguish.

Mum was all excited as demob day drew near. She would go on about the things they used to do together and how Dad was great fun to be with and I would really like him. I wondered if he would be like the man next door who was a wee fat man and came home drunk of an evening. No, my dad would not be like that – he was a soldier! On the day, I passed him on the road to school. I didn't know him and he did not recognise me.

The difficult part on the first evening of his return was the sleeping arrangements and I found myself in the single bed in my own room. This man with the muscular arms, deep voice and white teeth obviously intended to stay overnight. It appeared to be the plan that I had to sleep by myself, not that anyone had consulted me on where I wanted to sleep.

However, the next day Dad redeemed himself by declaring a school holiday. Off we sailed on the new *Waverley* up Loch Long to Arrochar and then to a cottage on the west shores of the loch. Dad hired a boat for the week and we fished, made fires on the shores, boiled mussels, dug potatoes out of a field and fried them up with the fish. We sang campfire songs, Dad played his bagpipes, locals came round to welcome him home. All in all, I had the holiday of my life. I'll never forget the week that Dad came home.

And, fifty years on, he will never forget that others were not so lucky.

My pal's dad did not come home. He had been a prisoner of war. On VE Day, the flags were up at her house but then the telegram arrived and her mother took the flags down. A year or so after that they received a photograph of a white grave stone. It was taken somewhere in Poland.[50]

A badge from any army beret and a torn telegram was all Janet Worton had to remind her of her father.

'Deeply regret to inform you of report received from Western Europe that Lt. T. H. Worton, Queen's Royal Regiment, was killed in action on 13th April, 1945. The Army Council desire to offer you their sincere sympathy. Under Secretary of State for War.'

Perhaps my mother underlined 13th. It's never been a good day. That was it. No counselling then. She was twenty-four. She never married again. There was no one else for her.

We had several photos of this handsome young fair-haired man, one on my mother's dressing table, and we were sent a photo of a white wooden cross marking my father's grave in Germany with his name painted on in black capital letters. He was blown to smithereens, but I suppose they found something of his twenty-six-year-old body to bury. Was that really his own badge they sent us?

One day my kindergarten teacher called my mother to tell the assembled children that I didn't have a daddy. Before these days of split families, everyone else had one, and they wouldn't believe at the age of five that I did not. Anyway I had never known him, being 14 months old when he was killed, but I did have two little dolls he bought me while marching across Europe.[51]

Tom Robinson's father was a railwayman who joined up with the Royal Engineers. When he was posted overseas in 1941 he left behind a family secure in its confidence of winning through.

I spent what I still believe was a splendid childhood, as the area is heavily wooded and I roamed the woods, bird-nesting and generally enjoying myself. I was in the Wolf Cubs and the church choir and went to school without any problems.

My mother brought myself and my older brother up with a keen sense of discipline. We knew what we could do and what we could not do as she was quick to box our ears. We did not want for food or anything else but I now know that my mother was hard pressed to make ends meet.

I never thought my father would not come back and of course we did not know where he was as his letters were censored.

Even when my uncle was reported killed in the Royal Navy and a cousin died in the Durham Light Infantry I never as a child thought that my dad would die. I thought that as he was in the Royal Engineers he would not be in any danger.

When he returned in 1945, we found that he had been in North Africa with the American 1st Army and then had been involved in the invasion of Italy. The convoy to North Africa had been torpedoed and the troops were kept below decks, some ships had been sunk.

Very quickly, it seemed, he started back to work on the railway and life continued. He took me on trips to 'the pictures' and spoke to the local ice cream man in Italian. Apart from teasing me, a thing my mother never did, there were no problems and we continued as a family. My older brother by this time was in the Merchant Navy and had left home.

My parents adopted a child, a girl, who immediately became my sister and we moved home to the town of Chester-le-Street where I went to a new school. I can never remember any of these occasions causing me any problems and I seem to have taken them all in my stride.[52]

Married in December 1939, Mary Dalton and her husband were together for just six months before he was called up. They met up occasionally over the next few weeks before the long-expected overseas posting.

We parted on the platform of Barry Station in Wales after an air raid. I just knew I was pregnant and didn't see my dear husband for five years, where he served in the Middle East and ended up in Basra in the Gulf.

He returned to us to see his son aged four and a bit, and going to school in the mornings. He had always written airmail and aerograph letters to our son, and a birthday or Christmas present when possible. If not, I would buy something and say it was from Daddy. I showed him photographs and he knew Daddy was a soldier (in fact he claimed a contingent of the Home Guard as they passed the house).

When they met it was very touching. My husband was naturally nervous, but knelt down to this handsome little boy who touched his face and said, 'You are a nice daddy.'[53]

When Aircraftsman Len Stirland came home, his three boys were given the day off from school.

I helped Dad unpack his kit bag – there was a small alarm clock for John, an aeroplane kit for Len, a beautifully embroidered tray cloth and bib in a packet for Billy, and for Mum and Grandma (who lived with us) there were lovely bronze ornaments, made in India, which I still have! The boys would not leave Dad's side and it was football in the garden and model-making and walking in the peaceful countryside.

A week later, Dad had to report to head office of the petrol firm he worked for (he was with them for 36 years) in London. We were able to go with him and stay at North Harrow with my brother and his wife. After the interview, John still remembers the Regent's Park Zoo and wondering why there was lots of barbed wire round the animals' cages and that we were able to buy choc ices (for the first time). People asked us where we got them.

We had a meal in Lyons Corner House, sitting near the orchestra, to the boys' delight. We had just reached the sweet – ice cream, of course – as the orchestra had their interval, so Leonard, a small boy for his age of six years, said to the waitress as she put a super silver-looking dish in front of him, in a very loud voice, 'Don't you have ice cream in *tubs* here then?' This was said in a strong Midlands accent. The other customers collapsed with laughter.[54]

We left Bert Spencer at his front door, having shared a taxi home with an Army captain. Bert takes up the story.

We closed the front door and a little more kissing and cuddling. Nothing else I assure you; my older spinster sister had made a point of being there, much against the family's wishes. She didn't realise, I suppose. When we got right indoors the wife came out with something she has never lived down. She had a big rice pudding for me saved out of rations. I'd just come from Burma, up to my knees in paddy fields, where no one eats anything else. I had eaten tons of the stuff.

The two children had been sent into the garden for a moment or two but now they came in. The eldest, now nine, could, of course, remember me and I got the expected welcome, but the young one looked bewildered. You could see it in her face, this man kissing my mum, what next? Anyway, I picked her up and treated her the same but she recoiled a little but later on she said to her mother, 'I like my daddy but I don't like his splinters.' I'd forgotten I hadn't shaved.

A good clean-up, and, yes, I had my rice pudding, then it was off to my mother's house about a mile away, with the eldest girl wearing my bush hat. I was the youngest of four and the only one in all the family to serve. Mother had had some heart trouble while I was away. She was out in the garden but she saw me through the window. It took her quite a while to compose herself before she could come in. She worried me; she didn't look very well.

After a lovely evening, it was back home to get the girls to bed. In the heat of India between the end of the fighting and sailing for home, all we wore was hat, shorts, socks and boots so we were very suntanned. When I undressed for bed the wife was very amused; she couldn't stop laughing. From my waist to well above my knees and from the ankles down, I was pure white; the rest like coffee. She kept kidding me to go on and take my pants and socks off. I'm not telling you any more about that night.[55]

The chances of building on a fragile relationship with Daddy were much improved when there was an extended and easy-going family to help soften any recriminations. For Marian Bryan, Dad's homecoming coincided happily with a wedding party that turned into a victory celebration.

It was a hot June afternoon the day after my aunt's wedding. All the grown-ups were eating their Sunday dinner and all the children were standing up around the kitchen table. From the kitchen I could see along the hallway to the front door and along the pathway. The door was open because of the heat. Up the path came a soldier. I ran into the living room shouting, 'A soldier's coming,' not knowing that this was my father. The lunch was interrupted and lots of hugging and kissing ensued. I can't remember being told that this was my father, or remember him kissing me. I remember looking up at this tanned and tall stranger, a little in awe I suppose as a five-year-old would. He must have felt ill at ease with me, he'd missed my childhood. We were in fact strangers.

That wedding went on for a week, as the men of the family came home. Each night another husband or brother would turn up, then off down to the pub to celebrate, then back to Grandma's house where we all lived (four sisters and several children), and another 'do' would break out. Next morning, we would find bodies scattered about on the floors and stairs. Some of these friends didn't go home for days and who could blame them?[56]

But all too often, the story ended less happily, with a family crisis brought about by some silly incident that in ordinary times might soon have been forgotten.

My mother and I stood at the barrier watching a stream of khaki-clad soldiers pouring from the train. I remember asking

my mother, 'Is that one Daddy?' over and over again as I had
no idea what he looked like. Then suddenly one of them stopped
and clasped my mother to him. My feelings were of surprise
and disappointment – he was my father, but he seemed more
interested in my mother – and she in him. I felt somehow I'd
lost both of them.

The close and easy lifestyle I'd had with my mother became
one of unfamiliar discipline and loneliness. Two had been
company and my mother and I had been very good companions.
I now felt excluded from their unfamiliar familiarity.

Going home from school was no longer the pleasure it had
been and one afternoon I didn't catch the bus home but, with
my friend Josie, bought a bun each and crossed the Finchley
Road to explore Woolworths. It was fun, exciting and naughty
but I felt sure my parents would be pleased to see me when I
eventually returned home.

Waiting at the bus stop later I wondered how I was going
to get home as I'd spent my bus money on the bun. A kindly
fat woman asked what someone so small was doing going home
on the bus alone – 'And I've spent my money on a bun,' I said.
'Your mum will be worried sick about you,' she replied and gave
me a penny piece.

By now I was looking forward to the welcome I was going
to get. As the door was opened I was horrified at the response.
Instead of the hugs and kisses I'd expected, my mother and
father were shouting. 'We called the police station but they
only had a little girl with a red ribbon in her hair!' and mine
was blue. I felt misunderstood and confused.

I was 5½ years old and from then on never really established a close relationship with my father, though I don't think he ever knew.[57]

For some, the differences were too great to endure. Dads came home and went away again. It was through the school railings that one young boy saw his father for the last time.

> I was nearly seven
> But
> We did not speak,
> My stranger
> and I
> I remember him now,
> as then,
> by the sadness of his eye
> and the tear of his look.
>
> I was too young
> Too young, to know
> We were captives
> Each to the fate
> of the other.
> He looked – and seemed
> to say,
> It's finished – over
> But I shall
> Love you ever.

He turned then and
walked away.
The glance pained,
A good-bye not said
And I never
Saw
My stranger
From that day.
Forgive me Father – my stranger –
If I find it hard to love you.[58]

CHAPTER FIVE

'Don't Be Jealous . . .'

Salvation Army's advice to women

I f it was hard for men coming back from the war, what must it have been like for women? Between August 1939 and June 1945, 619,000 women joined the auxiliary forces. At the peak of mobilisation, in mid-1944, the women's services – the Women's Royal Navy Auxiliary Force, the Auxiliary Territorial, the Women's Auxiliary Air Force, and the Auxiliary Nursing – had a combined strength of 466,000. What was to happen to them after the war?

The condescending assumption was that they should rejoin the family circle as wives, mothers and homemakers, as normal women, for heaven's sake. But the transition, even if it was possible, could be an agony of frustration, as a former long-serving WAAF testified in a BBC broadcast.

I have been taking stock of myself as a civilian. I do not altogether like the look of what I see, because I have made the unpleasant discovery that up-to-date I'm not much good as a woman newly out of uniform. You see, the service has provided me with everything for five years, and I've been taking a lot for granted, such as a roof over my head, uniform clothing, excellent food, drink at reasonable prices, cigarettes at a cheap rate, entertainment by Ensa, Cema, and film shows for the payment of a very modest sum of money, and four holidays a year on full pay and free warrants to any part of the country I was staying.

In fact life held no responsibility for me apart from my service duties. Service life is undoubtedly the most simplified form of existence provided one follows the rules. Men have always readily adapted themselves to a service career. The post-1939 regimentation of vast numbers of women has given the latter the opportunity to discover that they have the chance to follow a career without the responsibility of attending to hampering domestic details – a unique position for the average woman.

One of the foremost problems in a woman's life, 'What shall I wear?', is automatically solved the day she puts on uniform, and the wearing of uniform carries many privileges with it and opens many doors which remain closed to the woman in civvies. A fact I took very much as a matter of course during the five years I wore it. I find myself now sometimes walking into an officer's club for lunch and remember with a slight shock that I am no longer eligible for membership as I am a civilian.

One of the first things to consider on becoming a civilian – again something there's no need to worry about in the services – a roof over one's head. I luckily did a bit of thinking ahead as I laboriously started getting a home together two years ago for my husband to return to from the Far East. The windows of my house recently went out with a bang, but at least it is still habitable, so that is one problem I have not had to face.

Then – food. Queuing up by the servery hotplate in the mess for a nicely cooked meal three times a day is a very different proposition to standing in long queues for the odd bit of fish, meat and groceries. It is no longer a case of saying to oneself, 'I'm hungry, thank goodness it's nearly breakfast, lunch or dinner time,' not forgetting the odd cup of tea in the office or the canteen. I now have to think, 'WHAT shall I eat, WHERE shall I eat, and how often shall I eat?' My monthly mess bill for food would just about cover the price of two meals in a West End restaurant – it wouldn't cover my groceries for two weeks. The drink situation does not worry me as I get along without it very well, but it is an expensive proposition buying a friend the odd spot other than beer in a public bar in comparison with mess prices. I do however miss my ration of cheap cigarettes. I am finding that rather too much of the money I'm not earning at present goes up in smoke.

But what it boils down to is this one important fact, I HAVE GOT TO THINK FOR MYSELF NOW. Nobody is responsible for me in 'sickness and in health' but ME. The might and weight of a completely self-contained service of which I was a humble unit has been removed, and I face alone a world which frankly has no particular interest in my being alive or dead.[1]

Each of the women's services ran refresher courses on how to be a civilian. Domesticity took pride of place but there was some provision for vocational training.

This housecraft course includes cookery, rationing, budgeting, the principles underlying the use of paint, household repairs, making loose covers, rug-making, and a whole lot more. There are talks on dress design and embroidery – and for variety they have discussions on films, the theatre, and art appreciation. They're taken on visits to gas and electricity showrooms where they learn comparative fuel values, and they're shown good examples of utility furniture and modern kitchen fitments.

. . . Practically every kind of work is dealt with, and – what is pretty important, I think – girls are helped to make up their minds as to what they want to do . . . Those who are career-minded are given every opportunity to get at least a sound background training in whatever it is they want to do.[2]

Despite efforts to achieve a jolly 'all girls together' return to civvy street, ex-servicewomen who had had their taste of freedom were often, not surprisingly, reluctant to return to the old routine. Trouble was, those who wanted a career found themselves at a disadvantage.

I had had my own office in the services. Had been responsible for the interests and welfare of a large number of people. I had helped to feed them, paid and amused them; but when I told all this to the Labour Exchange, the Rehabilitation Officer smiled and shook her head, and explained that in order to do any one of these things in civilian life one must be trained, diploma'd and take examinations for which I might or might not receive a grant, nobody was then quite sure . . .

That was it. Nobody, least of all myself, was 'quite sure'.[3]

Ideas for career women were, to put it mildly, a little patronising.

I'm wondering if you might be interested in something to do with Horticulture? . . . There are specialised branches such as bulb and violet farming, herb growing, work in glass houses, etc. – there's sure to be an increasingly steady demand for women in this sort of work for years . . .

Or what about Industrial Welfare? . . . There are a number of good jobs going for the right sort of people in this direction, once you're fully trained, and I should think it's rather up your street! I had a chat with a Ministry of Labour official the other day, and he told me there are three or four Free Training Courses now available for ex-servicewomen. I believe two of these are Baking and the Retail Distributing Trade.

I think the war years have stabilised women's position in all sorts of industries in which they weren't very firmly settled before! You might like to take up something like

Electrical Housecraft – become a Saleswoman in the Electrical Industry or combine it with domestic science and become a Demonstrator.

I've even heard of women plumbers, paper-hangers, and garage mechanics – so you've plenty of scope![4]

Not surprisingly, by late 1946 more were rejoining the women's services than leaving them. According to the SSAFA:

The disappointments of civil life and the attraction of the life offered by the Services resulted in a big increase in new recruits.[5]

Exchanging a military uniform for civilian clothes was a minority experience among women. More common was handing in the overalls in exchange for an apron.

It is seldom recognised today that in the war years women were liable to be 'directed' (conscription by another name) into the auxiliary forces or the munitions factories. In January 1942, following a poor response to an advertising campaign to recruit women into industry, the government made a first tentative move towards the mobilisation of women, with the call-up of 20- and 21-year-olds. That the age band was so narrow indicated the sensitivity of the issue. There were traditionalists in the Cabinet, including Churchill and Bevin, who would have preferred to stick to voluntary measures. But the pressing need for labour overcame reservations and it was only a month before another directive ruled that those women between the ages of 20 and 30 already registered and available for work could get jobs only by going to the employment exchanges. The age level was raised to 40 in 1943.

Although mothers and housewives could claim exemption, the administrative structure now in place allowed for the direction of female labour into armaments, nursing, the Women's Land Army ('Back to the land, we must all lend a hand, To the farms and the fields we must go'), public transport (the female clippie was a familiar sight on urban buses) and civil defence.

When mobilisation was at its peak, there were 7,250,000 women (46 per cent of the age group 14–59) employed in industry, the military and civil defence. The 8,770,000 who remained full-time housewives had to put up with food shortages, rising prices, queues, the misery of the blackout, loneliness and fear of air raids. Of the 130,000 civilians killed during the Blitz, 63,000 were women.[6]

For younger women – unmarried and married – there was some compensation in being able to enjoy a more varied social scene. Unaccompanied visits to dance halls, clubs and even public houses, up to now the preserve of the male drinking classes, became commonplace. The arrival of American and Canadian servicemen with money to spend and a readiness to enjoy helped to lighten the mood. There was more sex outside marriage. It was bound to be so with split families – the women bored and restless at home, the servicemen free from domestic ties. Everyone knew someone who was losing a partner. Serving in the Far East, Bert Mullen recollects

> . . . friends and acquaintances who were victims of broken marriages and engagements – mainly due to their previous partners not waiting for them over the years (Dear John letters and Yanks in the UK, etc.), or sometimes it was due to our 'change of outlook' on life – caused by unusual experiences during the war years. This happened to me – a broken engagement.[7]

Women on the loose are a common feature of war-time memories, as in this collection garnered by George Campbell.

> My Uncle George came home after the war and brought a woman called Kitty with him. She was a Cockney from Bow and smoked like a trooper. She stayed about three months and then left after a blazing row.
>
> I remember my mum talking to another neighbour one day and she said that a couple of local women (whose husbands were fighting in Germany) had been out with men from the local workmen's club. They came home late singing and were neglecting the kids she said.[8]

For those who felt the desire to stray, the peculiar conditions of war offered every opportunity for military and civilians alike.

After the war my father stayed in London to work for two years to 'get experience' in his job before returning home. My mother was so green she believed this. She still does at 80 years old. But just in the last two years my auntie, my father's sister, tells me Dad fell for a WAAF and lived with her in London for two years. At the time all my friends' fathers came straight home from the war but not mine. He died six years after I was married, in 1965. I must have been green also, because I always believed he was in London for work.[9]

Stiff-necked moralists were quick to condemn what they saw as a descent into promiscuity. But there were sympathetic observers – among them Barbara Cartland, the romantic novelist, who acted as a war-time marriage counsellor.

It is very easy to say what a woman should do or should not do when she hasn't seen her husband for four years . . . They were young, their husbands were not fluent letter-writers – they started by not meaning any harm, just desiring a little change from the monotony of looking after the children, queuing for food, and cleaning house with no man to appreciate them or their cooking. Another man would come along – perhaps an American or an RAF pilot. Girls were very scarce in some parts of the country and who could blame a man who is cooped up in a camp all day or risking his life over Germany for smiling at a pretty girl when he's off duty?

He is lonely, she is lonely, he smiles at her, she smiles back, and it's an introduction. It is bad luck that she is married, but he means no harm, nor does it cross her mind at first that she could ever be unfaithful to Bill overseas. When human nature takes its course and they fall in love, the home is broken up and maybe another baby is on the way, there are plenty of people ready to say it's disgusting and disgraceful. But they hadn't meant it to be like that, they hadn't really.[10]

In his book, *Love, Sex and War*, the historian John Costello allows a correspondent from Manchester to speak for all those for whom romance was the only available antidote to fear and loneliness.

We lived in a world of uncertainty, wondering if we were going to survive from day to day. My husband was away in the RAF as an airgunner, and I'd conditioned myself to the fact that his lifespan was also limited and that our short, happy married life together was over . . . When 1942 came in with the hit-and-run air raids, I began to despair that the war was ever going to end. It was in this frame of mind that fate took a hand in my affairs.

The Yanks arrived and set up camps near Manchester, bringing a wave of glamour, romance, and excitement that has never been experienced before or since. They were not welcomed by the British men, but to the English girls they were wonderful. All I knew about Americans was what I'd seen on the films, but Fields Hotel, within walking distance from my home, became the meeting place where GIs danced under soft lights. Eating in secluded corners with their girlfriends, the GIs were able to forget the war for a few hours. There I was introduced to an American army captain. He was tall with blonde hair and blue eyes . . . I felt rather embarrassed at his flattering remarks about my long hair and attractive appearance. I felt even more embarrassed when we danced the American way, cheek-to-cheek. Outside in the blackout, Rick took my hand, clicked his heels together and bowed to me, saying how much he'd enjoyed my company, then he walked down the path towards the waiting jeep. If I was expecting a goodnight kiss, I was surprised and a little disappointed. 'And they say the English are a cold race,' I thought, and I didn't think I would see Rick again.

One weekend, as I prepared myself for another lonely sit-in, an unexpected phone call from Rick made my heart jump with pleasure. He came around about dusk in a jeep carrying a holdall and bounced it on the kitchen table. 'There,' he said, 'take a peek.' It was full of tinned goods, butter, sugar, sweets, coffee, sheer nylons, and make-up – not forgetting cartons of cigarettes. He had also thoughtfully brought two bucket-loads of coal.

So began another part of my life on the home front.[11]

The friendly invasion of Britain by American troops was a gift to enemy propagandists. Men serving overseas were subject to non-too-subtle hints that wives and girlfriends were finding comfort in the arms of American and

Canadian soldiers. Needling jealousy was sharpened by lurid tales of dissolute behaviour brought back by men returning from leave.

Uncomfortably aware of the effect on morale, the War Office urged broadcasters and film-makers, the two most powerful agents of counter-propaganda, to scrutinise 'every statement of fact and attempt to screw out of it any argument for resentment against Britain'. War Office records reveal a frank acknowledgement that anger against Americans was growing 'to such a pitch that every exaggerated story is rapidly circulated, and these allies are held responsible for all sorts of happenings – murders, rapes, drunkenness, thieving and so forth.'

Reasoned argument was a feeble weapon against the power of rumour.

It must be realised also that the resentment about the Americans' good pay, welfare, clothing and entertainment does not primarily spring from these things themselves. It is basically the result of deprivation of home life and its advantages which creates aggressive feelings against all more favoured brothers. Such resentment, of course, is glad to feed on any excuse of the others' ill-conduct (and these are not a few!) while silence creates a suspicion of the unmentionable.

So said a report in late 1943 called *Psychological Problems of Troops Overseas*. The suggested remedy was that broadcasters should show the humanity and ordinariness of the American and Canadian, to get the British individual to regard him as a brother and a comrade . . . Friendly intimate cameos of individuals will help. It will be useless to deny that Americans and Canadians have faults, for suspicion will grow on such denials. Mass reporting of praiseworthy allies only leads to further resentments of their privileges. Exaggerated anxieties on some scores may be removed by frank admission of the existence of the problems, by personal talks with and about individuals of these allies, and having established liking for the person concerned it will be possible to listen to him presenting or illustrating the case without exaggeration or justification. It may also be possible to show by rather too hard an objective criticism of a friendly American that Britons are not deserting Britons abroad for Americans at home.[12]

As to the portrayal of British women,

Infidelity and masculine fears must be faced and got over. The first by the soldier asking about it or hinting at it whenever he goes into a factory where women work or a woman's organisation, and being answered by a woman character in various ways – 'I'll bash your face in if you talk like that. Good heavens, what do you think we are!' or 'Well, yes, we've had two cases in this factory already in the last year and a half. It's absolutely scandalous. It lets us all down. You know, there are 900 girls working here, and all of us feel it. It isn't right, you know. I don't know what my husband would think if he heard about it.' The second, masculiniation, can be got over by showing the femininity of trousered women, and concern for their menfolk, and cups of tea, and the warm attitude towards their homes, even if they do wear trousers and wield spanners.

Radio and film

. . . can illustrate essential femininity (as a reassurance against the soldier's fears about this) and should give forth affection and the suggestion that they are waiting for the return of armies abroad. This need not be done by direct speech, of course; an unconscious glance at a photograph of a soldier on the mantelpiece, or a term of speech – 'If our Harry could see me now' – are the sort of things that can be both natural and implicit ways of conveying this attitude.

The women of England must be shown as having a non-anxious but non-hedonistic daily life. Their needs for men's company can be expressed by their wishes that the boys were back home, and by indicating their determined affection for their troops overseas. With extreme care a Canadian voice might talk to a female one, in a friendly fashion, but as a decided outsider. His politeness and his thanks for hospitality must be the medium of conveying his own strangeness and that his heart really lies in his own country.

On the wider front:

It might be possible to illustrate the small changes in England which make the soldier abroad feel that he might be a stranger, by such a trick as a dialogue between the soldier and the cameraman. On a bus, for instance, the soldier would ask, 'I suppose the stuff on the window is netting for air raids.' Of the conductress, 'So that's these bus women I've heard about. Not a bad job she does. Why is she shouting, "Workers only?" I bet that chap in the front isn't engaged on war work', etc. A shot of a soldier's hand throwing the ticket away can be answered by, 'Here! You can't do that. Pick it up. You get pinched for throwing paper away these days.' Episodes like these should be short or they will smell of education and propaganda.

The softening-up process may have worked for some but the fact remained that Americans' cheerful friendliness and generosity, qualities that made for popularity in peace-time, were less appreciated when wives and daughters were left unguarded. Resentment endured to the end of the war and beyond, a feature of domestic life recorded by J. B. Priestley in his short novel, *Three Men in New Suits*.

Eddie Mold returns to his farm-worker's cottage to find his wife out, his unopened telegram on the kitchen table and a heap of whisky and gin bottles in the garden shed. Listening to pub gossips brings realisation and the inevitable confrontation.

He stood there, looking at her, saying nothing. Something ought to have been there that wasn't there. And then he remembered – the bottles. They'd put them away. He could see them doing it, whispering together and shoving them back into the shed. Must think he was daft. Well, she'd see.

'Eddie.' She gave him a quick frightened glance, then looked away and dabbed at her wet face. She looked like somebody else. He hadn't come home to live with this one.

'Don't start telling any bloody lies now,' he told her. 'Didn't take long to 'ear it all. Proper knockin' shop. And you one of 'em. I 'eard plenty tonight at the Sun, and don't want ever to go in there again. Yanks. If they couldn't get it for nothing, then it was a quid for the whites an' two quid for the blacks. Them bloody bottles,' he shouted at her. 'They told me the tale anyhow – didn't need to 'ear any more. That's what I come back to. And my kid dead—'

'Don't bring her into it,' said Nellie, glaring at him. 'Leave her out of it. I didn't do anything till she'd gone – an' then I was so miserable, I didn't know what to do—'

'You knew what to do all right,' he shouted at her. 'An' you went an' did it, didn't yer? Well, go an' bloody well do it somewhere else now.'

'Eddie, what do you mean?' She was staring at him with her mouth wide open. Had something done to her teeth too. Probably paid for by what she'd earned on her back.

'What d'yer think I mean. I didn't come back for their bloody leavings. Bugger off!'

'Oh no, no, I can't!' she began, wailing.

This only made him angrier. 'I've told yer. Outside, sharp! Before I set about yer.'

She stood up, angry now rather than frightened. 'You won't touch me, Eddie Mold!'

'Touch you!' he repeated quickly. His anger was racing down his arms, quivering in his fingers, rising to his throat and nearly choking him. Then, quite suddenly, he felt sick. 'If I do touch you, I'll wring your bloody neck. So don't let me find you 'ere when I come back. I'm tellin' yer.'

He went out to the back and there he was sick, all the night's beer returning in a stinking flood. Down his new suit too, some of it. The terrible indignity of life, which the soldier knows better than most men, which he thought he had done with for a time, had him in its grasp again. He shivered above his vomit, then went slowly back into the cottage, his anger gone.

But Nellie had gone too.[13]

That reality was likely to be more prosaic did not make it any less painful.

I was married on my embarkation leave in May '41. Two days later I was on my way to the Middle East where I spent the next 4½ years. In late August '45 I returned to this country to find my wife had been living with a Yank for three years. There were no children so I divorced her.[14]

The shock of returning home to an unloving wife was an experience shared by all ranks. Quintin Hogg, later

Lord Hailsham, was invalided out of the army in late 1942.

In the nature of things, I had no opportunity of telling anyone the date of my return, though my family knew, I believe, of my illness and of the general nature of my intentions. I arrived in London late on the Saturday night in the blackout, dishevelled, tired after ten days' travel, twenty-three hours of which had been in the air, and still broken in health. Throughout all my travels, on the voyage out, in the desert, on night patrol, in Cairo, in Lebanon and in Syria, as a sort of talisman I had kept the key of my front door at 1 Victoria Square, and after stumbling up the steps in the dark, I put the key in the lock, and with a lump in my throat opened my own front door. I had no thought but to give Natalie a pleasant surprise, and the tiny gifts I had bought her. A startled voice from upstairs called out: 'Who's there?' I called out who it was, and went up to greet her. She was not alone. Fortunately, the full significance of what I found was not immediately apparent to me. I was introduced to a young French officer who – tactfully, I thought – made his apologies and left. Natalie gave me to understand that she was going to leave me, and I begged her not to. But the next morning she did and took the first instalment of her belongings . . . I was alone in London and alone in the house at the end of 1942, without ration card, identity card, clothes-points, much underwear, transport or immediate friends. The words I wrote in my diary some days later were: 'The kind of welcome I got when I came in had better not be described here.' My life was in ruins.[15]

Part of the anger against the foreigners' way with women and their rumoured prowess in bed sprang from guilty consciences. Whether on home bases or overseas, young servicemen were no angels. No one in Britain thought to try to measure the level of sexual activity in the armed forces – it was just not done to delve too closely into such things. But the liberal allocation of contraceptives to troops abroad suggested that the War Office was under no illusions. If there was anyone who still held to the chivalrous notion that the fighting spirit was a sublimation for sex, the rapid spread of venereal disease should have disabused them.

The declaration of war with Germany was the signal for the immediate release of a Ministry of Health circular to local authorities warning of an expected rise in VD rates brought on by the 'excitement of war conditions'. Within weeks the prediction was confirmed by hospital out-patient records but it was not until after the Dunkirk evacuation that the Treasury agreed to fund counter-measures, including mobile VD units. In less than two years, the national VD statistics soared by 70 per cent, with the biggest increases in London and the major ports. The graph climbed again after the arrival of American troops in Britain.[16]

In October 1942, the Ministry of Health embarked on

a campaign to educate the public. Advertisements appeared and pressure was put on newspaper editors to cover this delicate matter in editorials and news items. The Joint Committee on Venereal Disease noted:

> It is appreciated that space is valuable owing to the paper shortage and the Press having been responsive in the matter of the paid advertisements may not be readily prepared to give further space to this particular subject. Notwithstanding, the Committee feel that the possibilities in this respect should be explored.

Discussions were started with the BBC to explore

> . . . the possibilities of providing increased facilities for the presentation of the subject of venereal disease in their broadcast programmes, preferably in the late evening hours.[17]

The campaign continued throughout the war and into the period of demobilisation when the emphasis was on reminding married men of the possible consequences of their deviations from the marital straight and narrow.

> Venereal Disease – If you have ever suffered from any form of this disease be sure that you have completed the treatment and observations recommended by your medical officer; the observation period for gonorrhoea is a minimum of three months and for syphilis two years. Remember that

disappearance of signs and symptoms does not mean that you are cured. If you are not really cured you may transmit your disease to others, particularly your wife and children, so for their sakes as well as your own, make sure. If you are in the least doubt go to your own doctor or to one of the many treatment centres situated in most of the larger towns where you will receive advice free and in confidence.[18]

There was no advice on how to explain to a deprived partner why intimacy should be further postponed by months or years. Though presumably it would not have taken long for her to guess.

Another indicator of extra-marital sexual activity was the illegitimacy rate. Illegitimate births increased from an annual pre-war average of 5.5 per 1,000 births to 10.5 per 1,000 over the six war-time years, with a 1945 peak of 16.1 per 1,000.[19] It could be argued that the increase was artificial in so far as conditions did not allow for the usual number of shotgun marriages. Before and after the war it was quite usual for a detected pregnancy to be followed by a dash to the altar. But fathers in uniform were likely to be far away at the time when they were needed for a marriage ceremony. The figures must therefore allow for a category of what might be described as illegitimate by default.

On the other hand:

Babies born to married women in Britain were regarded as legitimate unless registered otherwise, and therefore children who were fathered by someone other than the husband were often not declared illegitimate and did not appear in illegitimacy statistics. That many British women married to absent servicemen did bear children is confirmed by the detailed investigation conducted by some of the larger municipal authorities. The records kept by Birmingham, for example, indicate that almost a third of all confessed illegitimate births were to married women and that the pre-war rate had trebled by 1945. Although this level was pushed up by the large number of American service camps around the urban area, a similar rise was observed in other large cities.[20]

The figures are further distorted by illegal abortions, the number of which is anyone's guess. Contemporary impressions suggest a big increase, particularly towards the end of the war.

Noting that illegitimacy rates were highest among the young wives of servicemen, John Costello argues that 'their work in war production encouraged an independence that often snapped the bounds of marital fidelity already strained by the extended absence of their husbands'.

And, one might add, the prospects for post-war reconciliation were correspondingly diminished. What happened to the children of these extra-marital unions depended on the permutations of family life. A correspondent from the West Country recalls a convoluted childhood with happy consequences.

I only knew and loved one of my three fathers. When my mother's husband arrived home from overseas he was devastated to find her 'with child', or, as Father would have it, 'with children'. My twin brother and I were born in the summer of 1945.

They were lonely days for the little wife left behind working in the factory so my mother sought comfort in the arms of another military gentleman (home on leave, I presume). My brother and I were the result of that war-confused union. Divorce was not a consideration in 1945, single mums were not in fashion, and a war-weary, unskilled man did not feel able to support alien twins. So my brother and I were placed for adoption. Though I have the documents and certificates to prove my origins and true parentage, I have never met either my genetic father or my mother's husband. Indeed, the saddest aspect of this triangle is that I have never met my birth mother. Something I would have dearly wished for, if only to have been able to say 'Thank you' for placing me, through adoption, with the most wonderful and loving parents any child could have wished for. My brother and I have been most fortunate.

The Second World War and indeed the events on D-Day changed world history for ever, but those events in the 1940s changed the course of my life immeasurably.[21]

A less happy story is told by Marilyn Harris, whose parents narrowly beat the legitimacy deadline, getting married five days before she was born. It was not enough to make a family.

When I was at school, my mother told me, 'Your father was no man to leave a woman and a child alone.' My life was hell with her taunts and lies about my father. I was always told, 'Go to your nan (her mother), I don't want you.' When Father came home, he was rejected and told by my mother to get out.[22]

Marilyn eventually tracked her father down, but he refused to see her. Years later when, as an old man, he was dying in a nursing home, she made another attempt at reconciliation. Again, refusal.

Years apart allowed suspicions to fester beyond help, even when there was nothing to justify a grievance.

My mother, alone during the years with three children, became neurotic and began to 'nag' my father about his alleged unfaithfulness when in the Army. She had no evidence of this and this behaviour resulted in their separation after we had moved to Sussex in 1945 when I was nine years old. All of us children, except my youngest sister, eventually left my mother because of her behaviour.[23]

Many of the old social values were destroyed by the war. It was a time for change and for all the worry and discomfort that accompanies a loss of certainty and a fear of the new.

It was precisely as T. F. Main had predicted as psychiatric adviser to the Army command. Two years after the end of war, he reflected on the problems he had so perfectly predicted.

> Many a returning serviceman knew that he had new viewpoints and ideas, and some were and are eager to practise their expression in civilian life, but few had any but a superficial understanding of the emotional strengths and weaknesses that service life had given them. Most men knew that they had a lot to learn, but few were prepared for problems of emotional adjustment in their very homes, and their own workplaces, and among their own familiar communities. In fantasy their civilian life was to be as they left it, with no closing of the emotional ranks when they fell out, and they felt themselves to be basically unchanged. The great barriers of unshared experience that grew up in the war years between them and their families in civilian life were and could only be half-realized. The blessing of freedom carries many burdens, and the feeling of these burdens had been forgotten.[24]

The emotional deprivations of service life intensified the hunger for home but at the same time romanticised what men would find when they eventually returned.

> Comfort, freedom, tolerance, affection, independence lay there. It was forgotten all too often that wives are not always obedient, loving, good-tempered and dressed in their best clothes, and it was not realised that a warm fire, an armchair, a book (and no bullying sergeants) become boring after three

or four hours. Friends are forgetful and may have grown new interests and other ties, and old familiar places are oddly unexciting and unsatisfying. It is both puzzling and disconcerting that the much longed for feeling of belonging at home can be so elusive, and that the old familiar places should feel so new. The feeling of strangeness, the growing fear of not now being able to grasp the prizes of old feelings and situations, the anxiety that after all it can never be the same, are forceful disappointments. A fear of meeting friends in case of failure, an inability to sense atmosphere in old places, and a feeling of emotional isolation from the relatively lawless and selfish civilian life is a terrible tragedy after years of longing. The difficulties are often about intangible and incommunicable deep human values, and the inability of others, wives and friends, to share a subtle but important viewpoint makes for distress and growing anger and a belief that they have forgotten what life is about. Men in such a state are restless, bitter and irritable at home, and feeling cut off from the very sources of understanding and affection go for long solitary walks or remain silent and morose for long periods. Alcohol is a commonly sought relief, and may help a man to talk to strangers without uneasiness, but sober mixing with crowds and inactivity at home are alike intolerable.[25]

The freedom and independence assumed by women of all ages did not accord with the serviceman's fantasy of easy suburban respectability. A wife who had acquired new tastes, new enthusiasms and opinions of her own was unlikely to want to backtrack on her experience.

Arguments, rows, violence in the home, hopeless impotent rage may follow the thwarting of the repatriate and his wife in their need to regain the homely understanding they so often cherished and yearned for in the past. These outbursts of anger are followed invariably by shocked repentance, and then the whole cycle may begin again on a basis of bitter despair at ever regaining emotional security.[26]

Warning signals were put up by those with a practical understanding of both sides of the issue. The WVS had this homily for staff dealing with the problems of men returning to find their wives had changed.

People who have been away from home four or five years have their opinions of women's work and capabilities still based on a pre-war conception. They are saying they find their women terribly independent! Put the following point of view across to them! If a woman has had to make decisions as to whether her children shall be evacuated or not; if she has had to do all the business over air-raid repairs for the house (figures showed damage or destruction to one in every three) and has perhaps herself kept the (husband's) farm or shop ticking over, she naturally does not now wait for her husband to decide whether to call in the plumber or not; she knows there isn't a plumber anyway, and she probably gets on with the job herself![27]

As a correspondent from Dundee puts it:

I think that it was Mum who was most affected by the enforced separation. She had found herself having to deal with all the family finances (which had never previously been her domain, and which she had not been educated for, through no fault of her own), raising two schoolchildren on war-time rations, and caring for her own elderly widowed mother. At the time of course I was sublimely unaware of her feelings, and largely unaffected by the war in my own small world of school and home.

Even now I don't really know what, if any, effect, good or bad, that separation and subsequent reunion had on the personal relationship between my parents. That part of their life was private to them, and never discussed in front of their children.[28]

While acknowledging that women had survived by their own efforts and deserved credit for their achievements, the WVS and others told them bluntly not to expect too much of their men too soon. 'The returned men are going to find it very difficult to adjust to home life again,' the WVS chairman warned her members. 'They have grown used to getting their food in pretty good quantity; now they will have to witness the shopping, the queuing, the contriving with rations that their wives must put into each meal. Talking to men coming into your clubs on their way back, I think you can do much by suggesting what is to be

expected. They will probably have been quicker in imag-
ining the results of bombing and air raids than in realising
the war's slow undermining of a woman's patience.[29]

It took time for war-weary soldiers to realise that women
at home had had their share of nervous exhaustion.

'When are you getting married, Jack?' I asked a friend just
back from Germany.

'I'm not,' he said. 'At least, not to Mary. Why, she used
to be a nice, quiet, thoughtful kind of girl. Now she thinks
of nothing but dancing and pictures. Drinks too much, too.'

I asked him if he knew she had suffered badly in the Blitz
and if he had talked to her about it.

Jack went away, and when I saw him again he told me
they were going to get married quite soon.

He found at first she had tried to avoid talking about the
bombing or even thinking about it. She couldn't stay at home
or be alone, must be 'on the go' all the time. Then she cried,
and after that it was all right.[30]

Any suggestion that ex-servicemen should exercise more
tolerance and understanding brought an immediate riposte
from homecomers who were disappointed by their less than
rapturous reception and disturbed by what they saw as a
society gone to pieces.

We disembarked, not expecting any particular acclamation,
but at least we hoped to find the work of the fighting forces

overseas had been realised and appreciated by our womenfolk.

What did we find? That any expectations we had of picking up the threads of our domestic life were lost in a wild fandango of pleasure-mad, sensation-seeking civilians. And somewhere in this chaos were our womenfolk.[31]

The possibilities for misunderstanding and unfounded jealousies were legion, as Margaret Wilson discovered.

A week or so after Harry got his demob, he asked me to go out, but I had never been to any clubs. But my father and mother, Harry and myself went to the club, and, as I was following the family out, an old friend, Mr Waters, whom I had known since I was a child, asked me if I had enjoyed myself at the Burns Hotel a few miles from here. I said I had never been there. Harry overheard him and he said to me, what did that mean? We had quite a row as we were coming home. My father asked what had happened. I told him what Mr Waters had said. My father told Harry it was all lies and that I had always been faithful, but I never slept that night. As a matter of fact, I cried all night because Harry didn't believe him. He had heard of too many wives going astray. Next day, my father took Harry down to the club to see Mr Waters, and he said it was only a joke. 'I've known her since she was born.' He came to the house to apologise with cigarettes and sweets, as he owned a shop. My mother never in her life swore until that day and she told him what he could do with the sweets etc. All the money in the world couldn't put things back to normal, as it could have caused a divorce. Harry went back to the mines after two weeks' leave, but after five years' absence he still had doubts in his mind and he suffered nightmares for a long time after the war. The coming home was not as I wanted it. Mr Waters set the seeds of distrust and jealousy crept in for no reason whatsoever. My life was hell at times. Harry has been the only man in my life since I was sixteen, and I'm proud of the fact, as everyone knows I loved him dearly.[32]

Shared visions of the future were altered by time and circumstances. A couple who thought alike in 1939 were liable to find themselves at variance five years on.

Before the war George was in an insurance office, an unexciting job, but since then his life had been full of danger, adventure, a highly colourful existence. Africa, Sicily, Normandy, and a race at breakneck speed to Germany.

He had just written to Sally, his wife: 'For goodness' sake find us a little place out in the country. The only thing I long for is a quiet life and time to grow things in a garden. Soon I shall be at home and *must* get away from people for a time.'

Poor Sally! This letter came as a shock. She had been evacuated to the country a week after the war began, four miles from the nearest town. All her dreams of good shops, gay friends coming and going, cinemas and theatres, were shattered.

What *was* she going to do about it? The common-sense way was to compromise – to have a house with a garden, not too far out, with a good train service.[33]

The gentle pursuit of compromise – putting concessions before demands – was as critical for relationships between mothers and their returning sons as between husbands and wives.

The Salvation Army had a few words of advice for mothers who might be inclined to overdo the welcome home for beloved children.

Don't be possessive. Maybe he went away a youth, but he has come back a man. Treat him as you would any other man of his present age. He will make his own decisions, plan his own time-table and choose his own friends. He will respect your advice much more gladly than if you present him with a cut-and-dried policy . . .

Don't ask too many questions . . . Your interest and concern are bound to be evident some way or another, but they've done with the Intelligence Officer and catechisings. Make the atmosphere of home conducive, and they'll talk all right.

Don't be jealous. You have no monopoly of their interests, and it is wiser to make their friends your friends too, if it is humanly possible.[34]

There were many women who simply lived for the day when they could be reunited with their husbands or lovers.

The idea of having to adjust came naturally as part of the progression of being together.

Enid Innes Ker gave in her notice at the BBC when she was sure that her husband, Tam, was on his way home from a Japanese POW camp.

The couple of weeks I had between leaving the BBC and Tam's arrival home was a very fraught time. I spent hours on the 'phone to various people in Norfolk trying to find a cottage to rent for the winter, and then later, when I had an idea of Tam's arrival date, trying to book us into a hotel for a couple of days after his arrival. I must have tried about 40 hotels in London before someone in the BBC put me on to a bed-and-breakfast place just opposite Claridges where I was finally able to book a room. I think it was probably not a reputable hotel, but it suited us admirably . . . I eventually managed to rent a semi-furnished cottage just by South Walsham Broad – for £2 a week. It had no running water, only a pump outside the back door, and no electricity or other lighting, but we were very happy there.

Maw has told me since that she did not know how she lived through that time with me, coping with my swings of mood. One minute I was on cloud nine and writing reams to Tam, and the next I was either worrying about accommodation, or cast into the depths because I was sure that he would meet and fall for someone on the way home, after all those years of never seeing a woman – there were bound to be nurses and other women on the ship and we all knew how quickly shipboard romances could flourish; or else I was very distressed because Tam's letters kept coming in saying he had not heard from me. I also became very depressed about my clothes, and suddenly came to realise how tatty my underwear was. How often it is that when one is in an overwrought state the break comes over something quite trivial. In my case it was the deplorable condition of my suspender belt that caused me to give way! I did not have enough coupons to buy a new one, and I told Maw in great distress that I could not possibly let Tam see me in that garment. Maw did not say much at the time but the next day she went out and bought a piece of stout unrationed material and some suspenders. With this, and taking the zip out of my condemned garment, she fashioned quite a reasonable substitute – and calm was restored.

The reunion took place on Euston Station – with little warning.

There was no question of having lunch, I just grabbed a taxi and dashed off to Euston. There was a great crowd of waiting wives and we were not allowed on to the platform but were kept back by barriers till the train came in. And then from every door there burst men with bright yellow faces (they had been dosed with mepacrine, a treatment for malaria, on the way home). I frantically leaped over the barrier and made my way along the platform amidst this sea of uniform and yellow faces, wondering whether I would recognise Tam, and then I saw him – fighting off the well-meant attentions of a WVS lady who was offering to carry his kit bag. He had spotted me vaulting over the barrier and could not shake off the WVS lady quickly enough.[35]

People had changed, life had changed, often in silly ways that were nonetheless confusing to a long-absent repatriate. Well before his arrival, Mrs Innes Ker had reminded herself to tell her husband

. . . that a penny stamp was now 1½d. and the minimum fare on buses had gone up from 1d. to 1½d.

This was a much greater change than you would think now when prices go up all the time. The charge for posting a letter to any destination in the UK had been 1d. ever since the inception of the 'penny post' in 1840. That had been the cost of a letter all our lives, and the extra ½d. seemed an enormous increase. Similarly the distance one could travel by bus for a penny was so great that we had become accustomed to offering up a penny on a bus and going as far as we wanted. Well, of course, Tam's first evening in London the cost of stamps and bus fares was not exactly a subject of prime importance and did not figure in our conversation. The next morning I emerged from my bath to find that Tam had disappeared. He was away such a long time that I was beginning to get quite worried. When he did appear he was bearing a bouquet of flowers for me. He had decided to pop out while I was bathing, thinking there would be a flower shop nearby.

Not finding one he had hopped on a bus, and of course automatically proffered a penny. The combination of Tam's uniform, his bright yellow face, the fact that he did not know the minimum fare was 1½d. and that he was seeking flowers for his wife bowled over the conductress. She would not accept a fare from him, told him where to get off and find a flower shop, helped him down with care and sent him on his way wishing him luck.[36]

The suddenness of many reunions often mirrored the abruptness with which loved ones had been sent to war in the first place. The call-up papers for Gladys Constantine's husband arrived one morning in February 1942, the same day she heard of her mother's sudden death.

My husband was due to report to the Army in three days' time. They graciously gave him an extra two days so that he could attend her funeral with me.

Our daughter was then five years old. He couldn't bring himself to say goodbye to her. He tried to write to us every day, though sometimes, depending on his movements, the letters came in batches. He always put in a separate letter solely to her so that she would not forget him, and he had a photograph of us both. When he was sent abroad, I did not hear for months and when I did, there was a black pencil through much of it. I just had to address my letters to him at 'PAIFORCE'.

It was one morning in June 1946 when a telegram came,

'Meet me at Radley Station at 11 a.m.!' . . . We were galva-
nised into action. The house was to be clean and welcoming,
and then we would dress up in our war-time best clothes and
cycle out to Radley Station to await the train, looking
glamorous!

I was on my last job, cleaning the kitchen floor on my
hands and knees with a scrubbing brush, when the kitchen
door opened and there was a soldier standing silently on the
mat. He had managed to get an earlier train. What a let-down
for me, but we used to laugh about it.

Of course, there were many adjustments to be made when
the men returned. I had 'grown up', so to speak, having
learned to cope and be independent, looking after a big
productive garden and even working at the local army depot
in a disused cinema for a few hours each day.

Our daughter, now nine years old, was a capable young
lady with a mind of her own – not used to responding to
army-like orders without question. So tempers would flare
and I was caught between two loyalties, but by thinking ahead,
I was able to avoid the situation arising. But when we had a
lovely little daughter in October 1947, the problem solved
itself; his attention was split between two of them. His
gardening became a real hobby and the nine-year-old joined
him. Later, when she grew up, the younger one joined him
in the garden.

There were, of course, financial problems after my
husband's return. The house needed repairs and replace-
ments. The Army pay in the war was a mere pittance and

I had 32s. 6d. to keep the two of us at home with rent of 17s. plus rates.

Those in the forces who were lucky enough to return to their old job found that promotions promised had gone to others who were already there. Again, others who had been in reserved occupations (like making beer) had made headway in their careers and had been well paid also during the war.

However, without ambitions we were just as happy.[37]

Dedicated wives were liable to become equally dedicated nurses for the period in which their husbands acclimatised to a life without terror.

Dad had survived the war without any physical injuries but in the months to come his body succumbed to numerous large boils which Mum had to bathe day after day for months. Also, as his nerves were rather shattered, we were not allowed to make any noise in the house. We had a piano, which Mum had inherited from her auntie, but we were not allowed to touch it when Dad was home, even though Mum scrimped and saved to be able to spend ninepence a week for me to have music lessons. Dad also smoked heavily.

Looking back, I don't suppose any of us fully realised the horrors he had experienced during those war years. There was certainly nothing like counselling for people then, to help them cope with the effects.[38]

Sheral Towler's father was a POW.

He arrived home and through my eyes he looked funny. A tall dark stranger that never spoke, he just sat in the chair and stared with an awful look in his eyes. My parents lived in two rooms with my mother's parents. Gran and Granpa still had a few of their sons living with them who also came home from the war. Their homecoming was so warm but my father's wasn't the same.

Over the months that passed I can remember being woken by my father's screams. To me he was speaking silly, but it was him speaking the German he learnt.

Mum's marriage was very up and down although they had five more children. He never came back the same man. Over the years he drank, and said awful things. The one thing I realise now is really he should have had help, but didn't receive any.[39]

Marriages made in haste to beat the deadline of an overseas posting, and based on little more than a spur-of-the-moment physical attraction, were at risk of one or both partners repenting at leisure.

The Morrells had more to go on but Alma was not entirely free of worries that her marriage might not survive.

I have always resented the fact that the war took quite a few best years of my life away. We married in 1940 after a long courtship and were only married two weeks when he was called up. 1940–1945, my husband was sent abroad and I never saw him for four years. He left from Scotland around the Cape to Iraq, back to Egypt, across the desert to Italy. I wrote to him every day and in return (he liked poetry) I have a book full of beautiful love poems. When he came home in 1945 I met him at the station. Would he still love the girl he had left behind previously? Fortunately he did, because we celebrated our Golden Wedding in 1990, but alas he died the same year. Had we not had a true foundation from the courtship I don't think we would have survived the long separation.[40]

It took huge strength of purpose on both sides for a war-time marriage to survive, particularly given how little time many couples had had together.

We got engaged the first Christmas of the war. He was 27 (just), I was 25. We didn't intend to get married straight away as we had very little money – however, he got his call-up papers in 1940 early, so we decided to get married before he went, then I would save the separation allowance (which was about 30/ [£1.50] a week). We arranged the wedding for June 1940 – however, he was called up early so we had to bring the wedding forward. He had to go five days after the wedding. After that, we had a 48-hour leave about once in three months, and once or twice I managed to go see him for a weekend. (Travelling on unheated trains, usually packed with people sitting on their suitcases in the corridors.) You couldn't read as the lights were so dim.

Then he was sent to North Africa, later Italy. We never set eyes on each other for three years, only censored letters. However, on demob we took up where we had left off. We had a very happy marriage, it got better as time went on.[41]

That many family crises were waiting to be discovered is suggested by the frequency of cases where one or other of the branches of the voluntary sector was able to pre-empt domestic calamity.

A WVS representative in Malaya heard of a sergeant who was frantic with worry yet had been refused compassionate leave.

He had had word that the grandfather with whom his wife and three children lived in a remote country place had suddenly become totally blind. The young mother had to look after him as well as her trio of under-fours; she could leave none of them long enough to do the two-mile walk to the shops. A member living near her was alerted and secured a reliable Home Help to go in regularly, while Kuala Lumpur WVS secured a promise to have the father's case reviewed.[42]

It was another family breakdown caused by grandparents losing control that set a young soldier in the Far East worrying about his six-year-old brother.

Grandfather, a house painter, had broken his hip falling from a ladder and was unable to work; debts were piling up and

Grandmother, overwhelmed, had taken to drink. In the neglected home a WVS member saw the boy looking 'more like an animal than a child; untaught, unfed, unwashed and with no idea of manners'. It happened that the writer kept a small private school. Without fee, she called for the boy every morning and kept him for the day at her school, providing clothing and meals. A Home Help got the house cleaned up. Granny was persuaded to stop drinking. The small boy became a perfectly normal child. And his brother was content, though before he had been clamouring to go home.[43]

Relationships crashed when the reality took over from the fantasy created to help sustain a prolonged absence.

I found many prisoners of war very distressed because their wives had aged a lot in their absence – they hardly realised that they had aged too – and one man said to me rather bitterly, 'I left behind a pretty young wife and have returned to find an "old soldier", hardened by four years' factory work.'[44]

Judging by talks to groups of employers, Army Welfare Services had a grasp of the often cruel realities of starting again as a civilian.

I dealt recently with the case of a Durham miner ex-prisoner of war who returned home to find his 15-year-old daughter, whom he had last seen as a little schoolgirl of ten, walking out with a soldier. He took her home and walloped her and she left the house. This man still further complicated his family affairs by accusing his wife, quite unjustifiably as it turned out, of carrying on with another man in his absence, and dragged her down to the local police station to have the row there, to the gratification, of course, of the village gossips![45]

Rows, even when violent, could be contained within the family if at the cost of individual happiness.

My father spent the war with the 8th Army Royal Artillery, starting in the deserts of Egypt, moving up through Sicily to Monte Casino, and ending the war with the partisans in Yugoslavia. He sent me ribbons and dresses, and almonds. In later years he talked nostalgically about the war after he had had a few drinks. He was, I discovered a few years before he died, a very sensitive, artistic man, whose nature rebelled at what he had had to do.

My mother, Lily, a nurse, worked at the munitions factory at Aycliffe. She brought me shortbread, and I can still recall the wonderful smell! In the evenings she taught me to read: I knew all my nursery rhymes and could declaim a number of vaguely unsuitable poems, such as 'The Highwayman', long before I started school.

When Dad came home, Mother and I were at home, in Angus Terrace. I was almost five and had never seen my father.

She was exceedingly fussy about the house, and I seem

to remember she was polishing a chair when there came a knock at the door. I can remember reaching to open the door, finding a strange soldier on the doorstep, complete with kit bag. I did not know who he was, so he must have arrived from the Italian-Yugoslavian border unexpectedly. What my actual reaction was I do not know, but I must have resented this intrusion into my life. I had always slept with my mother. Now I was ejected and probably felt rejected.

My father soon went away again to train as a teacher at Freckleton near Preston, but when he came back, there was permanent warfare in our house. My parents rowed and fought viciously for the rest of my mother's life, and most of the time they did not speak to each other. I did what I could to protect my mother in the fights, but I usually came off worst.

A new baby was born in 1952. She was very premature and very sick for a long time. My father doted on her, and to me the contrast between this relationship and his and mine was stark.

My father and I never got along together. He hit and punched me frequently for no good reason that I can ever remember. I know he knew he was cruel to me. I know this because I found him once weeping by my bedside. He swore he would change, but nothing did . . .

In my father's later years, after my mother died, I learned to love him. He was a kind and loving grandparent to my children, and we miss him dreadfully.

His was a life wrecked by the war. As was my mother's

and my life up until my marriage. And there was no compensation for that![46]

It was much the same for Avril Middleton, whose father, a Royal Marine, was away for the first six years of Avril's life. In the war it was her mother who took the brunt, 'a highly intelligent, self-sufficient person' who made a living as a teacher. When her parents came together again in 1946, it was a meeting of opposites.

My father has always not been quite as articulate as her and they have rowed almost every day in their 56-year marriage. She believed in a personally oriented family with everyone having the right to a say. He believed in an authoritarian family with his word as law. Having been brought up by her for six years I found it impossible to accept this 'interloper' as boss. He had had amoebic dysentery whilst in Burma and whenever he drank heavy-gravity beer it made him angry and violent. He didn't drink often, but seemed to think it manly to drink this kind of beer when with the boys. I hated him for what he was doing to our family. One of my strongest memories was one Saturday. My mother had got lunch, there was still rationing. Our kitchen was in the basement of an early-Victorian house, it had a flagged floor and a scrubbed-top large table which was laid. My mother just said quite lightly, 'You're late, Ted'; my father without a word kicked over the table, breaking all the crockery which was very difficult to get, and I went over to him and kicked him on the leg and told him how much I hated him. My mother was kneeling on the floor picking up the broken crockery and crying.

This pattern of events went on for many years. My mother tried to commit suicide when I was 13. They never got to know one another because of the war. My mother would have lost her job if there had been a divorce. It was impossible to teach then if you were divorced; the woman was thought to be 'scarlet'. It was bad enough being married.

When the relationship was not violent it was cold.

My mother told me that he was unable to get an erection for six months or so when he returned from the war.

The impact on Avril was lasting.

I never married as I had such bad role models, and my relationships have been stormy. Most men find a strong woman difficult to deal with, it frightens them. I only had strong women as my role models in my formative years. I was forced to be a 'substitute husband' for my mother as my father refused to take responsibility for anything, either financial or personal. He should never have married and should have stayed in the Navy. He was excellent as a leader, being dropped behind enemy lines to set up resistance cells, winning medals and being a hero. It was the everyday life he could not handle. He expected everyone to be honourable and took their word and therefore got kicked in the teeth time and time again. He never had a chance to grow up in a normal environment.[47]

The reverse situation, with a mother descending from frustration into helpless anger, was experienced by Dorothy Bullock.

My father was called up in 1939 and fought in the North African campaign for six years. I was five years old when he left and eleven years old when he returned. I was playing in the street when he arrived and he didn't know me. He was a stranger to us all. He had one demob suit on his back and a few bob in his pocket. Mother was angry and crying when she saw him. Apparently, he should have arrived a week earlier, and she wanted to know where he had been. When he told her she was still angry. He had been to a camp somewhere in England to be checked out . . . He said all the men had to go through this but my mother wouldn't believe him. She accused him of having some sort of disease from abroad and that's why he didn't come home. She made life very difficult for him and us, always angry, always crying, always shouting at him. They sent these men home after six years of fighting, no help for them, no counselling, no one to talk to, no one to help them adjust after the hardship suffered in the war. They both should have had help, they certainly needed it.

   . . . I remember my mother burning all my father's

photographs of him in uniform. It was as if she didn't want to be reminded of him in the Army. It was not a happy time for us when he returned. He loved us but my mother's bitterness and unhappiness all the time made home life difficult.[48]

After a long separation, much depended on the way the reunion was handled, by both partners. Was it nervousness or sheer insensitivity that led Derek Bradley's father to behave as he did?

We knew from his letter when he would arrive home after the nearly six years' absence, i.e. early a.m. on a specific day. Mother hung bunting, 'Welcome home – Laurie,' all over our little back-to-back, inside and out, and all our neighbours were aware.

We were both up early that day and waited all through the day till I was put to bed at 9.30 p.m. I was awoken an hour later by shouting and swearing etc. I came down to find two men in khaki in the room with my mother in tears. Father had just walked in drunk with his friend. They had spent all day up at his mother's with family and friends and had a wonderful time. What a let-down, poor Mother.[49]

Another less than happy homecoming is recalled by Betty Colven.

WHEN DADDY CAME HOME

We were living in Peckham, and married, with two daughters aged three and one. After six years in the Army he was finally to be demobbed. The date was April 27th, 1946, and it was Cup Final Day. We put up 'Welcome Home' banners and waited for the big moment of his arrival, complete with demob suit etc. The time was 1 p.m. After a brief greeting, he turned on the radio and settled to listen to the Cup Final, ugh.

He couldn't understand that he was now a family man, welcomed and needed.[50]

Fortunately, as Betty Colven says, she 'worked on it'.

Every now and then he would say that he was going out. No not to the pub, but to musical concerts, the pictures, or a football match. The latter I didn't mind, he has always been a football fan. He couldn't understand that I felt hurt. This situation went on for about a year while we both adjusted. We have now been married for 52 years and are still together.

The readjustment was all the more difficult when the wife had stepped into the husband's shoes.

There were tensions between our parents but we were not aware of them until later years. I learned that my mother wanted my father to get out of the pub trade, particularly as his health had been ruined in the war. My father had been a notorious gambler before the war and was a very familiar figure at racecourses. He was red-hot at mental arithmetic.

My mother reckoned that he would have been a good book-maker. I have no doubt that she was right and my father's refusal to change career undoubtedly contributed to his early death. What made this tension worse between them was that my mother had run the pub for four years with some success. She had put money away whereas my father would habitually take his spending money out of the till. I can remember fear-some arguments – not the words but the noise and the hurt on my mother's face.[51]

For the typical couple, the welcome home, bringing in family and neighbours, was the big event that broke the psychological barrier of years of self-containment, allowing two people to rediscover each other in the conviviality of something like a wedding party. Valiant efforts went into those events, with the re-emergence of long-hoarded scarci-ties of food and drink. All contributions were gratefully received.

An old uncle who lived with us died just before VE Day, so when we had the street bonfire his mattress was hauled down-stairs and put on the fire. As they got to the bottom of the stairs, the big stair knob fell off the banisters and Gran said she thought it was his head, even though he had already been buried.[52]

But after the parties came the inevitable feeling of anti-climax.

After four years apart, Mabel Harrison was unable to find out exactly when her husband was coming home. For three nights she waited up until the early hours, listening for the sound of a taxi pulling up at the front door. The burst of celebration when he did arrive was all the greater for the agony of waiting. Soon enough it was time to start the hard slog of rebuilding a life together.

He was given £75 demob pay and we were on Army pay for three months. I had saved coal as I worked all day in a library but he was so cold, it was deep snow in January, that the ration soon dwindled. March was exceptionally warm and we had a week in Scarborough, then he got his old job back as painter and decorator. I gave up my job, women didn't go out to work in those days. The food was a problem, making the rations spin out, and I had difficulty finding cigarettes for him. He had toothache and was refused by three dentists for not being on their panel before he found one to pull his tooth. It was hard adjusting after so long but we didn't have counselling in those days, you just had to work it out. The soldiers were very bitter about their lost youth. My husband was 27 when he joined up and 33 when he came home. I was three years younger. The house needed decorating but there wasn't any wallpaper at first. Life was hard because we had lots of electricity cuts and they usually happened at teatime so I was cooking our dinner by candlelight, very miserable. One thing we enjoyed was hiking in Wharfedale with our friends. We went every Sunday in 1946. No cars in those days for us. The men were a bit depressed at Civvy Street, it wasn't what they expected, no one seemed to want to know about their war, and to us who stayed at home it went sort of flat when the war ended. The excitement of air raids etc. was over.[53]

The Harrison family came through in one piece. Many others collapsed in the squeeze of personal, social and economic pressures.

CHAPTER SIX

'An Immeasurable Effect On Married Happiness'

War – according to the Denning Report on divorce law

I was in the land army in 1945, stationed just outside Grimsby in Lincolnshire where my mother and family were living at that time. I returned to my home for a weekend leave, a few weeks before the end of the war, to be told that my mother had left home and that my brother and sisters were at my aunt's house awaiting collection. I was to take them home as soon as possible.

As the oldest of six children and with a father serving in Italy, Dorothy Skipp bore the full force of her family crisis.

I was devastated and vividly remember walking to the Post Office, sobbing, with people staring at me. The clerk counted the words on my telegram to my father and, seeing how distressed I was, tried to comfort me with kind words. I have never forgotten him. Obviously, I had to return to my billet to request leave and my aunt agreed to have the children while I arranged this. My father's telegram reply came after a couple of days and said that he was trying to bring his demobilisation forward. Meanwhile, he asked that I try and keep the children together and pay the rent and insurances until he arrived home. This I did with the few pounds I had saved.

On his arrival home, my father's first task was to make friends with the youngest children who did not remember him at all. We then all sat around the table and discussed how we should handle things without our mother there to supervise us. We decided that my father should return to Barking, in Essex, where we had lived previously, to try to obtain a house for us. I was to be in charge during his absence and the various household chores would be shared between us all. Even my youngest sister, who was only four years old, had to take her turn to do the shopping.

During this difficult time, my mother decided to take my 14-year-old sister away. She did this by meeting her at the school gates one afternoon. My father was furious and was determined to get her back, to keep the family together. He did not know where to start looking as we had no idea where my mother had gone. We found a piece of blotting paper in the house that my mother had used, and by holding it up to a mirror we were able to decipher her address in Coventry. This was a pure piece of luck! My father duly brought my sister back after some unpleasant and difficult scenes with my mother.

We eventually obtained a house in Barking, but prior to this move we were temporarily split up. My youngest sister and I went to an uncle, one sister went to my grandmother, and my father and remaining three children stayed with an aunt. Once we were all together again we continued our routine of keeping house collectively. On Friday nights, we all stayed in to clean the house from top to bottom. This did not always suit everyone, as the elder children would have preferred to be out with their friends on Friday nights![1]

The steep climb in the number of divorce petitions – up from 9,970 in 1938 (in England and Wales) to 19,155 in 1944 and 34,443 in 1949 – was wholly predictable. The same trend had shown up after the First World War and since then divorce procedure had been simplified by the 1937 Matrimonial Causes Act. That the apparently inexorable rise caused little dismay in government circles was less to do with an ignorance of statistics than with an exaggerated faith in the war-time machinery set up to allay family conflicts.

At home, it was the probation officers who were in the first line of reconciliation, being involved in family disputes either by direct appeal from wife or husband or by request of a magistrate with a matrimonial offence to resolve. The back-up to the probation service, and its natural successor in the business of marital repairs, was the Marriage Guidance Council. Set up in 1938, its progress was interrupted by the onset of war but it was reconstituted in 1943 with centres in London and other big cities. Its consultants were largely middle-class professionals ready to give their time for modest payment or no fee at all and their valuable contribution was acknowledged by a government report in 1947:

> Our experience shows that when we are able to deal with conflicts in marriage at an early stage, it is possible for the skilled helper to resolve them in the large majority of cases.[2]

For the armed forces there was the option of taking marital troubles to a representative of the Soldiers', Sailors' and Airmen's Families' Association, which boasted a network of 20,000 representatives round the world. Even so, such was the need for the avuncular shoulder to lean on, SSAFA was at risk of collapsing under the weight of tribulations.

In the Mediterranean area, work also increased rapidly, the Middle East branch dealing with 8,500 inquiries in the last six months of the year from serving men and women regarding their family problems at home. Of these, 5,000 were conducted by personal interviews with the men. The Tripoli Inquiry Bureau had a particularly busy time after the cessation of the Tunisian campaign. Travelling SSAFA officers visited hospitals, convalescent depots, detention barracks, base depots, and other static formations, and in certain special circumstances – as, for instance, just before the opening of the Sicilian campaign when units were confined to camps in the desert for security reasons – SSAFA went out to them by car and interviewed men from dawn till dusk. These travelling officers often had to undergo considerable hardships and discomfort.[3]

By 1942, the pressure for help from servicemen with domestic troubles had reached a point where it was considered to be a threat to morale. As a remedy, legal aid sections were set up throughout the Army and the Air Force. Though prepared to give practical advice on dissolving relationships that had gone sour, their first objective was to encourage reconciliation.

Men away from home are inclined to act on impulse sometimes at a time when there is still some hope that they might become reconciled. It is important that no man should take the irrevocable step of bringing his marriage to an end while there is a reasonable chance of becoming reconciled. It is right and proper to give advice and assistance to a man who has decided that after full and careful consideration and with all due regard to the future to institute divorce proceedings. It is essential, however, in order that he may give the matter earnest thought before taking the irrevocable step, to advise every such applicant of the seriousness of his proposed action and of its effect and consequences to his wife, himself and to any child they may have . . . While any improper pressure will not be exercised, and while it will always be borne in mind that the final decision is for the applicant and nobody else, it should be remembered at all stages of the case that an applicant might change, or begin to change, his mind, and that such change of mind might not crystallise into a full attempt at reconciliation without encouragement.[4]

On paper, the results were impressive, with an estimated 27,000 reconciliations, 'but it is only right to say that there is no record of how many of these reconciliations proved permanent'.

Quite so. Notwithstanding the combined efforts of SSAFA and the military legal aid service, the pressure on the divorce courts intensified. By 1944 there was a backlog of 25,000 cases. And divorce statistics tell only part of the story. Magistrates had wide powers to grant a wife a maintenance order – in effect, an acknowledgement of separation and marriage breakdown – on the grounds of her husband's desertion, cruelty, adultery or neglect to provide for her or their children. These orders, which totalled 10,538 in 1938–9, had increased to 25,400 in 1945–6.

In December 1943, the Cabinet took note that the spate of divorces was not likely to fall off for some time.[5] New judges were assigned to the Divorce Division and there was a move to extend the power of assizes out of London to hear divorce proceedings. But these were no more than stopgap measures. With no sign of an easing of the legal bottleneck, the idea was mooted of allowing the county courts to try undefended cases. Lord Jowitt, the Lord Chancellor in the post-war Labour government, had his doubts. While recognising the merit in reducing delays in hearing cases – some petitioners were faced with the prospect of years of waiting – and in reducing the cost of obtaining divorces, involving the county courts 'would give rise to acute differences of opinion and to violent controversy, particularly in the House of Lords.'[6]

Given that the huge Commons majority enjoyed by Labour and the urgency of the matter in hand, it might have been said that Jowitt was acting overcautiously. His timidity may have had something to do with facing up to the stony disapproval of Geoffrey Fisher, the tight-minded Archbishop of Canterbury, who believed that 'each single divorce, however understandable, however tragic . . . creates an area of prison and a centre of infection in the national life.'[7]

It was Fisher who was the self-appointed leader of a crusade for moral regeneration, calling upon the country to reject 'war-time morality' and return to living Christian lives. And it was Fisher who would lead the opposition in the House of Lords to any shortening of the divorce marathon.

But Jowitt's fears of a clerical assault were dismissed by the Cabinet with an endorsement, in principle, of extending the authority of county court judges. Meanwhile, a committee of inquiry, set up under Sir Alfred (later Lord)

Denning to recommend 'procedural reforms . . . with special reference to expediting the hearing of suits and reducing costs',[8] also came out in favour of using the county courts. Jowitt still dithered, seeking clearance from the Chancellor of the Exchequer before taking the irrevocable step. His letter to Hugh Dalton suggested that it all came down to a question of who was paid what.

> I am worried to death over this beastly question of divorce . . . I am recommending the Cabinet to accept the recommendations of the Denning Committee and get the County Court Judges functioning as soon as possible; but according to that Report the County Court Judges are to act as though they were High Court Judges, and . . . they are to be treated while doing divorce both in the matter of robes and payment as though they were Judges of the High Court. This will involve some fairly substantial payment out of public funds, but I am satisfied that it is the cheapest way to meet the difficulty. I might otherwise have to resort to drastic steps and appoint a whole batch of new High Court Judges at a salary of £5,000 a year each; whereas under this scheme once I have got it working I hope I shall be able to cut down my High Court Judges from the present seven sitting in divorce to something like three or four.[9]

Dalton was suitably relaxed at what he saw as a minor imposition on the national budget.

I have had a quick look at the Report and I am glad to say that I shall have no point to raise at the Cabinet about the financial implications. It seems to me that, if the proposal enables the bulk of the outstanding cases to be cleared away rapidly, it will be cheap at the price.[10]

The full Denning Report was published in February 1947 with recommendations for grants to voluntary bodies offering marriage guidance and the appointment of trained welfare officers to work in co-operation with the divorce courts to persuade worrying spouses to patch up their differences.

The Court Welfare Officer should have special duties to perform in cases where there are dependent children. The children are the innocent sufferers from any estrangement of their parents, and it is in their interest that every possible attempt at reconciliation should be made. We realise that an unhappy home may be worse for the children than a home with one parent only; but true reconciliation means a happy home with both parents which it is desirable for every child to have.

Adopting the popular consensus that 'the marriage tie is of the highest importance in the interests of society', the Denning Committee nonetheless sympathetically acknowledged the 'external difficulties which strain the marriage'.

'An Immeasurable Effect On Married Happiness'

The recent war and its consequences have increased these greatly. It has removed men and women from their accustomed environment, separated them for long periods, and subjected them to severe physical and emotional strains. There is a housing shortage which often prevents married couples from living together; or huddles families so closely together that the strain of constant association becomes almost intolerable; or subjects young couples to the interference of relatives. The mere mechanics of everyday life have become so exhausting for women as to have an immeasurable effect, through sheer weariness, on married happiness.[11]

Those with settled relationships – being of a certain age, perhaps, or of firm convictions – were liable to give short shrift to the moral backsliders, who were urged to pull themselves together. The Salvation Army knew what had to be done:

But it is no use people getting sorry for themselves instead of being sorry for their sins. The married man who 'can't leave' the girl he has met, the woman who 'doesn't want' to sort things out and face life afresh often need truth more than sentimental sympathy.

Things have gone far enough in finding excuses. It is far more important that the structure of society shall be kept secure than that individuals should perpetuate their straying fancies.

Of the need for pity and understanding, I have spoken

often during the past few years. But a clean cut with a spoiled past is the first condition of restoration. The men and women who admit they have played the fool and must end it now are far more likely to get back to healthy security in their human relationships than those who find excuses for their sins.[12]

But it was not just sexual aberrations that led to family break-ups. The causes of incompatibility came in many guises. This account from a WVS worker is a heartbreakingly sad snapshot of the times.

Over a year ago, in a batch of exchanged invalid prisoners, a man I know of came home. He was taken prisoner at the time of Dunkirk. He had been in a prison hospital close on four years. When he went overseas he left a wife and two babies, one of a few months, the other two years old. The husband and wife were desperately in love, the parting was torture to both.

What happened during the years they were apart? He was in bed and in great pain much of the time and he thought of her and the children. He saw, as is natural in a dream, their little home slightly glorified. He saw his wife running her house and looking after her babies and, of course, always looking as he loved her most. All through his suffering he was comforted by the knowledge that one day he would get home again, that then everything would be perfect. Back where it used to be, except that his wife would be sweeter even than before, waiting on him and petting him, making up as best she might for all he had endured.

And the wife? She had to leave the little house to take the children away from the air raids. She shared a house in the country with another woman and her children for two years. At last, unable to bear sharing any longer, she brought the children back to London. Her furniture and curtains had suffered damage from neglect. As a sergeant's wife she had not much money, but she did not want her husband to come home to a shabby house. She took the children daily to a war-time nursery and got a part-time job in a factory. She put the children in the nursery by seven a.m. She worked in her factory until mid-day, had dinner in the canteen, came home past the shops to get her food and about three began her housework and cooking. At half past four she fetched her children. After a little play she bathed them and put them to bed. As soon as they were asleep she got down to washing and mending their things. In between these chores she paid the rent and the insurances, filled in Government forms, got new ration books and all the other odd jobs that fall on the householder. She grew more tired and dragged-looking each year; just one thing kept her going. Some day her husband would come home. She had her dreams too. He was coming home the gay, strong young man who went away. He would hate to see her tired and worried and he would kiss her and pull her head on to his shoulder and say: 'You relax and leave everything to me.'

The end of this particular story is a tragedy. I heard it from the man's side. 'It was as if we were strangers. We sat night after night facing each other across the fire. We seemed to have nothing to say. It was as if a wall had grown between us. We couldn't go on like that. We're getting a divorce.[13]

Another way of settling marital disputes, more drastic than divorce or separation orders, was resorted to with increasing frequency in the mid-forties.

Charged with wounding his wife Ivy, Craftsman Harold Booth, aged 37, was committed for trial . . . Mrs Booth of Underhill-street, Leicester, said her husband was the father of two of her children, but during the four years he had been in the Middle East she had twins, and a boy by another man. Her husband did not know of this until he returned home from overseas on Oct. 8. He had been drinking, and when she told him the twins were hers, she alleged he picked up a knife from the table and stabbed her. Det-insp. McMurdo alleged that when charged, Booth said: 'That's quite right. I saw red and stabbed her.'[14]

After a courtship in the course of which a total of 372 poignant love letters were exchanged, a 23-year-old RAF warrant officer was alleged at Exeter to have confessed that he had shot his fiancée. For the prosecution, it was said that the airman, who had received neuro-psychiatric treat-ment, felt that he was being pushed into marriage with the girl (an expectant mother) against his will, that he had made three attempts to break off the engagement, and then, feeling the position to be hopeless, he had shot her.[15]

The behaviour of his wife, to whom he was devoted, while he was in Burma was suggested at Willesden to have preyed on the mind of a returned soldier who stands committed for trial at the Old Bailey on the charge of murdering her. He said that what had happened to him was the general fear of all the men in Burma.[16]

A letter quoted at the trial of a newly demobilised soldier accused of murdering his wife must symbolise what young husbands feared most.

Dear Jack – I have no rights to call you husband ever again, and I know what I am going to tell you will shock you. I have a son a few days old. I don't want to make excuses as I know there is no excuse for a mistake like that.

You told me years ago going out boozing would be the ruin of me. Well, it has ruined our lives. I know you are too hard a man to ever think of forgiveness or that I would have made the greatest mistake of a woman's life in one night. Please don't stop my money until you arrive back in England for Barbara's [their daughter] sake. Then I will get out for good. I won't bother you ever again, and I know you will take Barbara from me. With that, and what I have been through these last months, I think I have suffered for what I have done. I could have run away with the man. He offered to take me, but, Jack, even though I know what to expect from you, I wait for you to come home and at least have done my duty as a mother to Barbara. Tell me if you want me out of the way before you come home. I will find somewhere to leave Barbara, if that is the way you want it. I have learned my lesson. I hope, some day, you will find loneliness is the hardest thing in the world to fight. I guess I am not fighter enough. Oh, Jack, tell me what you want me to do. You see, I happen to love my husband and his daughter.

It will break my heart to leave you both, but debts must be paid, and not with money. I paid with months of torture.

Well, Jack, it took me a long time to tell you, but I would rather confess than have someone meet you and delight in telling you. Goodbye for now, Jack. Barbara is wonderful. I hope she never finds out what her mother done. All my love, Lily.[17]

Judges were surprisingly lenient when they detected extreme provocation. Lily's husband got five years for manslaughter. A soldier of the 14th Army in Burma who 'dreamed of the little house in Yorkshire and lived for the day when he would return to his wife and two children' went to prison for seven years after he found that his wife had been unfaithful.

He failed to straighten a domestic tangle, and finally cut his wife's throat with a razor.[18]

Another 14th Army veteran was bound over for two years after he arranged an abortion for his wife who was pregnant by a lover. The abortion went wrong and the wife died. The manslaughter verdict was accompanied by words of comfort from the judge.

I am sorry for you. I think that by stress of circumstances you were finally goaded into doing this, in order to retain the affection of your wife. You have suffered terribly already, and by your own act have lost this woman you loved.[19]

And a 24-year-old soldier who strangled his wife in the interview room of a Nottingham hospital went free after the judge told him: 'In all my experience I don't think I have ever had to try a more tragic case than this.'

The defence had claimed that right to the end his client believed his wife was loving and faithful.

When they met in the hospital he wanted to put his arms around her and kiss her, but she was 'cool with him'. He was not bitter towards her.

When the others left the room his wife suddenly said to him, 'It's not yours. It is another soldier's.' That was the first time he knew the child was not his.

He asked his wife the father's name, but she refused to tell him.

'I put my arms on her shoulders and told her she must tell me. She still refused and I held her by the neck and said,

"You have got to tell me." I had no intention of killing her. I hoped to frighten her into telling me who the father was.

'She still refused, and I shook her with my fingers on her neck. I found she had collapsed and laid her down on the floor. I thought she had fainted. I was nervous and put the handkerchief in her mouth to prevent her coming round too quickly before I could get away.'[20]

This was described as 'shock after shock – provocation after provocation'.

Public interest in the plenitude of sex offences which stopped short of murder was heightened by the frequency with which they were committed by 'returning heroes'. 'River Plate Sailor Assaulted Widow – Girl Tells of Scar'; 'Paratrooper Said to Have Used Broken Glass – Officer Don Juan Deceived 5 Women'; and, intriguingly, 'Sailor Came Home a Changed Man'. This last was a case in which a young naval rating, home from service in the Far East, took to ripping up women's clothing, a harmless pursuit until he started assaulting female shoppers in a Birmingham department store. He was sent for medical treatment.

Here was the stuff of drama, and the dramatists duly seized on it. Shuffling trial records, it is easy to spot cases that might have served as inspiration for the emotionally deprived major in Terence Rattigan's play, *Separate Tables*.

In a plea at Lewes Assizes on behalf of a civil engineer, who last November was demobilised with the rank of lieutenant-colonel, reference was made to his distinguished Army record . . .

The ex-officer, Ronald F. [name withheld for legal reasons], aged 43, pleaded guilty to improperly assaulting a 15-year-old assistant nursemaid between Nov. 12 and 20, and was sent to prison for 12 months.

Mr W. Hugh Evans, prosecuting, explained that on the evening of the assault F. and the nursemaid, who were alone in the house together, played a game of shove-ha-penny. Afterwards F. suggested that the girl should pay a forfeit or kiss and make friends. Soon afterwards the offence took place.

The girl's mother had stated that her daughter was not allowed to associate with men, and was quite ignorant of sex matters . . .

Mr Eric Neve, KC, defending, said that after having been a Territorial officer F. was called to the colours. Unfortunately, he introduced his wife to a brother officer, and when he returned from the Far East he found that she had gone off with his friend. This had the effect of demoralising F.

It was alleged, Mr Neve continued, that his wife said to him, 'This is a criminal offence. You know you will go to prison.' He replied, 'It will be somewhere to go. I blame this all on you.'

He was a fond father and husband, and he had now filed a petition for divorce . . .

'You have pleaded guilty,' the judge told the accused, 'to debauching a child of 15 who was in your employment, towards whom you stood, or should have stood, in the

WHEN DADDY CAME HOME

position of her father. I don't want to make your position more painful than it must be. There may be many matters between you and your wife which might account for your being unfaithful to her, but as you know you have been brought up as an officer and a gentleman. You know nothing can excuse an educated man for such conduct of which you were guilty.'[21]

The statistical record of sexual offences goes back no further than 1946 but the steady increase from that year, when there were 9,329 prosecutions, to 1950 when the figure was 13,185, must link across to the problems of young men who had spent critical years in an all-male military environment. As ever, Colonel Main was quick to spot the problem.

It is common to hear from these men of the fear of going into public places, an embarrassment at going to church, the cinema, the dog-track, and of difficulty in joking and feeling at ease in company. Among unmarried servicemen contacts with women of their own kind, friendship, affection and marriage may have been a deferred delight, a fantasy elaborated during service life whenever the unsatisfied needs for tender relationship were felt. Now, sheer ignorance of womankind may make for awkwardness and shyness and fear of the very people who were worshipped from afar. Violent feelings may be noted – a belief that women should conform to his fantasies of perfection in understanding and friendliness in their recognition of his needs in public conduct and in private conversation. The fact that women are ordinary human beings, now wise, now foolish, often tactless, often without intuition, may be felt by him to be a wicked infuriating failure on their part. Again, the feeling of being cheated of a thing he felt sure he was to get may give rise to angry desire to destroy all womenkind as monsters, cocottes, harlots, drunkards, foolish, empty-headed, hard-boiled gold-diggers. So his approach may vary from inability to speak in their presence and a shy avoidance of women in general to a despairing attempt to achieve ultimate relationships with prostitutes and brash attempts at affection-less seduction, with violence if his advances are spurned. Many men who have got as far as escorting a girl home from a dance are in terror when it comes to say good-bye. What is the proper thing to do? Can he kiss her? If he tries and fails he may feel again anger and foolishness. If he succeeds he may be no better off. Has he got to go further? Will she think him slow if he does not? What is the correct thing to do?[22]

Several of our correspondents refer to schoolteachers, scout-masters and fathers with wandering hands. Maybe their frustration would have been just as intense if the war had never happened but the victims tell a different story.

Not long after my father's return I developed eczema. I had it all through my childhood and in later years often joked I was allergic to my father. I was covered from head to foot in spots and quite often shunned and ridiculed by children and adults alike. If I ran home there was no sanctuary there because every day of my life until I was nearly 16 years old my father abused me – sexually, physically and mentally. Everyone thought he was great, sociable and the life and soul of the party. But he had two faces. One for home and one for the outside world. The neighbours suspected what was going on and many times took me in for a few hours to comfort me but in those days no one contacted the NSPCC, if indeed it existed. My sister suffered the same treatment on a smaller scale but . . . was luckier than I was as at seven years she went to boarding school and only came home in school holidays.

I remember going to school at three years old and the headmistress sent for my mother. She said, 'Are you aware that your daughter is exceptionally intelligent and can read, write, fasten shoelaces and tell the time?' I suppose I was intelligent and in spite of my daily ordeals at home I even managed to sail through my 11-Plus and go to high school. But as I got older and developed my life was unbearable and I couldn't concentrate on school work. The scandal broke just before I was 16 and I left school without even taking my 'O' Levels. Had my home life been good I maybe could have gone on and made something of myself.

It's not good even telling anyone about the things that happened to me as I know myself it is horrific and too hard to believe. But I managed to grow up reasonably sane and married a good kind man who understood my problems.

This lady's father is still alive.

He lives in the past and is always talking about the war. The war obviously affected his brain and left him with no conscience about right or wrong and even to this day he has no guilty feelings.[23]

Between 1938 and 1955, homosexual offences known to the police increased by 850 per cent compared with 223 per cent for all indictable offences.[24]

Prosecutions for various homosexual offences doubled between 1945 and 1950. The crackdown coincided with the appointment of Sir Theobald Mathew, a homophobic Director of Public Prosecutions, whose views were shared by Herbert Morrison, a Home Secretary renowned, incidentally, for groping women whenever opportunity permitted. But to put all the onus on Mathew and Morrison for the upsurge of persecution of homosexual affairs is surely to confuse cause and response. It is at least arguable that in bringing together men in close companionship over a long period, the military had provided the circumstances in which there could be a realisation of sexual preference.

The ambiguity of macho man arm in arm with his best buddy was not lost on the military leadership, who tempered efforts to remove 'a foreign body in the social microcosm' with a reluctance to bring formal charges except in cases where transgressors 'had committed a flagrant breach of discipline, especially between officers and other ranks, or civilians.'[25]

Back on Civvy Street, strenuous efforts were made to contain what orthodoxy saw as a malignant growth. Fear of the law and, for those not of the inner circles, fear of social ostracism made for repression and private misery. Of a sample of gay young men in the 1950s, 40 per cent were too frightened to seek advice. That was hardly surprising in a period when, as an example of the excesses of intolerance, homosexual offenders could be ordered to accept hormone treatment, with uncertain side effects, as an alternative to prison.[26]

Nonetheless observers of the post-war fashionable social scene noted the readiness of homosexuals to declare themselves to their friends – men and women.

For the first time I heard young women in London discuss homosexuality with great freedom, some tolerance, and apparent knowledge. Indeed, the women seemed to recognise homosexuals far more quickly than men . . . My younger lady friends spotted very quickly what they called 'queers' in almost every walk of life.[27]

Today, would they not agree that they were witnessing the first stirrings of Gay Liberation?

There are other social changes to consider, too. Women's contribution to the war effort, in the services, factories or at home, enhanced their self-respect and self-confidence. There was nothing they could not do. Was this the spring-board for modern feminism?

Direct links are not conclusive. At the end of the war, it is clear that most women were happy to give up their lives in the factory, even if, with the men coming home, the choice was not always theirs. In the late 1940s, sex equality had few friends among the governing classes. In the Labour administration, elected with a thumping majority to bring about a social revolution, views on women's place in the home were positively nineteenth century. As soon as the war was over, a determined effort was made to herd women back into the domestic corral. Few objections were raised, least of all from the trades unions, to returning servicemen assuming the right to take back the best jobs, even when it was accepted that women could compete on equal terms. Children of working mothers were consistently refused priority for day-care or nursery education. For ten years after the war more nurseries were closed than opened. As a standard-bearer of the social ideal, the Institute of Houseworkers was set up in April 1947 with government backing, to embody 'all the ideals of domestic service advocated since the first decade of the century.'[28]

Everywhere there was encouragement for women to throw off the image of masculine capability in deference to the traditional concept of feminine beauty (for the young) and maternal warmth (for the not so young). The first group was targeted commercially by such as Christian Dior, who dismissed what he called the Amazonian look in favour of clothes 'with rounded shoulders, full feminine busts, and willowy waists above enormous spreading skirts.' He was supported by a contingent of fashion writers who looked to women to bring a little brightness into dull austerity Britain.

This country is starved for gay, bright tones. These colours need courage – and, of course, taste. But better live and dye (forgive the pun) – better live and dye dangerously than play safe in timid beige. I hope, too, that without going all frou-frou, you will plump for femininity – though 'plump' is possibly not the right word. Have you noticed how much nicer the ATS and WAAFS look in their battle blouses than in their tunics? It's because a blouse is a feminine garment, and a tunic a masculine one. I expect your recent way of life will have given you a preference for suits, but don't let your post-war suits be too severely tailored. When Austerity Regulations permit, let yourself go on pleats and flares. Let fashion come back, so to speak, with a swing.

Finally, I hope the ex-service girls will follow the good example that civilian women have set in this war, by doing a lot more home dressmaking. That's the way the girl with a little money can get individuality into her clothes. It's the best way, too, to find out about your figure and its needs.

Knowing how to make clothes teaches you how to buy clothes. And knowing how to buy and make clothes – and wear them – is one of the great contributions women can render to the return of a gracious, pleasant post-war world.[29]

It is easy to be dismissive but for a country short on individuality and style, fashion was important. So too was the restoration of family values, weakened by years of parental sacrifice to the greater good. However much prejudice was lodged in traditional anti-feminist arguments, the case for giving more attention to the family as the essential cog in the social machine had great force.

The divorce statistics told their own sorry tale, as did the figures for juvenile delinquency. The only bright note for a government that linked economic recovery to an expanding workforce was the reversal of the trend towards smaller families. Fears of an ever-accelerating decline in the birth rate had taken hold in the 1930s when the gloomiest forecast envisaged the population of the entire country falling to less than ten million by the end of the century.

A Royal Commission set up in 1945 reported four years later with a tranche of proposals to encourage parenthood, including generous family allowances. By now birth rates were on the increase – and though the baby boom was short-lived (by the early 1950s, births had dropped back to the level of the 1930s), it was enough to invalidate the doom merchants. But the Commission was taken seriously nonetheless as a blueprint for social stability. Something had to be done, it was argued, to help the family recover from the disruption of war. State, Church, and a new breed of child psychologists combined to promote the virtues of motherhood and the central role of the mother in bringing up children. Their arguments were strongly supported by the police, who had plenty of evidence to show what happened when young people were let off the parental rein.

Recently I interviewed Donald Thomas – now undergoing life imprisonment at HM Prison, Wandsworth, for the murder of PC Edgar. As a result, a number of firearms and a quantity of ammunition was recovered, resulting in the sentence of his younger brother for possessing firearms etc. without a certificate. Amongst these was a sawn-off .38 revolver, to which they had tried to fit a silencer. Both Donald and Stanley – who are illegitimate – admitted that they had lacked the control and care of a father. No truer case existed of 'Spare the rod and spoil the child'.[30]

Crimes of theft increased by 78 per cent between 1938 and 1947, with the sharpest rise occurring in 1944–5. Of the various categories, breaking into shops and warehouses topped the scale with a 172 per cent increase in the decade up to 1947.[31] The culpability of young people was a matter of debate over incomplete figures, but research in the late 1950s showed that children born just before or early in the war gave most trouble in each year of their growth from age eight, when criminal responsibility began, to age 20.[32] The trend was spotted early on by the police, who identified the critical factor in the increase in juvenile crime.

> During the war years children have lacked fatherly control and restraint and in a large number of families mothers have obviously tended to allow too much freedom to children. It will be understood, of course, that in these cases the child was left to the care of nurseries etc., finding invariably that when he or she returned home that some time must elapse before mother returned. This must have tended to mould the children into gangs, crime following before the child had realised the position. It is a fact today that the majority of children lack parental control and in nearly all the cases the parents are to blame.[33]

Material conditions exacerbated the problem but no one doubted the root of juvenile crime. A Metropolitan Police report in 1948 pinpointed the moral breakdown brought by war, and not just the one that had recently ended:

> Years ago, we were troubled with serious cases of warehouse-breaking. In every case, the actual amount of property stolen was comparatively small but the terrific amount of wilful damage done suggested that the crime had been committed from motives of spite. Windows had been deliberately

smashed. Rolls of expensive silks and similar fabrics had been unrolled and ruined by ink and paint. Expensive pipes, fancy goods etc. had been put into presses and deliberately smashed to pieces. The damage amounted to thousands of pounds.

Observation was kept and two small boys under eight years of age were discovered smashing all the windows of the warehouse with hammers. Questioned, they admitted having deliberately caused all this damage and had thoroughly enjoyed themselves in doing so. It transpired they were members of large families, living in slum conditions in the Clerkenwell district. Obviously this was a case of lack of parental control. This happened shortly after the 1914–1918 war and similar crimes are happening today.[34]

The Teddy Boys of the 1950s were in training. Distrustful of their elders and of adult values, the teenagers of the urban working class were about to show, in an orgy of vandalism and gang warfare, what they thought of the war and its aftermath.

The heavily promoted revival of domesticity was rarely questioned by women. For a great number of war-time workers, pushed into uncongenial, low-paid jobs, the call to home came as a welcome release. A 1943 survey of women's work showed 58 per cent against work after marriage (though professional women were heavily in favour). When it came to a question of taking what were regarded as 'men's jobs', less than a quarter of those questioned felt that women should compete on equal terms.

Such was women's eagerness to sign off from the factory benches, the Ministry of Labour tried to slow the process to give returning servicemen a better chance to re-establish themselves.

A recruitment campaign launched in 1947 was pitched at mothers with grown-up children, who were urged to take up jobs in transport and hospital catering. It is significant that the Women's Land Army was not disbanded until 1950. By then, there were about a million more women in employment than there had been in 1939 – but most were part-timers out to earn a little extra to top up the housekeeping. It was still rare to find a woman in a position of responsibility. Even rarer was to find one who gave orders to men, as a former ATS officer reported to the British Legion. The war had left her disabled but

I eventually obtained the Rehabilitation Officer's permission to take up a post as Lady Housekeeper in a small hotel in the country, and here I must say, all Rehabilitation officers I have met are concerned that the employers will allow one to continue hospital treatment, and that the work is not too much for the disability.

However, the post of Lady Housekeeper was a snare and delusion. I had been asked if I could control staff, and having been a messing officer, I thought I could. What staff we had flatly refused to be bossed by a 'chit of a girl' and some walked out on the spot . . .

Not a cheerful beginning, nor did it become more so. After

a month of waiting at table, clearing and cleaning the dining room for every meal, opening and closing the bar, typing madly in place of a typist in between getting the rooms ready for the occupants, I was heartily sick of the game.

It made me laugh to think that I had been discharged from the ATS as Unfit . . . I was now working harder than I had ever had to work. And what for?

Suddenly I realised that this was a game that ceased to appeal, and that my health was not improving. What was I to do? The discipline of four years 'sticking to it' broke down finally and it was with light-hearted relief I realised that one advantage of Civvy Street was that I could give notice – and give notice I did![35]

Demobilisation brought a rush to the altar and the registry office, with marriage rates exceeding those of the immediate pre-war period. The trend continued upwards until 1972.

Often with these early post-war marriages, the responsibility for creating a family home was left to the women. In the days before technology eased the effort of cooking and home care, housewifery could be a full-time job and more.

In 1941, I was engaged to a soldier. I was in the Women's Land Army and my fiancé had to go abroad in 1942. We wrote to each other nearly every day – from 1942–1945. During those three years, I of course never could be certain that my fiancé John would return to England – he could have been killed, also, if he did return, he could have been injured. But we were extremely fortunate that John returned thankfully in good health. Our marriage was arranged through our letters – and we were married on September 8th 1945. Unfortunately, for both of us, John was not demobbed. He had to go to Austria for six months (was in the Army of Occupation). I carried on working on the land. We still wrote to each other nearly every day. During those six months I set about finding accommodation for us. In January 1946 I was able to find a furnished little cottage in Sussex, very near to where I worked on a farm. I knew John would not return until some time in March 1946. To secure this little house I paid the rent – £2.10s. from January. During those two months I prepared our house for John's homecoming. I had to wait during the February for a telegram telling me what day in March John would arrive back in England. During the weeks of uncertainty I found casual work on the land in order to leave at a day's notice. The telegram came at last, the waiting would soon be over – March 6th was the date of his arrival. We had a month together before John went back to his work.

We settled down in our little house very happily. I had become used to some of the food being rationed and became a good housewife (I must say that). Actually, I attended a homecraft course – five weeks in a hostel organised for engaged and married Land Army girls – it was free – that is all the Land girls got it for free, apart from the uniform.[36]

It was toughest, of course, for women whose husbands did not come home. Charles Fraser's wife was in hospital when she was told that he was 'missing as the result of enemy action'. The story is taken up by her daughter.

Her recovery was slow and erratic. The first few days were helped by what I imagine now must have been 1940s tranquillisers. When she was discharged from hospital, she staggered the whole family by announcing that during her convalescence, she had given a lot of thought to her future. We were moving to Cambridge. She and my father had loved their time there and had talked of returning after the war. The youngest daughter of a protected family, the cosseted wife of a loving husband, a newly widowed young mother, she revealed a hitherto unsuspected strength and set up a whole new life. First, rooms in a house near the Round Church, next a school for me. Her pension was adequate, but she had ambitions for me. She found work and was good at it. Later she bought her own house.

Had my father lived and come home, life would certainly have been different, it might even have been better. My mother is now over eighty and the best comfort I can offer her for fifty years without my father is that she has given me and her grandchildren a role model without equal.[37]

Few women in the forties had time or opportunity to consider the advantages of a life outside the home or to wonder if their talents were best occupied in domesticity.

There were simply too many day-to-day problems to worry about. It is said that the recovery of the Conservatives from their 1945 nadir can be partly attributed to the clever targeting of the women's vote, with the promise to build more houses, improve gas, water and electricity supplies and other measures to 'strengthen family life'. In the 1951 election, Labour votes were lost 'in the queue at the butcher's or the grocer's'.[38]

But there was one area where feminism did make progress. An effect of war-time work was to bring forward the question of equal pay. As early as April 1940, the Industrial Court ruled that women over 21 on the buses and other transport services were to be paid the male rate after six months on the job. Local government employees – at least on the higher grades – were the next to crack the mould, but it was not until 1952 that the London County Council introduced equal pay for teachers, eight years after the House of Commons had voted (by one vote) for pay parity in schools.

It is significant that the Beveridge Report did not mention equal pay, and while a Royal Commission reporting in 1945 recommended equal pay in occupations where the sexes clearly performed the same work, it played down expectations by warning that an increase in women's pay could bring about a fall in men's wages and a reduction in the number of women employed. It was an argument much favoured by the craft unions, which resisted equal pay in manufacturing and engineering as an employer's ruse to dilute the skilled and semi-skilled male workforce. The good example had to be set by the civil service, education, health and the nationalised service industries, all of which made substantial progress towards equal pay (if not equal status) by the mid-fifties.

The early post-war generation of feminists were frustrated on two counts – the demands of running a house at a time of austerity and the demands of industry which pushed women into unskilled and low-paid jobs with no career structure. But economic and technological change was on the side of feminism. With improvements in the home and the shift from heavy service industry, from muscle to intellect, the artificial disparities between the sexes became all the more ludicrous.

The process was accelerated by the rise of the consumer society. The release from austerity stimulated a desire to spend and the need to increase the family income, if necessary, by having two earners instead of just one. This in turn opened up opportunities for young people, young women in particular, to assert their independence. It is not by chance that it was the children of the war and its immediate aftermath who made the great leap forward to sex equality.

It would be wrong, though, to see this equality solely in terms of job opportunities. Just as important, perhaps more so in truth, was a change in attitude by women – towards men and towards themselves. When and where did this begin? Girls growing up during the war saw for themselves in their everyday lives that it was possible to exist without a man about the house; many, as we have seen, deeply resented him when he reappeared. They watched their mothers work, run a home, pay the bills, organise their lives in the most aggravating circumstances. How could this impression not leave its mark? And the father who eventually came back, ill, authoritarian, a stranger, may not have commanded much respect. Certainly, they were entitled to think that, if this was the foundation stone of a patriarchal society, maybe there was something wrong with the whole edifice.

For Germaine Greer, the link is direct and personal. Less well known than her pioneering feminist book, *The Female Eunuch*, is the one she wrote 20 years later, *Daddy We Hardly Knew You*.

Just when he should have been dandling me on his knee while I searched through his pockets, he went away. He wasn't there to see me turn from being a baby into Daddy's little girl. It was the war he left me for.

Like thousands of other Australians, Reg Greer had been called up. For his daughter, like so many others, his return was vividly recalled:

I was five when my mother and I went to the station to bring Daddy home. I was sure I would recognise him from the photograph on the sideboard . . . distinguished features, dark hair brushed back from a high forehead, a relaxed smile and an ironic glint in the eyes. I knew the exact proportion of the ears to the head, the precise bend in the narrow nose, the set of the long head on its square shoulders.

We trailed up and down the platform peering into every face. The heavy skirts of the men's greatcoats kept knocking me off my feet. The kissings, hugging knots of people began to gather up their belongings and disperse; the platform was emptying and still we hadn't found Daddy. I began to drag my feet and daydream. Mother grabbed my arm, nearly wrenching it from its socket, as she became more agitated. Suddenly she stopped and dropped my arm.

An old man was standing sightlessly by a pylon. His neck stuck scrawnily out of the collar of his grey-blue greatcoat. His eyes were sunken, his skin grey and loose. I ran up to look at Mother's face. Surely she wasn't going to take this old man instead of Daddy. She was standing with her head cocked, peering like a wary bird. If she was shocked, she made no sign. She bundled the old man up and took him home and a year later my sister was born.

By then I had learned to match the old man's features with the photograph and to admit that this distant, speechless wreck was indeed my father. I would rather have had one of the handsome big Americans who used to hang around my mother. So would she, I wouldn't wonder.

Time together only emphasised the gulf between father and daughter.

During the years and years that we lived in the same small house, he never once hugged me. All the Australians who served overseas had a difficult war, too far from home to touch base for years on end. Thousands of them came home to live out their lives as walking wounded, carrying out their masculine duties in a sort of dream, trying not to hear the children who asked, 'Mummy, why does that man have to sleep in your bed?'

Australians don't whinge. There was no way these damaged men could explain their incapacity for normal emotional experience except by complaining, and they would not complain.

But their children must.[39]

CHAPTER SEVEN

'Are We Going Back On The Dole Afterwards?'

D-Day soldier's fear for the future

When Dad came home he expected changes in the way the country was run. Ernest Bevin got a personal reminder of this in June 1944 as he joined Churchill at Portsmouth to watch men embarking for the D-Day invasion of France. 'Ernie,' they called out to him, 'when we have done this job for you, are we going back on the dole?' Memories were still fresh of the chaos after 1918 and of poverty in the twenties and thirties. There had to be another way. It was all very well to revere democracy, but 'we have come to question the value of the sort of freedom and democracy which can find a place for chronic unemployment, bad housing conditions and underfed children.'[1]

The words are from an army education booklet, one of

a series that encouraged discussion on the rights and obligations of post-war citizenship.

Army education played a big part in crystallising ideas of how life could be improved. It did not start out as a radical programme. The original idea was to motivate the front line, to convince the armed forces that the causes of the war were worth fighting for.

The concept had its origins in the First World War when mostly vocational courses were organised to relieve the tedium of massed troops waiting around for something to happen. The success of the enterprise led, in 1920, to the formation of the Army Education Corps. In 1939, on the outbreak of war, AEC officers were allocated to intelligence duties and the Corps virtually disbanded, 'surely,' wrote Lord Gorrell, founder of the AEC, 'one of the most retrograde as well as short-sighted steps ever taken by rulers of democracy.'[2]

Gorrell's blunt assault on the War Office ('Has nothing been learned?') was supported by the historian H. A. L. Fisher, Warden of New College, Oxford.

No one will pretend that the soldier's life under siege conditions is devoid of its hours of boredom, or that boredom is helpful to military efficiency, or that during the last war the troops both in France and at home did not welcome the well-planned courses of instruction which were arranged for them by the Army Education Corps, which has now unhappily ceased to function. Both in respect of adolescent education and in respect of education in the army the country might do worse than to recur to the plans which were then made.[3]

It was advice the War Office could not afford to ignore. After the Dunkirk evacuation, tens of thousands of troops in camps up and down the country were forced to idle away their time, or spend it, none too profitably, on square-bashing or kit inspections.

Sporadic efforts to provide forces education via the universities, the Workers' Educational Association and other civilian bodies were overtaken by an inquiry led by General Sir Robert Haining. His report, approved by the Army Council in August 1940, argued

> . . . that care for the needs of men's minds is a factor that contributes quite definitely to military efficiency; that mental contentment is essential to the maintenance of morale; and that the soldier removed from civil life may, after the first adjustment to his military environment, succumb to a measure of mental torpor, against which education, aimed at the development of individual initiative and intelligence, is a safeguard.[4]

Haining proposed a voluntary scheme with lectures, classes and correspondence courses linked to vocational subjects, hobbies and the humanities, including economics and citizenship. It was this last one that turned out to offer rich possibilities for social debate, which really got going when the voluntary element was reduced in favour of incorporating education into regular training activities. This allowed for a weekly discussion of current affairs.

The aims of army education were now pretty well established.

> To increase the fighting efficiency of the soldier by enabling him to study subjects which will improve that efficiency, by exercising his mind and by training him to think quickly for himself.
>
> To fortify his loyalty and morale through an understanding of the cause for which he and our Allies are fighting.
>
> To keep him mentally fresh and prevent the 'staleness' which may result from too long continued intensive military training.
>
> To make him a better informed and more responsible citizen. To give him, where possible, some opportunity to prepare himself for a vocation on his return to civil life.
>
> To afford opportunity for him to make a better use of leisure time and develop some interest or talent which may be of value to him.[5]

The parameters for good citizenship were set by a series of booklets, prepared by the universities, and published under the collective heading *The British Way and Purpose*. Bearing in mind the innate conservatism of the military command, these teaching aids were refreshingly broad-minded. Hindsight reveals a fair amount of nonsense, particularly in matters relating to our Soviet ally ('the Soviet Government has devoted special care to the preservation and strengthening of the various natural cultures') and to Britain's international standing ('Any power which wishes to rule the world must first conquer Britain').[6]

Equally, there are enlightened sentiments which must have come as a welcome surprise to those raised on pre-war political cant. It was something to know that the war was a struggle 'to make a decent life genuinely possible for all'. And who among radicals could argue with this updating of the democratic idea?

Every man, whatever his race or colour or creed, should be given an equal opportunity of realising the best that is in him.[7]

Not surprisingly, there were some who felt that the Army was losing sight of the target. A War Office memo of 1943, author unknown, though Colonel Blimp comes to mind, notes:

I am getting a little uneasy about the general question of education in the Army. On the one hand there is the school of thought that, since the education of the community as a whole is of vital importance, the education of a large part of it, namely the Army, is certainly of no less importance; and on the other hand there is the argument that the Army is being trained to fight what we hope will be the concluding campaign of the war and that it is not a proper charge upon Army Votes to educate the Army beyond the stand requisite for its success as a military machine.[8]

But education was a morale-booster and as such raised the efficiency of the Army as a military machine. In any case, education was value for money.

The amount spent on education for the whole Army is roughly the equivalent of 20 bombers or 35 tanks, i.e. the losses of bombers that might take place in one night are financially equivalent to the education provided in a year.[9]

Interest in politics and what politics might do for servicemen when they returned to civilian life was further stimulated by the wide circulation of the Beveridge Report with its promise of a free national health service, child allowances and full employment, or rather unemployment at less than 8.5 per cent.

The report was an immediate best-seller. A hundred thousand copies were sold within a month of publication. That was before a cheap edition was distributed to the armed forces.[10] If Army education set out the broad terms of a society in which unity of purpose could be put to use in peace-time reconstruction, it was Beveridge who filled in the details. His report became the manifesto for hundreds of thousands of returning servicemen.

A commonplace of modern history is that the Labour government elected in 1945 had no clear idea of how to achieve its objectives. Policies were cobbled together to produce an election platform that was strong on promises but shaky on implementation. No matter, the formula for change was there in the Beveridge Report. When the forces voted overwhelmingly for Labour, disappointing the expectations of the right that it would be carried home on loyalty to Churchill, they were in fact voting for Beveridge.

It is no coincidence that in the aftermath of the report's publication, every Gallup poll showed a comfortable Labour lead.[11] It was hardly the fault of the pollsters if no one then took them seriously. If they had done so, the biggest movement in votes recorded in any British election since 1918 would not have come as a total surprise – to Conservatives and Labour politicians alike.

A Mass Observation survey published in 1943 reported unequivocally, 'People *want* full-scale Beveridge' but detected also an underlying frustration: 'Many dare not hope for what they want'.[12] There was a fear that the old guard would somehow reassert themselves to defeat reform. By the 'old guard' they meant the Tory party, not its leader, for whom the adulation was immense. There is a strong memory among the voters of 1945 that if they could have had Churchill and the Labour Party, that dream ticket would have been overwhelming. It was a misreading of the great man, however, whose reservations on post-war social reform we have already noted.

In the armed forces, the popular mood veered from general optimism (this time it would be different) to personal anxiety at the prospect of missing out on life's chances. At best, the feeling of comradeship, of working together for common ends, of shared achievement, quite simply, of winning, raised hopes of transforming Britain into a democracy capable of making 'a decent life genuinely possible for all'.

The pace and volume of forces education increased as the end of the war came in sight. Continuing emphasis was given to debating current affairs and thinking constructively about the future.

Undoubtedly the question that constantly occupies the minds of men now fighting for a democratic civilisation is that of social security and progress after the war. These common aims are not to be achieved merely by the diffusion of goodwill and a spirit of comradeship, nor do the publication of Government reports, and the acceptance of them by Parliament, suffice. It is necessary to include among the subjects of study the methods and machinery of government, the methods of industry and commerce, the balancing of industry and agriculture, social legislation, taxation, the administration of the nation's finances, health, our educational system, and other such topics. These are all studies which will create a new interest and purpose in the lives of men who are about to fashion the future.[13]

Part of the enthusiasm for the subject of citizenship derived from a lack of confidence as to what else to provide in the way of practical education. Forecasting the peace-time demand for particular skills was a chancy affair.

Only in few industries is there likely to be any rapid expansion requiring the training of large-scale additional labour. It seems reasonable, however, to assume that, while a large proportion of the population has, during the war, been retained in essential civilian work, and that after the war many of these will be available for the new peace-time industries, there will be opportunities in expanding industries for the employment of men and women from the Services. The extent to which training for such industries can usefully be given to individuals before they begin to work in the expanding industries is a matter which needs much more examination than has been possible hitherto. Such examination must evidently be conducted in the light of increasing knowledge of post-war plans.[14]

One way round the problem was to ask the servicemen themselves what they wanted. The opportunity came in March 1944 when the Army carried out a survey of qualifications for specialist duties. A number of questions were added concerning 'the worry which is probably uppermost in most of their minds, i.e. what is going to happen to them after the war'.[15]

The exercise brought in 6,248 completed questionnaires. The major finding was that 60 per cent not only requested further education but specified the subject in which they most wanted instruction. Of these, two-thirds asked for technical courses. When it came to preferred choice of occupation, there was a distinct trend away from mining, textiles, wholesale and retail trades, catering and domestic work, in favour of ship-building, engineering, transport and communications and the professions. In other words, away from low-paid, unskilled or semi-skilled jobs and towards better prospects.[16]

The official response was encapsulated in the 1944 Army Release Scheme. In the period leading up to demob, servicemen were to be given vocational training to 'tune up their old skills'. In all, 130 subjects were offered in weekly sessions of four to six hours, in addition to time spent discussing current affairs.[17] The centrepiece of the scheme was for residential 'formation colleges' to embark on 'the most advanced and specialised courses for general and technical studies which the Army resources of instructors and equipment can provide.'[18] One and a half million men were expected to participate, for whom 2½ million books were required.

It did not happen. And for the best possible reason: that the war ended far sooner than anyone expected. The plan needed at least a year to get off the ground. Japanese surrender gave it less than two months. Thereafter, demo-bilisation took away the instructors on which the formation colleges depended.

An appeal was made to the BBC to help plug the gap. From September 1945 to January 1947, the BBC Light Programme and Overseas Service carried a weekly series of 18 forces education programmes. Judged to be 'one of the biggest experiments in education by radio so far attempted', the BBC pursued its objectives with characteristically high-minded zeal.

> It is natural, indeed, that in these non-militarist and only spasmodically bellicose islands, service in the Forces should be generally regarded as a deviation from the ordinary run of things and the years spent away from home as so much 'lost time'. Whether it is in fact 'lost time' is another matter; every individual will draw up his own balance sheet of new skills and experience gained to offset the many hardships. But that the feeling exists there is little doubt. The broad purpose of these educational provisions is to reduce this feeling to as low a point as is possible in a world where a sense of waste and frustration has affected many people, civilians included, for too long. Any suggestion of a continuing 'two-nations' society – civilians and ex-servicemen – would be a disaster. United in war, we must strive to maintain at least something of that unity in the days ahead.[19]

In other words, let's get back to Citizenship. Clearly, no one had any idea of how to put across vocational subjects on radio. Apart from an industrial magazine programme, *The World of Work*, which proved its popularity by running uninterruptedly for two years, the programmes were heavily angled towards personal development and community matters.

CLEAR THINKING: A series of talks on the avoidance of slipshod habits of thinking. Illustrated by quotations read by another voice.

CURRENT AFFAIRS: Barrack-room arguments often stop short, or should stop short but don't, at a point where neither side knows the relevant facts: how does the population of Germany compare with that of the Allies? How many children do go to secondary schools? Is every lease-lend item a book-keeping entry in a ledger intended sometime to balance? The aim of this series is to encourage factual and quantative thinking as a necessary basis to, though not the whole of, argument.

JOB IN HAND: A series of talks and discussions with leaders in trade and industry, who will speak of their job in its setting in the post-war world: what changes have the war years made, what technical advances have there been, what developments are likely?

Servicewoman had their own programmes, which were intended to be 'practical enough to interest family men as well'. Topics ranged from 'What Ought We to Know About Food and Health in the Home?' to 'Carpentry and Running Repairs' and 'The Weekly Wash' – the latter a severely business-like presentation by F. Courtney Harwood, Director of the British Launderers' Research Association.

There was some evidence to suggest that the BBC was over-estimating the intellectual capacity of its audience.

I visited the Household Cavalry yesterday, Thursday 8th, and listened with a group of about twenty other ranks to a Music programme (which in fact was turned off just before I arrived in the middle of a broadcast) and the Current Affairs programme. The instructor said (and the class agreed with him) that seventy-five per cent of the people who listened found the music above their heads. The instructor suggested, and the class agreed enthusiastically, that if we were to use music which the average other-ranker hears (i.e. what is played in cinemas or frequently on the radio or in such things as 'A Song to Remember') they would willingly listen to an analysis of the work which they heard, or other of the composer's works or the story of his life, and so forth.

The instructor also said that the Clear Thinking course was quite unacceptable. Members complained of the professional voice of Dr Burt and said that the subject was far too remote for the experience of the class. I found later, however, that he was referring to a class of Life Guardsmen, who are, I understand, selected more for their physical than for their mental dimensions.[20]

That programme-makers needed to lower their sights was also deduced from complaints that programmes were transmitted between 10.00 and 11.00 in the morning – which coincided with NAAFI break – and on Saturdays.

But there was an alternative explanation, one that was not considered. It could have been that servicemen had had their fill of general education. The real demand was for knowledge that had a direct connection to job-seeking.

The buck was passed back to the government. Could it deliver?

As Minister of Labour in the coalition government, Ernest Bevin had a vision of a technically proficient workforce, enjoying full employment and high wages, leading the world to economic recovery. He and his successor, George Isaacs, scored one out of three. The heady growth of the world economy in the late forties put paid to fears of an early return to mass unemployment. There was plenty of work to do, more even than Beveridge had anticipated when he defined full employment as 8½ per cent or less on the dole. The trouble was, from the point of view of ex-servicemen, the jobs available rarely measured up to the expectations voiced so clearly in the 1944 survey of educational preferences. British industry was still in the age of labour-intensive mass production, with its dependence on a ready supply of semi-literates prepared to spend their days at the conveyor belt engaged in routines of mind-bending tedium. It was a future that was unlikely to appeal to men who had fought Rommel in the desert, survived hand-to-hand combat in Burma or been part of D Day.

It was not simply the fact of putting on a uniform that raised career expectations. Young men and women had gained in experience and maturity in ways that were not feasible in peace-time. In their late teens and early twenties, they might be officers – non-commissioned or commissioned – in charge of others, taking life-or-death decisions. They had carried responsibilities and performed deeds that earned them admiration and respect. Thereafter, joining the crowd at the factory gate to clock in on a Monday morning was, to put it mildly, an anti-climax. Often, the frustration of ex-servicemen bored with their civilian jobs was worked out on their families.

Dad was restless after the war, he couldn't settle down, or get a sufficiently well-paid job, enough to finance a family of six. He wanted to emigrate to Australia on the £10 Assisted Passage scheme. He had seen the country and made friends there, he was sure that we would have a better life.

I don't know why we didn't go, but perhaps Mum was against the idea. The compromise that they settled for was that Dad left Liverpool to find work in Coventry, which was booming with industry in the early 1950s. He stayed in a men's hostel in Coventry, worked on the buses to save a deposit for a house, so that we could join him.

Mum was left alone again in Liverpool with four young

children. She stood this for a while but when the loneliness became too much, we were boarded out in Bootle with strangers, and she went to Coventry to join Dad. They eventually found a suitable house, a three-bedroomed semi-detached, which was in the process of being constructed.

Mum missed us so much, we were brought to Coventry and boarded out again for a short time with families that the local priest had recommended, until the house was habitable.

I think the long-term effect all this had on me was to turn me into a very bossy older sister. I had to take a lot of responsibility for my younger siblings while Mum and Dad worked hard to establish a home for us. I had to learn to be self-reliant and adaptable, and became 'an old head on young shoulders'.[21]

Emigration was considered and rejected by another Liverpool family where dissatisfaction at work led to domestic discord.

Returning to civvy street did not suit Dad. He had been 'someone' in the army and now he had returned to his dull clerical job in Liverpool on virtually the same wages he had left in 1939. Money was tight and of course this caused all the usual domestic problems. We discovered my father had a quick temper, he swore and banged doors, totally alien things to us. My mother excused this on the injuries and suffering he had endured but we found it very hard to understand; we had had a quiet and happy home life until now.

We especially didn't like it when our dear sweet Mummy cried. Dad was disillusioned with peace-time – so called – and wanted to emigrate. Mum wouldn't hear of it, she had had enough upheavals and besides, she had two elderly parents to care for. Resentment set in all round. I really did love my dad, especially when he was in a humorous mood, he was very witty and a great mimic, I thought he was the life and soul of the party at times. Unfortunately, Betty (my sister) never developed a rapport with him at all, she tolerated his charm but openly hated his 'other side'.[22]

General disillusionment was some time in coming. Plans for reassimilating skilled men into civilian work were reasonable, at first sight. While it was assumed that those who had steady jobs before the war needed no more than a short refresher course, there were training centres for any who had been called up before they had learned a trade. Maintenance allowances for six-month courses were set at £3 a week for an unmarried man and £3.15s. for a married man with one child. A deal with the trade unions allowed these workers to be employed as fully trained craftsmen, though there remained opposition from union die-hards who preferred to believe that nothing less than the traditional seven-year apprenticeship should be allowed. The unions' reluctance, as they put it, to 'dilute' the labour force affected also the Interrupted Apprenticeship Scheme whereby the unexpired period of an apprenticeship was reduced by a third for ex-servicemen who had practised their trade in the armed forces. The concession, though welcome, was mean-spirited when applied to men whose military training and experience justified their immediate acceptance into the ranks of the fully qualified. To have to resume an apprenticeship, even a curtailed one, was a humiliating put-down. Many who were eminently capable of skilled work found themselves shunted into inferior and unsatisfactory jobs. Sybil Hurcomb's father was a sapper who found that his knowledge of bridge-building was no help in getting him a job in the building trade.

Eventually he got a job as a delivery man for a firm of chemists but delivery in those days meant by bicycle, not van. He used to be exhausted when he finished work each day. Also, he was paid only about £2.50 a week. Previously Mum had had to feed four of us on the army allowance but now she had to feed five on about the same amount, which meant we were even poorer.

Dad tried hard to help by having an allotment and providing all the vegetables he could. Then we had some chickens and Mum had to cook a big saucepanful of mush from scraps for them every day. She also worked at our local junior school as a dinner-lady. That was good for her, as it meant she had one reasonable meal a day. At home she was giving Dad all her share of the rations to give him enough strength to keep working.[23]

Marian Morgan's father was one for whom a return to an unfulfilling job caused domestic discord.

I will never forget my mother's cry of joy at the sight of the handsome, uniformed young man walking up the garden path, and the way in which she ran towards him and threw herself into his arms.

Such a loving reunion should have augured well for the years to follow. Sadly, the opposite proved to be the case. From that day the tranquillity of our domestic scene was shattered. My father returned to his employment as a coal miner, so presumably our economic position, although harsh, was not as dire as that of families dependent upon an unemployed breadwinner in those days. However, he was restless and unsettled, hated his job and projected his dissatisfaction on to his family, particularly my mother. The scene in Lawrence's *Sons and Lovers*, in which he describes the misery and horror of listening to parents quarrelling violently downstairs whilst he lies in bed listening to the shriek of the wind in the ash tree outside the window, always comes to mind when I think of the nights when my brother and I lay wide awake in bed, unable to sleep because of the voices beneath us raised in bitterness and acrimony. Our lives were now ruled by this patriarchal figure who found it very difficult to demonstrate the love and affection which I know was in his head.

Looking back, I am aware that my father was a deeply unhappy person, dissatisfied and, I think, hankering after a way of life which was always to be denied him. This, ironically, worked to our advantage, in that he ensured that his children benefited from a very good education.[24]

Those who did manage to join government training courses were liable to find a mismatch between qualifications and job vacancies. This was particularly true of the building trade. The problems were highlighted in an official report on ex-service employment in 1948:

The Government Training Scheme had completely fallen to the ground because they had trained men in such trades as plastering and bricklaying and now there was no work for them. Moreover, employers were not keen to take on men trained under these schemes because they had little practical experience; the same remarks apply to some employers towards 'Service trained' men.

Mr Evans (Royal Artillery Association) said he had cases of men being sent to the Exchange for permission to take a particular job, the Exchange refusing permission but filling the vacancy themselves with a man from their own books, not necessarily an ex-serviceman. As a result of this he now told men to go to the employer first and the Exchange afterwards.[25]

The universities were overwhelmed with applications from 'mature' students who had either had their studies interrupted by the war or had missed out entirely on higher education. The government was liberal with grants but could do nothing in the short run to satisfy the demand for places. Even with the introduction of shortened degree courses, up to a third of eligible students failed to get in.

It was the same story with the three-month business management courses offered by the technical and commercial colleges. Only about half the number of suitable applicants were accepted. If more places had been available it might have helped to dissuade ex-servicemen from hasty investments in dodgy small businesses. After years of obeying orders, being one's own boss had distinct appeal. But the circumstances for setting up as an independent were not promising, as British Legion records reveal. Falling in with the wrong sort was a common failing.

An ex-serviceman desirous of setting himself up in business answered an advertisement in a London evening paper, wherein a lorry was offered for sale for £140. The advertisement also stated that a 'B' licence could be arranged, so that, in effect, he would be able to start work immediately.

Upon inquiry the vendors told him that a petrol licence would be arranged for, and that, furthermore, adequate and remunerative work would be found upon which he could embark with the lorry . . .

Nothing transpired, and after many fruitless approaches he informed the vendors that he was consulting solicitors and placing the matters in the hands of the police.

As a result of this threat he was given work of a kind

which was quite unsuitable, did not require a 'B' licence, and which, furthermore, resulted in serious injury to his health.

Being destitute, he was forced to carry out this work. He then made independent inquiries and discovered that the lorry was not worth much more than £20, and was of such an age and condition that there was never any possibility of a 'B' licence being obtained in respect of it.

The usual warnings were directed at those tempted towards the fantasy of a rural idyll.

An ex-serviceman answered an advertisement in a Lancashire paper of highest repute, wherein a cottage and holding was offered for sale and an agreement to be signed to the effect that the purchaser should retain the vendor as a lodger.

Any lawyer would probably have advised against such an arrangement, knowing full well the friction that would be likely to arise, and particularly having regard to the inexperience of the purchaser in running a small holding of this nature.[26]

The lawyer would have been right. There *was* a falling out, and while the British Legion did what it could, the moral for anyone answering an advertisement was to 'beware the hidden dangers'.

But the biggest obstacle to creating a profitable business was the bureaucratic rule book – a volume so dense (in size and intelligence) that few who had it thrown at their heads ever recovered. Rules and regulations had grown out of all proportion during the war, and they were slow in being lifted. Nor were those regulations designed to do any favours for men who had done their military duty.

Ex-servicemen who have set up as greengrocers in Civvy Street are finding that, having been given 'A' licences to trade as retail greengrocers, they cannot deal in tomatoes or imported fruits, with the result that customers go elsewhere.

A full licence is only granted to men who were in business on their own account before the war. This restriction is made because imports of fruits are limited and if there is a large increase in the number of retailers among whom the imports have to be shared it would operate unfairly against men who were in business before their call-up.

Men are warned, when they apply, of the restrictions placed on them by an 'A' licence, but most of them do not realise what effect this has upon business.[27]

A further hazard for the potential retailer was the rule making the granting of a licence dependent on having a suitable address to trade from. But having acquired premises, ideal in every way, there was no guarantee of getting a licence. Here was a British situation to appeal to Captain Yossarian, Joseph Heller's American war-time anti-hero, a true Catch-22. The consolation was supposed to be in knowing that if one was pushed into bankruptcy by bureaucratic order, it was all for the good of the country.

Obstruction and petty-mindedness were endemic to a system managed by civil servants who had no experience of business life. At times it was almost as if the comfort of a secure job fostered a bureaucratic contempt for anyone outside the ranks of government employees.

A Liverpool man, a qualified pharmacist, with a wife and children, was discharged with a pension of 23s. a week. He had the chance of taking over a suitable business for £1,200, and the National Pharmaceutical Union agreed to advance him three-quarters of that amount.

His application to the local Labour Exchange was turned down because he was not in business on his own account before being called up, and he was still subject to direction into other employment.

A protest from the British Legion pointing out that the labour exchanges were charged with special responsibility for assisting 'those disabled by war service to set up their own business for the first time' drew a curt refusal to reconsider the case. There could be only one conclusion. Local officials were interpreting government schemes in whatever manner they thought fit.

Grants were available to help set up small businesses or reestablish old ones that had failed when their proprietors had been called up. But little account was taken of wartime inflation.

We have had several cases of discharged men who have been forced to abandon their previous business . . . A man with a small haulage business for instance sells his lorries and with them his goodwill. On return to civil life he must prove that he has sufficient customers to justify a licence whilst lorries, even if available, have increased in price by 100%. In order to start again, therefore, he will need, for replacement of lorries and recovery of goodwill, about double his former capital; this is what floors him and it is money for which he asks.[28]

Other examples of insensitivity, not to mention sheer incompetence, came thick and fast.

A discharged Marine who applied for a grant was first told that 'the scheme had not yet started', and later that 'the forms had just arrived but had not been opened'.

In South London an ex-RASC man, discharged with a pension of 12s. a week, had two cars, which he needed assistance to get ready for the road. He then applied for a grant to start his own business. That was two months ago. Since then, to use his own words, he has 'done nothing else but fill in forms'.

From Brighton comes the story of a plumber who before the war was in business at his private address. Discharged without a pension, he applied for a grant. Answer: No pension, no grant.[29]

One of the few small businesses the British Legion felt able to endorse was that of operating a taxi service. With over half the London drivers heading towards retirement (nearly 10 per cent were 70-plus) there was room for newcomers. Inevitably, there were drawbacks, notably a petrol ration that did not permit double shifts and a shortage of spare parts. The Legion had its own Taxi School to initiate drivers into the mysteries of urban geography. Six months' training were as challenging as any Army endurance test.

Fred Marks, ex-Sergeant Major in the RAOC, has joined the ranks of London's cabbies in the almost record time of six months. Today, with his coveted taxi-driver's green badge on his coat, from the seat of the cab he bought with his gratuity, he will tell you: 'Any man training for this job has my sympathy. If I thought I had to go through that six months again I'd sooner go back to my one-man shop.'

Green badges are not easily won. Scotland Yard tests make it a nightmare memory.

First thing a man has to do is to fill his police form PC04, giving personal particulars, including all convictions, however trivial, a photograph and a medical certificate. A rough test of your knowledge of London follows, and you are told (without mincing words) just how good or how bad you are.

A fortnight later you are called before experts of the London Carriage Office, Scotland Yard, to be tested in more detail. This is where the nightmare begins.

For a taxi-man, before he can ply for hire, must have an encyclopaedic knowledge of the quickest routes between any two points in London. If he fails the first three times to point out the route at a moment's notice on the map, he is told to come back in 28 days; if he answers ten questions successfully he must also come back in 28 days, but this time to answer ten harder questions.[30]

Nonetheless, demand for places far outstripped supply. At its peak of activity in 1947–8, the Legion's Taxi School catered for no more than 125 trainees at a time. Those who passed could be sure of a steady job. Outside London, a taxi-driver career was more problematical.

I came home from Milan on New Year's Day 1946, having survived the actions at Dunkirk, North Africa, Sicily and Italy, and was given a demob suit and £90 for my six and one-third years' service.

I had married my wife on 3 April, 1943, and on the 10 April I was on board the troopship *Franconia* at Liverpool, bound for North Africa. My wife was in the WAAF, stationed on the aerodrome at Redhill (Surrey). I used to worry overseas as to what my wife did amongst all the airmen, but later on had to put it at the back of the mind.

My wife was demobbed before I was, and was waiting for me at my mother's house. We had no house, no furniture or other things and no jobs. We put our name down at the Housing Office, but no houses had been built.

There were no decent jobs going, so I went back to driving a taxi. I was an ex-grammar school boy but still could not get a good job. I did however make good money with the taxi job as Blackpool was very busy with all the men and women being demobbed, but the job meant working very long hours.

I tried to get a licence to operate my own taxi but there was a ban on any extra licences being granted owing to the petrol shortage.

We had a son in July 1947 and were allocated a new house in 1949. In 1950, I changed my job to be a driver for a local biscuit company and stayed with the firm for 29 years.[31]

Some of the saddest cases of failed expectations were to be found among commissioned officers, young men who had succeeded on merit, often starting as private soldiers, and who were now brought to realise that the qualities for which they were justly praised were no guarantee of preference in civilian employment.

The disillusioned hero, unable to find a place in a society that seemed to him to be cruelly indifferent to his fortunes, became a stock figure in the post-war literary output. One such was the young fighter pilot, unable to come to terms with his own emotions, in Terence Rattigan's *The Deep Blue Sea*. A little later, the widespread frustration of the officer class was used by Bryan Forbes in the film, *League of Gentlemen*, in which a group of former comrades-in-arms took to bank-robbing as revenge on an ungrateful society.

True to post-war conventions, wickedness was not allowed to prevail on screen but as the black maria drove away in the final scene, audience sympathy was entirely with the criminals.

There were many excuses, not all of them specious, for failing to accommodate the officer class. For one thing it was by no means axiomatic that military leadership carried over into business management or the professions. To take an obvious example, the trade unions, cushioned by a Labour government, did not take kindly to commands from above. Negotiation and consultation were two essential skills that many ex-officers had to learn from scratch. They were simply not used to having their orders questioned.

Learning the art of two-way communication should have been a prerequisite of school teaching, seen by many ex-servicemen as a passport to middle-class respectability on a modest income. Here, at least, there were opportunities galore. A government emergency scheme aimed to attract 70,000 entrants to the profession, a figure soon increased by 13,000 to provide for the raising of the school leaving age in 1947. A year's intensive training was offered to those with basic educational qualifications. Getting a teaching diploma was dependent on two further years of practical teaching.

There was little attention to academic achievement. 'The best we can do is to introduce you to the subjects you would like to study,' said Walter Sheppard, principal of Leavesden Green Training College. But not to worry. We know 'that the majority of our pupils have neither the inclination nor the ability to appreciate the academic approach.'[32] It was a commonly expressed view and one that was to have a long-lasting and disastrous impact on British education.

The emergency scheme is generally reckoned to have been a success, though the customary verdict of social historians might be challenged by some of those on the receiving end. A correspondent recalls an army captain turned primary school teacher who marched about the classroom, swagger stick at the ready to whack recalcitrant pupils. Then there was a 'pray, damn you, pray' major who presided over morning assembly as if it was a parade of new recruits.

> Our Father which art in Heaven – (Stand up straight boy, don't loll about) – Hallowed be thy name – (There's a boy talking; see me afterwards) – Thy Kingdom come, thy will be done – (What do you think you're doing? Keep your hands to yourself) . . .

And so on.

A sad tale is of a bomber pilot who kept his class mesmerised with tales of derring-do until the discovery of his paederastic tendencies brought his career to an abrupt end.

Some former officers were taken on by large companies able to make use of their leadership qualities.

Nevertheless, the capacity to absorb men of the type required at a level commensurate with their war-time responsibilities and experience is limited in even the largest undertaking, for they must compete with an existing staff qualified by technical experience as well as personal ability, and no employer will wish to disturb his staff relationships by blocking all hopes of promotion for his existing staff by the introduction of a large number of newcomers at a high level.

This was R. Gresham Cooke, Secretary of the United Steel Companies, writing to *The Times* in September 1947. In the same issue, an officer's wife put in a plea for the disabled.

My husband, on leaving hospital, was advised to get a not too strenuous job to help him back to health and strength. In spite of excellent credentials and a splendid Army record, it has been hopeless. The only reply received informed him they had 500 applications.

It is to be hoped things are not going to be the same as after the last war. We have a small son to educate and something ought to be done for those men who can for a time no longer be classed as fit men.[33]

The criticial age group was 34 to 45, as the British Legion knew only too well.

The situation which is causing all of us deep anxiety is the growing waiting list of names that we have of men of 40 years or over, without special qualifications, all of good educational and administrative background, for whom apparently the only employment available is with a pick and shovel. This is, of course, particularly true of men who were in the Regular Army before the war and who have no special qualifications . . .

There are two sides to this, not only the unnecessary and painful distress for the families of men who have served the country overseas in the fighting forces, but the monstrous waste of first-rate man-power.[34]

In a period when a career in sales and marketing required little more than the gift of the gab, Captain Smith and Major Jones took to the road with their sample cases or were to be found behind high street counters, or in car salerooms. But opportunities were hardly plentiful since there was little enough to sell. It must be remembered that rationing was more severe after the war than during it. Bread was rationed for the first time in 1946, while potatoes were rationed at the end of 1947, two impositions that came to symbolise the misery of austerity. Everywhere there were shortages and queues.

Shop windows were boarded up. To buy a packet of cigarettes or even a decent pint of beer it helped to know the right people. Trains were dirty, draughty, jam-packed and invariably late. The failures of social and economic planning showed up at every turn. Last week there was a shortage of sardines; this week there were plenty of sardines but no openers for the cans. In 1948, the average family income was less than £7 a week.

It was this heavy greyness that somehow absorbed much of whatever energy and enthusiasm servicemen had in reserve.

Civvy street was unimaginably drab in the late '40s and early '50s. I was repelled by the way people seemed obsessed with getting hold of things which were in short supply – mostly things which, in the army, I had thought unnecessary, or obtained as a matter of course (like cigarettes, food, transport, free tickets to concerts).

The culture shock of civvy street was considerable. The most unsettling thing was that nobody ever told me what to do next, so for about two years I did nothing much. As a Rifleman, every hour of the day – and sometimes the night – was regulated by orders and priorities. After six years of this I was a mass of conditioned reflexes, able to react positively only to being told what to do and where to be at any given time. As a civilian, nobody seemed to care what I did or where I was. People got on with their own business and left me to mine. It wasn't so much the attention that I wanted, but a structure in which to function. Also, civilians seemed far more snobby about rank than soldiers, and I didn't like telling them I had been a Rifleman. The girlfriends I had before joining up had all found somebody else; a few were quite stroppy about my coming back at all.

The army was, among other things, a big, noisy, energetic and purposeful crowd; civvies seemed listless, preoccupied and aimless. My mother was completely incurious about my service days, which I slightly resented because I wanted to talk about them to her. If I did something wrong or daft nobody gave me a bollocking. There was no point in being obstreperous. The feeling was one of unfocused resentment at the theft of six years of my life (from age 19 to 24), but it didn't appear to be the army's fault. Apart from the gift of the gab I had no saleable skills, and no ambitions. For about two years I drank too much and swore a lot.[35]

It was not all bad news. As Margaret Wadsworth writes:

Sometimes the services had opened his eyes, taught him a new trade, encouraged him to spread his wings. Training Centres were opened. New careers were started, and providing a man was intelligent and his family willing to help, the way ahead was promising.[36]

Diana Bites was five when Dad came home. Her brother was eight.

My brother had attended a private preparatory school where he had been taught to knit. This horrified my father who immediately moved him to an all-boys school. He was always disappointed that my brother was not sporty like he was.

He had worked for Lloyds Bank when he enlisted and when he came home he had to take his Banking Exams whilst those who had stayed behind were much 'higher up' than he was. I remember a very tired, strained, bad-tempered Father, with my mother continuously saying, 'Don't bother your father.' I am pleased to say that he did become a manager with his own branch.[37]

The best that could be done for those who found it hard to readjust to the old routines was the advice handed out by the Directorate of Army Welfare Services to employers who were liable to encounter problem cases.

. . . It is most unreasonable to expect these men to be able to get fully into the new routine of life at once. You must be prepared for the first few months to ride them with a loose rein and be generous in allowing them days off and time off until they are settled in. The manager of a department of J. Lyons & Co. at Cadby Hall gives the following example of how necessary this sort of handling is and how well it works: two men invalided out of service overseas returned to his department. After a fortnight they came and told him that though they badly wanted to keep their jobs and stay with the firm, they just could not stick with the daily grind. He suggested to them that they should go on half time for a couple of months and see how that would work. They agreed and at the end of two months were able to come on full time again and have now settled in quite happily.[38]

In every community there were families whose thoughts were less of getting on than simply surviving. For them, living in miserable conditions with the worry of scraping a living was the only sure prediction. They put up with it all with extraordinary good humour.

We lived in a two-bedroom terraced house, no bathroom, no hot water. My mum used to carry the cold water upstairs from the yard, also no coal for the fire. I was the youngest of four children, three girls and one boy. We used to wear clogs for school and second-hand clothes. My mum used to sell some of our clothing coupons to buy food.

When Dad came home from the war he kept going to the council and we eventually moved to a three-bedroomed council house.

My brother always had his own room, the three girls shared, the three of us sharing a double bed. We were very poor but Dad worked hard to keep us all. He always felt it was a woman's place to stay at home and look after the children.

Dad always made a great fuss of me, I think really I was his favourite although I shouldn't say this. My brother managed to go to Grammar school and Grandmother helped buy his clothes and books he needed. He has done very well for himself. And we all own our houses.

There was always many rows over money, sometimes we had no coal and it was very very cold. We used to go to bed wearing socks and coats to keep warm. We did not feel deprived as there was a lot of people in the same boat.[39]

317

After the optimism engendered by army education, Beveridge and the election of a government pledged to transform society, there was by 1946 an unmistakable feeling of let-down. It was not just the predictable rest-lessness of men who felt like strangers in their own homes; or even that living conditions and employment chances were less favourable than the demob boys had been led to expect. The chief cause for resentment was the realisation that servicemen could not expect any preference over civilians.

The issue was debated in Parliament as early as April 1945 when J. J. Lawson, MP for Chester-le-Street, spoke for Labour against the idea that ex-servicemen should have priority in the distribution of jobs. The great mass of people had been in the fighting line, he argued. Preference for servicemen would be unfair to those who had lost sons or husbands in the bombing. He was opposed by a Conservative, Sir Ian Fraser, who spoke for the British Legion when he demanded preference on the grounds that 'it was more dangerous to fight at the front than do war work at home'. Later in the debate Sir Ian took a step back, admitting that he and his friends in the Legion were not anxious for a fight on the question. In view of the fact that the Minister of Labour was intending to mark the employment register to show which men were ex-service, he was happy to postpone the battle until after the election when there would be many more ex-servicemen on both sides of the House. He was right in predicting increased political representation for the military but wrong in assuming that they would all go his way. The new Labour government held to the principle of equality of treatment.

Its case was put by Colonel George Wigg, MP, in the *British Legion Journal* of March 1946. Preference in employment for ex-servicemen and women (Legion policy) was, in his view, short-sighted. It ignored what he regarded as axiomatic, a government capable of delivering full employment and 'a square deal not only for the ex-serviceman and woman but for the whole community.' The article attracted a reply from Captain Quintin Hogg, MP who, in typically barnstorming style, launched an attack on those who maintained 'we are all in the front line now'.

If the saying means that there has been in the main any comparable degree of sacrifice or hardship between those who worked in civvy street and those who underwent the rigours of life in the field, or the prolonged heartache of separation from their families, I must say I have yet to hear more pernicious and dangerous rubbish . . . The point is that real equality of opportunity between one who has spent the last six years in the service and one who has not is only pious humbug unless some degree of preference in the early stage is given to the ex-serviceman and woman.

The 'early stage' was critical, for no one, not even the staunchest Labour supporter, believed that Utopia was so close that it alone would solve the problem. The British

Legion felt that preferential treatment was the immediate answer to an immediate problem.

> Does Col. Wigg suggest that the ex-serviceman and ex-service-woman, many of whom are signing on at the Labour Exchanges up and down the country, should get at the back of the queue waiting for jobs? Surely until there is a job for everyone, all things being equal, the ex-serviceman and woman should get preference. Until full employment obtains the British Legion must retain preference as part of its policy.[40]

A few concessions were made. Around 15,000 vacancies in the administrative and clerical grades of the civil service were reserved specifically for ex-servicemen.[41] The BBC agreed, when filling 50 per cent of its vacancies for manual workers, to give preference to ex-regulars. The Building Societies' Association offered 'special consideration' to suitably qualified forces applicants ('candidates should not be more than 26 years of age, of good personality and address') and the Caterers' Association agreed that ex-regulars 'should have opportunities of employment appropriate to age, experience and ability'. Generosity of concessions was greatest in Northern Ireland where the civil service and local authorities gave preference to ex-servicemen in filling all posts for which they had the necessary qualifications.

But it was the rule on reinstatement in former employment that should have given ex-servicemen the best chance of asserting their claims. Unfortunately, the scheme was totally unworkable.

A lot of problems arose when a returning serviceman wanted his old job back. By law an employer had to take a man back, but in the meantime had to replace him with someone else. By law the substitute had to give way, but what a predicament: if he left where could he go? He, or she, had carried on as best as he could and was then thrown on the scrap heap. It was difficult for the ex-serviceman to put him in that position, unless it was a retired man who was willing to retire again, or a woman who knew she was only temporary. Then again, the serviceman didn't always want his job back.[42]

The British Legion went in hot pursuit of employers who were thought to have circumvented the Reinstatement Act.

When ex-Petty Officer Edward James Murkin, 46-year-old veteran of two wars, resumes his pre-war job, he will get a cheque for £80 from his employers. This is the sum fixed by the deputy umpire as compensation for having been discharged on the ground that his absence on war service had rendered him 'incompetent to deal with new devices'.

Murkin, the father of five children, was a boiler-house charge hand at Felsted (Essex) sugar-beet factory when he was called up as a naval reservist in July 1939. He was reinstated at the factory, his salary being £7.7s. a week, and discharged two months later, and offered a labourer's job.

Chelmsford Reinstatement Committee, to whom he appealed, decided in favour of the employers, and with the support of the British Legion he took the case to the deputy umpire.

The employers were ordered to reinstate Murkin in his old job, pay £80 'for loss sustained through the employer's default', and provide him with instruction in new devices introduced during his absence.[43]

Even when employers played by the rules, there were always those who behaved with ill grace, handing out jobs as if they were favours to a charitable cause. Trained as a farm manager, S. F. Hay was lucky with his employer. Others were less fortunate.

Some farmers did not want to know. I must make it clear only some were like this, they either would not take on ex-service people or if they did they treated them like dirt. I was speaking to an old shipmate of mine the other month and this happened to him. He left the land after a couple of years; he would not put up with it.[44]

In all, the reinstatement committees adjudicated on 443 cases in 1945 before entering on the period of maximum activity in 1946, when 4,277 cases were heard. The following year they were down to 1,777 cases and in 1948,

1,387 cases. Returning ex-servicemen rarely made trouble. If they were lucky they received a cheque from their former employers by way of thanks for not aggravating an already difficult situation. Others simply turned away.

I left the army on February 27 1946 after nearly seven years of service. Initially, I received a few weeks' paid holiday in order to 'climatise'. It was an extremely difficult period of time for my wife and I, and our son David, who was born in March 1944. We had no home of our own and had to live with my parents in their small cottage. Money was also scarce, the family allowance my wife and I received when I returned home.

One of the greatest shocks I encountered was when I returned to my old employer. One of the assurances I had during the war was that my old job as a transport driver would be available if I was lucky enough to come home. However, after a chat with my former boss he informed me that there was nothing he could give me. After spending over six years in the army I was very disillusioned and very disappointed. At one stage I was even tempted to rejoin.[45]

The group everyone thought should have preference – more as a pious wish than a firm proposition – was the disabled. They had their own employment register and rights of priority in job-seeking enshrined in the 1944 Disabled Persons' Act. The following year, Remploy Limited was set up under government auspices to provide facilities for the employment of the severely disabled. The original plan was to open a hundred factories, each specialising in a particular range of products. But shortage of building materials and difficulties over Board of Trade licences slowed the plan so that by the summer of 1947 only 10 factories were functioning.[46] Eight months later, the number was up to 16, with another 23 in the process of being built. But still there were problems in persuading the Board of Trade to grant licences to sell goods on the home market. As to exports, it was said that Remploy factories 'had not yet reached a high enough standard of workmanship' except in the production of Christmas cards, cardboard boxes and utility furniture.[47] So much for preferred treatment.

As to the employment register, barely 100,000 signed on as disabled in the first year, when it was reckoned that one million were eligible. One difficulty was that personal application had to be made at a local employment exchange – and a lot of disabled ex-service people had no way of getting there. The Minister of Labour promised to make registration simpler.

Pensions for war wounded were derisory. When fixed in 1939, they were lower than during the First World War. Dunkirk casualties were awarded the equivalent of 48p a week.[48] The level of payment was raised towards the end of the war but applications for pensions took for ever to process and voluntary bodies like the British Legion had to use their own funds to support claimants while they waited for an official declaration of the obvious. A welcome concession, sought by the British Limbless Ex-Servicemen's Association, introducing an entirely new allowance payable to men whose disabilities made them unemployable, took eight years of lobbying to achieve.

There was less success in securing treatment for, or even minimum understanding of, psychiatric cases.

Many men come to the British Legion who joined up in the early days of the war – perhaps were wrongly passed by an overworked medical board – and were out again in a very short time. They say they cannot hold down the jobs they did before the war or get other jobs because of their nerves. Certainly they are distressing cases.

We cannot let them walk the streets, losing hope with every day that passes.[49]

That was precisely what the government seemed intent on doing. The degree of official ignorance was such that in at least two areas of the country, known sufferers of psychiatric disorders were given grants to set up small businesses.

Apparently this was considered the easiest or the only way out in the case of men who were unfitted for ordinary industry.[50]

In early 1946 the Ministry of Labour mooted the idea of a rehabilitation centre, basing it at the resettlement college at Egham. But the staff there were chiefly experienced in physical rehabilitation and were not qualified to cope with mental disabilities. As a way out of the quandary, the War Office suggested the conversion of six of its own resettlement centres, 'which can be more suitably staffed and equipped for dealing with these psychological problems.'[51]

What followed is such a classic study of bureaucratic muddle that the civil servant at the Ministry of Labour charged with planning the operation must be allowed to tell his own story.

It started with an offer of War Office Resettlement Unit premises made by the late Adjutant General to the Secretary. We jumped at the offer and went to the Treasury who agreed in principle to our negotiating with the War Office to take six CRUs for use as Industrial Rehabilitation Centres when the War Office had ceased to use them for their own purposes. Then the quartering people in the War Office who are concerned with premises came into the picture and after considerable comings and goings between us and the War Office and the Ministry of Works, it emerged that the War Office were not prepared to let us have the CRUs at all; the AG had no authority to commit the War Office to giving away War Office premises. The Secretary and the Minister then took up the matter with the new Adjutant General and the Secretary of State for War followed by further negotiations with the War Office which resulted in an offer of four CRUs – not the same ones as we had originally hoped to get. Meantime, we had surveyed and prepared plans to adapt the premises originally offered and those had to be scrapped and plans prepared for the adaptation of the new premises.

The Treasury agreement to the scheme had been on the understanding that we secured their approval to proceeding in each case when the cost of the adaptations were known. So, having given the Ministry of Works an account of our requirements for each Centre, we had to wait for them to produce estimates. Meantime, squatters, not appreciating from their peculiar angle what was happening in Whitehall on these matters, occupied two of the premises. We hurriedly mobilised trainees at great inconvenience to occupy the Centres and hold the squatters at bay. We succeeded at Caerphilly (where, incidentally, the Ministry of Education who had part of the camp were ousted by squatters) but we failed at New Washington, Newcastle-upon-Tyne. The reason why we agreed to give up the New Washington camp was that the squatters had nowhere else to go and the Ministry of Works turned up at the Inter-Departmental Committee on Squatters, where these things were fought out, and said they could offer us alternative premises in the region. The premises offered at Beamish Hall appeared rather more suitable to our needs than New Washington, so we gave up New Washington and started all over again on surveys, getting out estimates, etc. on Beamish Hall.

Then the Treasury shot its next atomic charge! These places were all held on requisition; in some cases considerable sums had been spent on them by the Army. The Treasury were not prepared to agree to further expenditure unless the premises could be secured for a long period by purchase or on a long lease. This put us in some difficulty because we did not want to be saddled for ever with these places – which are by no means ideal for our purpose but are the best that can be got in present circumstances, but the Ministry of Works agreed that they would be willing to try and secure them for a long period for their own purposes.

Ministry of Works then began negotiation with the owners to secure a long tenure. The owners of Caerphilly are the Glamorgan County Council who have plans for doing something else with the camp and are not prepared to sell. The owner of Sudbury (Derby) wants the camp to be cleared away and the place restored to agricultural land and the persuasion of our Regional Controller and the Regional Director of the Ministry of Works has failed to move him. In the case of Beamish Hall, Newcastle, and Wightwick Hall, Wolverhampton, where the owners seem to be prepared to enter into a long lease and to sell, respectively, the Treasury are being in touch on the terms and the matter is being thrashed out between them and the Ministry of Works.

In two regions, North Western and Scotland, we have not got nearly as far as this, however, because it has not been possible to find any premises in these regions to replace the CRUs which we had hoped to get from the War Office but had to give up.

When all these difficulties have been overcome, if ever

they are, the Ministry of Works will have to put the adaptations and building work out to tender and when the work actually begins all the usual problems of shortages of labour and materials will undoubtedly delay matters. The most hopeful view which the Ministry of Works felt able to take was that we might be able to move in and begin operating the Centres six months after the adaptation work starts and in no case are we within measurable reach of starting the work at the moment.[52]

Two rehabilitation centres were eventually opened but, like so much that was happening in that 1945–7 era, it was too little, too late.

CHAPTER EIGHT

'Tough Going These Days'

BBC advice programme on finding somewhere to live,
1945

Finding a means of earning a living was easier than finding a home.

House building proceeded apace in the 1920s and 1930s. Around four million houses were built between the wars. In 1939 alone, the housing stock increased by 350,000. If that rate of building had continued into the 1940s, slums and overcrowding would soon have been evils of the past.

It did not happen, of course. On the outbreak of war, building labour and materials were commandeered for the military. German bombs put the building programme into reverse. They destroyed or made uninhabitable around half a million homes. The price of the average semi-detached quadrupled in three years. By the time Dad came home there was a housing famine.

The government promised immediate action. Ernest Bevin spoke confidently of building five million homes 'in quick time'. Party policy was to erect 300,000 new houses in two years. The politicians were way off target. A shortage of materials and widespread bureaucratic muddle combined to exacerbate what was described by the SSAFA vice-chairman as 'the greatest single welfare problem today'.[1]

In his recent study of post-war Britain, Peter Hennessy draws back from his otherwise blanket approval of Labour reforms to describe the housing débâcle as an 'un-Attlee-like muddle'.[2] As Hennessy concedes, the muddle started at the top with the failure to agree on who precisely was responsible for housing. The Chancellor paid out housing subsidies, the Minister of Works issued building licences, the Minister of Labour provided manpower, the Minister of Town and Country Planning approved building sites, and the Minister of Supply controlled the distribution of materials. To cap this mess, the minister with overall responsibility was Aneurin Bevan who, as Minister of Health, had quite enough to do in setting up a national health service. At the other end of the chain of command were the local authorities, many of which had little or no experience of building programmes. They were not short of advice. Instructional circulars were issued by the Ministry of Health at the rate of five a week.

Meanwhile, the waiting list for homes grew ever longer. Complaints were loudest, and rightly so, from couples who had never had a home of their own. A marriage that took place early in the war, to pre-empt an overseas posting, say, invariably left the wife lodging with parents or in-laws. It was a sensible option, providing security, mutual support and companionship at a time when all three were badly needed. Demobilisation changed everything. Now, the young couple wanted to move out. In many cases they *had* to move out to rediscover the love that had brought them together years earlier. Parents were not always sensitive to their needs.

> I think the hardest part for me was after the war trying to find somewhere to live. I lived with elderly parents and of course they didn't want me to go because of the little girl. It took my husband and I 18 months before we finally got our first home.[3]

Edith Brian lived with her parents in Islington after her marriage in 1942. Her husband was demobbed in 1946.

> We found it very difficult to weld together after such a long absence, having both matured and gone through many different experiences. My husband returned to his job as a motor engineer for £12 per week, and I continued at the War Office. Finding somewhere to live was a major problem. The area had been badly bombed being so near the city. Willow herb grew on many flattened sites. Our names were on three different housing departments; Islington, the

London City Council, as it was then, and Loughton in Essex. In five years we were offered nothing, despite having two children by that time.[4]

Elderly parents could be Jekyll and Hyde characters, helping and hindering young people trying to make a life together.

It so often happens that a young couple have been separated inevitably during the greater part of the war, the man has been serving for years, the girl has got employment, they have been going different ways, they have been developing a different background, and the one hope of keeping that family together is that as soon as possible they should have a common interest, a common home, a common activity together in the upbringing of the children. Instead of that, they are crowded in one or the other of the in-laws, and those in-laws are hardly human if they do not take the part of either the husband or the wife, whether of their own relationship or the other one, that is just luck! But at any rate you have the fact that husband and wife do not even get a room together, she is doubled up with the daughters, and he is doubled up with the sons, and it is quite impossible for the children to be properly brought up, or that the marriage will remain happy.[5]

On the question of moving, children were not always of the same mind as their elders.

I was born at my grandparents' large home and lived there with Mum and various family members popping in and out until Dad came home and we were put in a tiny council house in another part of the city.

It must have had a long-term effect on me, suddenly leaving a big family home to live in a small one with Mum, a new strange dad and crying baby sister. I always wanted more brothers and sisters but never got them, and used to love to visit other people with large families. I ended up with four of my own children and that was the happiest time of my life. Sadly, for me, all four now live in other towns. I am destined to be alone.[6]

But Evelyn Jones, who was just five when the war started, was only too eager for her parents to break free from the extended family.

After D-Day, Grandad died and in 1946 my brother was born. I used to sleep in with Mum next to the baby in the cot. When Dad came home (he is 83 now), I was put in with Grandma. I found it very horrific. The bed had two ditches, one each for Grandma and Grandad. I was lying in a dead man's bed. There was no one I could tell how horrified I was. It was a self-preservation instinct. Gran used to have terrifying nightmares and talk and scream over incidents in the past and add up grocery bills in her sleep. Of all the strange houses and people I'd met and lived with nothing was so frightening. It was 1948 before Mum and Dad got their own home in a prefab, which Dad still lives in.[7]

It was in 1942 that George Yorke, then an officer cadet in Wales, met an ATS girl from the Forest of Dean.

We knew each other for seven months, married on embarkation leave, had three days' honeymoon, then shared my billet near Birmingham for two weeks. In February 1943, we said 'Goodbye' when I embarked for North Africa.

Three years, 150 air mail letters, sundry pictures, and a small thin gramophone record of my voice later, I arrived back in England. There, greeting me, was my wife and a young daughter, born towards the end of 1943. They had spent the three years with my wife's mother and her two younger sisters in their cottage in the Forest of Dean.

My little girl had been for the first two and a half years of her life fussed over by an adoring grandmother, two aunts, and sundry other equally adoring relations who all lived nearby.

All she knew of her father was the voice she had heard constantly on the record that was played on the gramophone that stood under the couch when not in use. 'Daddy's under the couch,' she told visitors. The record was made courtesy of NAAFI in Athens.

My wife, to me, was almost a stranger, and little Christine completely so. We had to get to know each other. It didn't help with my wife's closely knit family, to know that within a month I would have to report to my pre-war employers, a Town Hall in London. This would mean finding somewhere for us all to live in London, a process well nigh impossible at that time, and then, much to the family's distress, uprooting my wife and child and taking them 200 miles away.

All I could offer my country-bred wife and daughter, used to complete freedom in the Forest of Dean, were two furnished rooms in a suburban street.

No, life was not easy, my wife finding life in London so much more hectic than at home, where a visit to the village shop was an opportunity for a chat. We managed, though, and without any major upsets. In six months I made a move to another council by the seaside in Kent, and they gave me a requisitioned flat. A humble place, looked at today, but heaven to us at that time.[8]

The BBC did its part in boosting morale, though in trying to make a virtue out of necessity the message came across with more than a hint of desperation. Here is John Morgan discussing the imaginary case of Bombardier Johnson, discharged after five years' service. Has he got problems. His home has been destroyed by flying bombs, his wife has died and he has five children to care for. But not to worry, Bombardier, John Morgan is ready with a few answers.

First he's got to get a house, and I don't have to tell you that's pretty tough going nowadays. However he's been down to his local council and put his name down and he comes pretty high on the list because he's got a good claim to priority.

But what's to be done in the meantime? His wife's mother

is going to take him and the eldest and the third child, but she hasn't room for any more. It's very important that the eldest should settle down as soon as possible; while she's been evacuated Sheila has won her scholarship to the local Secondary school and is now well on the way in her studies for School Certificate . . . That means that Bombardier Johnson has had to pay a visit to the Education Offices and see about her transfer from the school she's been at to the Secondary school in the home town. For the same reason – the importance of his education – arrangements are being made for the second child to stay out in the reception area because he takes his scholarship exam next March and it would spoil his chances to start chopping and changing just now.

So far so good. But there are still the youngest two children for whom no arrangement has been made and who've got no home to go to. Now in this particular case a voluntary society is going to help. You'll have heard of the Soldiers', Sailors' and Airmen's Families' Association. That's a voluntary society with representatives in all parts of the country, and also they now have representatives with the Forces overseas. Well, they were asked by the Resettlement Advice Office to see if they could help Bombardier Johnson in his difficulties . . . SSAFA runs a number of children's homes where they can put a limited number of children of service or ex-servicemen for a short period in times of domestic emergency. And Joan and Margaret, the two youngest, are going to one of SSAFA's homes temporarily until other arrangements can be made for them.

Now, you'd think that was the end of the immediate difficulties, but it isn't quite. First of all there's quite a sticky economic problem to solve. While he was in the Army, of course, Johnson was getting children's allowances as part of his Army pay and allowances. Now he's got to work out a new budget to keep himself and his children on his civilian pay. I'm not saying he can't do it – he's pretty sure he can – but it does mean some pretty careful planning. That's something which a good many of us will find when we get back to Civvy Street. The whole of our personal economic situation is different. It needs thinking out pretty carefully – with prices being what they are nowadays and so many things to buy that have been provided for us while we've been in uniform. And after that, he'll have all the usual headaches we all have nowadays – clothes, coupons, rations, queues and what have you.

Well, I think we'll leave that set of problems there![9]

Forces' charities were convinced that bad housing or no housing at all were the chief causes of broken marriages.

Thousands of young couples with children are being forced to live in one room. That is bad enough, but at least such couples have a place they can call 'home'. Far worse is the plight of young couples who have to share accommodation . . .[10]

'Tough Going These Days'

The files of SSAFA, a forces charity closely involved in housing problems, were crowded with examples of horrendous deprivation.

One man's wife has recently had a second lot of twins within sixteen months; they live in a perfectly clean basement in which there is not room now to put the additional cot to house the babies. The husband himself is home at the moment dealing with the fifteen-month-old twins, and when the wife comes home she will have these four children to look after with no one to help her, because in the present world there are no unemployed sisters.

The next case is a man who has never lived with his wife since they were married; he lives in a slip room in his mother's house. In a few months' time his sister is coming back from a sanatorium, this is her home. He will then have to leave or sleep on the floor, either of the dining room or somewhere else. His wife lives with her mother with her two children in a slip room. He pays his mother 30s. a week and his mother-in-law 70s., and there is not a great deal of money left. The man has even bought furniture for his home and is paying storage while he is looking for a home.

The third case is that of a Petty Officer, a serving man who was given fourteen days' compassionate leave by his officer to find accommodation. This man went to the Houses of Parliament to his local Member of Parliament, to the Housing Committee of the LCC, to the Sanitary Inspector,

339

and then to the National Society for the Prevention of Cruelty to Children. He has not been able to find anything.

All these people are in regular employment, all of them are in receipt of a good salary, and not one of them is able, through no fault of his own, to have the ordinary decencies of life, the ordinary happiness of life, all these things are denied them. What is the result? What is the good of making elaborate health arrangements if you are going to shut up four babies in a damp basement? What is the good of our calling upon a man to work hard, to put his back into it, when he never sees his wife? As he said himself, 'My nerves are all on edge, is it worth it?' That is the question.

As to the Petty Officer, he made exactly the same remark. He said, 'Now they are talking of another war [the Russians were blockading Berlin], and after fifteen years I have only got one room.' I must tell you this room is so small that they are afraid to have a fire on because the cot might catch fire. It is not much of a lookout for the wife because the child cannot sleep with a light on, and therefore she has to sit in the dark.[11]

This account leaves out what is possibly the most significant point – that all the cases relate to 1948 – three full years after the war ended.

Clearly, the only solution was to build more houses. The government was urged to lift restrictions on private building – the rule of thumb on the issuing of licences was to allow one private house for every four built by local authorities.

The free enterprise lobby was told there were not enough building materials to go round and when it came to a choice, local authority housing for rent, rather than purchase, must have priority. In any case, a free-for-all would lead to a collapse in standards.

It is hard now to recognise that those uniform rows of dismal concrete two-up-and-two-downs that blight the outskirts of towns and villages were designed to be superior to anything that went before. Bevan insisted on 900 square feet of living space for each home – 150 square feet more than the pre-war council house. His good resolution did not last beyond 1951, when the government allowed economics to prevail over ergonomics, but the new houses did at least have running water, indoor lavatories and a connection to gas and electricity. It would have been perverse to criticise local authorities for their aesthetic failure. Dull uniformity was the price to be paid for speedy construction.

Once that argument was conceded, there was no case at all against the ubiquitous prefab, the product of the 1944 Temporary Housing Act which empowered the government to spend £150 million on emergency housing to replace war-damaged property. In five years, 150,000 prefabricated homes were built. They were intended to last for ten years. Some are still standing.

Bevan called them 'rabbit hutches' but they answered a need and they broke new ground in building technology. Each steel-framed unit with asbestos sheets consisted of more than 2,000 components. Dispatched from the factory in kit form, they were put up in days. To a WVS representative they seemed like every woman's dream come true.

To begin with, all the cupboards are built in and there is plenty of space in the cupboards. How exquisite today when cupboards are unobtainable except at some fabulous price. Most ingeniously, the centre wall of this temporary house we saw does not arrive as a wall, but as a set of cupboards, one side being cupboards and the other side flat.

Then there are two forms of heating. This will be (unless we are very much mistaken) a godsend this winter when the coal shortage will make heating a tricky question. It may be necessary, in winter, to cut off gas or electricity for certain hours of the day. It will certainly be difficult to get coal or coke. In these Government houses you can use a fuel-heated stove, which at the same time heats all your water, or you can use an electric fire, and there is an electric immersion heater with thermostatic control to heat your water. The fuel stove, when it is lit, heats a splendid linen cupboard.

The kitchen produced groans and sighs of envy from even the most generous of us. They are so compact. Cooking is by gas or electricity, and apart from the cooking stove there is a large clothes boiler. In some of the houses there is even a refrigerator, unobtainable today. Over the cooking stove there is a built-in ledge to hold saucepans, and in those houses where there is an electric cooking stove the fortunate owners are allowed to rent special saucepans for a penny or so a week. (The price seems to vary according to the saucepan and its size.)

These temporary houses are much roomier inside than they look from the outside. They have two good bedrooms and can comfortably house a small family. There is a nice-sized living room and admirably arranged plugs for lighting, wireless, etc., and a very nice bathroom and a separate lavatory. Finally there is space round each house for a garden. Actually in the houses we saw at Clapham there was space for a handsome garden where gardens had been before. In one house which we visited there were two old pear trees in the garden bowed down with fruit. We looked at the pears, and we thought of the house, and we said to ourselves: 'All this, and Heaven too!'[12]

The prefab was most certainly an advance on many of the available Victorian and Edwardian houses, particularly those in rural areas.

I remember what a 'carry on' it was to have a bath in 1946. After leaving the forces my late husband and I lived in a cottage in Kelsale; no mod cons, cold water from a pump in the garden. The bathing itself beside a lovely warm fire was great but then came the emptying in reverse order. We were more worn out than relaxed after all this. When electricity came my husband went to Ipswich, bought an electric copper and carried it home on the train to Saxmundham. Then it was on his bike to Kelsale. We thought that copper was wonderful. In 1956 our landlord put in a bath with a cold tap and run-away in the kitchen. Same method of filling. Our old tin bath was put in the barn and used as a store for the apples from the orchard. That's what they call the good old days![13]

Some families found a novel way of creating a home – in converted railway carriages. A correspondent remembers an aunt and uncle who could not afford a house but could just manage to buy a patch of land. They then acquired a railway carriage for next to nothing, put it up on blocks and called it Mon Repos. Their young nephew was a frequent visitor. He brought along friends to play trains.

Ordinary domestic facilities were something of a problem.

I was married on December 1st 1945. The only accommodation we could get was a converted railway carriage where my eldest daughter was born. The hot water needed was boiled in a kettle on a Beatrice Oil Stove. Now to the loo. I joined the railway at Acle, and, doing my late turn of duty one night, a young girl going by train to Yarmouth evening classes asked if I would like a piece of chewing gum. I said yes and she gave me two pieces. I started to chew. On arriving home about 11 p.m. I had a hot drink and went to bed. But not for long! My tummy ached; I had to get dressed and dash to the loo. It was a bitterly cold night and some 27 yards to the loo. This happened three times during the night, by which time I was chilled to the marrow. It was a long time before that young girl told me the chewing gum was a laxative. I could have strangled her![14]

Allocation of prefabs was restricted to families with one or two children. Here, at least, ex-servicemen were given preference; they moved to the head of the queue. That was about the only concession made to them, although the government made vague promises that 'special attention should be given to the housing needs of ex-servicemen'.[15] A year on, the British Legion was noting that 'the unhappy result, as might have been expected, is that local authorities adopt different schemes and conflicting devices – some good, some bad – often irritating to ex-servicemen and blitzed-out families alike.'[16]

What this meant in practical terms was explained by the SSAFA representative from Sheffield, 'one of the most ghastly places in the country in respect of housing'.

The Housing Committee have 35,000 names on the list. We have taken deputations to the Housing Committee over and over again, and they will not give us any priority for fighting men. All we can get is that out of the prefabricated houses they will share fifty-fifty. They thought that was a great concession. In Sheffield they will tell you the servicemen did not win the war, it was the munition workers, so we cannot get any priority for servicemen as a reward for their services.[17]

In vain did the British Legion and SSAFA officials protest at having to tell men returned from the war who have 'been willing to sleep under the desert sky, in barn or field, that they are to take their place in the queue and their claims will be dealt with at an unpredictable time in some unknown year'. The government had a clear duty, the Legion insisted.

> We want to know the order, and we want it to be defined in legislation. We think it is placing an impossible burden on local authorities if each has to settle the order for itself. We believe that direction should be given, and that local authorities would welcome it.[18]

The government thought otherwise.

Not surprisingly, homeless families decided to act on their own account. Throughout the country there were military camps, collections of Nissen huts, that were now unoccupied. The idea of making use of them was initiated by SSAFA with an application to the Ministry of Works. The letter was sent on 19 October 1945. There followed a lengthy correspondence and numerous meetings before the Ministry came back on 2 October 1946 with an offer to sell one of the camps for £20,000, a fortune in those days. The mean-minded response hardly warranted a reply, not least because by then over a thousand camps were occupied by 50,000 squatters who did not give a damn for the Ministry of Works. What happened in Northwich, according to SSAFA, was typical.

> We had hutments which housed about 200 Americans. These hutments have been absolutely void of tenants since the last American unit left, which must be fully 12 or 18 months. The hutments are built of wood and are deteriorating. I was visited by several ex-servicemen about two months ago who asked me whether it would be right for them – I was going to say 'to become squatters', but I do not use that word. I said the better thing to do was to go to the local council and ask what authority they had over the buildings. It then appeared that the local council had been offered by the Ministry of Works these hutments at such a price that the local council turned it down. In about ten days or a fortnight the whole of the hutments were occupied, and the majority of the occupants were ex-servicemen who had just become demobbed.[19]

Thus was the housing shortage solved – huts for heroes?

CHAPTER NINE

'You're In The USA My Son . . .'

Verses on emigration – *British Legion Journal*, 1946

There was an alternative to austerity Britain, and between 1946 and 1949, 1¼ million young men and women took it. They emigrated to Canada, Australia and New Zealand, and Southern Rhodesia. In addition, 57,000 war brides left the country, mostly for North America, and nearly 8,000 servicemen and 200 servicewomen chose to be demobilised overseas.[1]

The exodus caused some worries at the time. There was a fear that the cream of British youth was being skimmed off, at inevitable economic cost to those who remained. The blame was put squarely on a government that promised training and well-paid jobs, then failed to deliver.

It is little wonder that many are deciding to try the Dominions. Already a first batch has left for Australia. A second batch

goes this month. Many more would be on their way if ship-
ping were available.

We wish them well. It is no part of our policy to export
'the unwanted', but those who are leaving these shores are
in the opposite category, young, single, trained to skilled jobs.

Much as we like to see them starting a new life with our
own kith and kin overseas, our thoughts are with those who
are denied opportunities to which they have every right in
the homeland for which they fought.[2]

In the event, the impact was more symbolic than real.
Letters home were reminders that the good life was achiev-
able. People began to realise that rationing, shortages and
making do on very little were not of necessity permanent
post-war features.

Commonwealth servicemen had even had a better
demob deal than British servicemen, as those who went
out there discovered.

New Zealand, with her proud tradition of well-funded
social services, provided a welcome home that was generally agreed 'to be the most lavish that any government
has felt able to afford.'[3] For every month of overseas
service, the New Zealander was entitled to two days'
leave on full pay up to a maximum of 91 days. Gratuities
were the same for all ranks – £3.15s. for each month of
service – the equivalent of the rate for a British field
marshal. The clothing allowance was £25, sufficient for
a head-to-foot civilian outfit.

The difference between the new and the old country showed up yet more dramatically in the catalogue of grants and loans for starting up again after the war. A family man discharged from the New Zealand Army and in need of a home could borrow up to £1,500 – the price of a five-bedroomed house in a quarter-acre holding. The contrast with Britain where ex-servicemen had to wait for years for half-decent accommodation could hardly be over-stated. Some concessions available in New Zealand were simply beyond the British imagination (as well as the British pocket), like the £6,000 loan on offer to any would-be farmer in need of land and stock. Other benefits, such as the free one-year rail pass, might easily have been duplicated in Britain, had not the government taken the view that servicemen should not be seen to be enjoying advantages over civilian war workers.

The schemes operating in Australia and Canada followed the New Zealand pattern in all but detail. An Australian serviceman looking to finance a house purchase could rely on £950 as a cheap loan. This was less than two-thirds of the start-up available to New Zealand Anzacs but the repayment terms were easier in Australia – 4 per cent interest and a pay-back period of up to 50 years.

Canada imposed the strictest rules on work reinstatement. An ex-serviceman was entitled to his old job, without conditions. Moreover, if he was better qualified as a result of military training, his employer had to pay more for his services. Educational opportunities were also greater in North America.

Whether a man intends to be a bricklayer or a university professor the procedure is the same. He has to state his case to a committee and show how his training has been interrupted. Then they will arrange that he goes to a technical school or a university, according to which will best serve his needs.

Maintenance allowances will be paid during this training. The scales are rather complicated and vary much on a man's circumstances, but they will do for him all that will be done anywhere – enable him and his family to live while he trains himself for the task of earning his own living.

In addition, there was a re-establishment credit for those who did not take immediate advantage of educational or vocational training.

This credit is the equivalent of the basic gratuity and may be used at any time during a period of 10 years for many purposes, including: acquisition of a house to an amount not exceeding $2/3$ of its value; repair or modernisation of a house; purchase of furniture and household equipment not exceeding $2/3$ of the cost; and the purchase of a business not exceeding $2/3$ of the value.[4]

But what was enshrined in law was not necessarily the full story. Living conditions in the Dominions could be much better than in Britain. This was hardly surprising given that these countries had not been devastated at home by bombing and rationing; their economies had not suffered in the same way. Equally, conditions could also be much worse, as many war brides discovered. Arriving with her infant daughter at a settlement in north-west New Brunswick in November 1944, Dorrie Lloyd felt that she had stepped back 50 years.

. . . no indoor plumbing, going up a hill to pump a pail of water, a big monster sitting in the kitchen called a wood stove, no paved roads, in the spring up to your ankles in mud. The worst thing I found was the outdoor toilet, marching through the snow and sitting while the icy wind whistled around you. I learned to cope and by the time my husband arrived back in Canada I had settled in, more or less.

We began our married life together in a small wooden house and the early years were far from easy. The returning veterans were finding it hard to settle and a number of war brides just could not cope and returned to their own countries.[5]

It was hard too for Canadian-, Australian- or New Zealand-born wives who had seen their husbands go off to fight a far-distant war in a part of the world of which they knew little.

My father was a train conductor. There were three of us children. Terry, the eldest – named after our dad, Joy, 13½ months younger, and me, Aline, four years eight days younger than Joy.

I remember the day, when waiting for a tram to go to town, a family friend stopped to chat to Mother. Adult conversation usually bored me but my attention was alerted when I heard, 'I see in the paper Terry's name amongst the latest intake.' Then the voices were hushed and they spoke in whispers . . . It seemed no time at all before Nana moved in to look after us children while Mother went north to Auckland to spend time with Dad who did his army training at Trentham Camp.

She was pale, quiet and thoughtful on return – Nana said, 'You've dark rings under your eyes, Edith.' I would hear her crying when she was alone in her room.

It was soon necessary for Mother to go to work, she had taken in sewing, ladies' overcoats and suits too in woollen herringbone which was then the fashion, wedding gowns and bridesmaids' frocks, and I particularly remember the airforce wedding when the five bridesmaids wore gowns of different colours and we always referred to it as the 'rainbow wedding'.

Her first job was with the Bell Tea Company. The dust from the tea and being indoors all day did not agree with her and she became ill. A friend with a milk round offered her a job. She would leave home in the small hours while we slept and walk two miles to where she met Jack and his horse and cart, and delivered milk from huge milk churns into billies and jugs.

Then she went to work at Cadbury Fry Hudson where she

353

was part of a team packing huge cakes of chocolates to send to the boys overseas.

While Aline's father was in Egypt, her older brother Terry landed himself in trouble with the police.

I have never forgotten the night I awoke and knew something was wrong. I climbed down from the big green wooden bed I shared with my sister and stood in the hall and listened. A light shone under the kitchen door. I felt my way along the dark hallway and quietly opened the door. There she sat by the coal range in our Morris chair steadily hand sewing although she must have been blinded by her tears. I put my arms around her and asked why she cried. It seemed Terry had been up to 'no good' and was being sent to a home in Invercargill. It was winter and he needed a coat which she was up making all night so she could take it to him at the train as he passed through Dunedin.

When we were older, she told us how she met Terry at the train. He was handcuffed to a policeman. He was only 13 years old! What was happening to her beloved first child? She was devastated.[6]

The expectation that all would be well when Daddy came home was cruelly disappointed. It was not long before the family split apart and Aline and her mother moved to Christchurch. Looking back, Aline does not blame the war for the break-up. Rather, she believes that her father volunteered as a way out of a hopeless relationship. 'They were incompatible.'

The distance factor and poor communications could put an intolerable strain on Australasian families caught up in the war. Helen King feels 'a great sadness for the young men whose lives were taken over by fighting'. Her own father returned a semi-invalid in 1943. He took to drink and was violent to his wife and children.

My brother tried to stop him one day but Dad threw him out. Mum didn't stay long after that. She took us two girls and we came to Perth. She had to get a job and we had no home life. Our earlier problems caused havoc in our teenage years and later in our marriages. My sister has grown up hating me simply because there was no love. Everybody had so many problems they didn't know we children existed.

Reconciliation between daughter and father had to wait for over 30 years.

Three years before he died we found him in the RSL War Veterans' home. He was 80 then. He was very self-sufficient but lonely . . . I learned to love my father. At his funeral many of the old regiment were there and I have a letter which was written by his comrade on the Kedak trail. His regiment had to leave Dad because he was too ill with dysentery to walk. The Japs were everywhere. He was so ill his friend did not expect him to live. They were helped by natives to get

355

him to hospital then he was shipped home. As children we were victims. When he came home we didn't understand what was wrong.[7]

For the feminist writer Germaine Greer, understanding what her father had been through took years to discover. Only during research for her book about him after his death did she come across the truth. He had not been a victim of Japanese atrocities; nor had he been a flyer facing heroic death on adrenalin-pumping missions. His war had been ordinary and uneventful by those standards: as an intelligence officer, based on the besieged island of Malta during the worst of the bombardment, listening in to enemy radio broadcasts for clues, codes, anything. He cracked under the strain and was sent home, narrowly (and by his own cunning) avoiding being marked down as a coward.

From his daughter, rightly, comes only sympathy for what he faced and how he coped with it. It is an unusual insight into the realities of war.

Military mythology has to pretend that real men are in the majority; cowards can never be allowed to feel that they might be the normal ones and the heroes insane. Real danger provokes a real response: the human organism goes into over-drive, giving the frightened one a high, making him feel cool, detached, superhuman. And so the flying aces pull off those legendary stunts. Actually, flyers were a small élite, served by a squad of earthbound individuals like non-flying Flying Officer Reg Greer.

The flyers were the ones who had the satisfaction of getting a crack at Jerry; everybody else had to sit tight and take the bombardment. The constant stress of irregular alerts, of months of interrupted sleep and of appalling noise levels gradually wore down men and women to different degrees. On a poor diet, in crowded conditions and with little sleep, they had run out of endurance. The authorities compounded their distress by accusing them of fear. They were actually too tired and too dispirited to feel fear.[8]

Readjusting to a loved one who had been through this sort of experience was never going to be easy.

There were familiar problems of children having a man about the house for the first time. When Elizabeth Wright's father reappeared, 'I was frightened of him, and whenever he came into a room where I was playing, I would collect all my toys together and leave. Which must have been quite upsetting for him – and my mother.'[9]

Joan Benson had three children old enough to remember their father's departure. He was invalided out shortly before the end of the war in Europe.

There was no problem with the girls. Dad may have been a bit strange but he was the man they prayed for every night and he gave Mum cuddles and that was good enough for them as they got cuddles too. Our son would have nothing to do

with him and went as far as saying, 'You are not my father.'
Start of trouble. It took me some time to realise that I was
the voice of authority in their young lives and in a way we
all tended to resent this new voice of authority . . .

I suppose we all saw the situation as it affected us individu-
ally. No one gave a thought to the man who had spent a few
years of authoritative army life amongst adults who was suddenly
tossed back into the rough and tumble and noise of family life.

The happy renewal of their father-son relationship was
engineered by a simple association of ideas.

On our family excursion to the corner shops we sometimes
saw a Salvation Army captain ride past on his push bike.
My son used to chase after him calling, 'Daddy, Daddy.' It
became a joke in our small street. As my husband did not
ride a bike the only thing they had in common was the
old-style officer's hat with the solid peak in front. My
husband wore such a hat in a large framed photo. But he
came home in a modern, what we called, lemon squeezer.
One of those cosy little hats that could be taken off and
slipped under the shoulder lapel.

So Dad went out in his lemon squeezer and came back in
his old formal officer's hat and was immediately accepted by
his son.[10]

Family tensions were heightened by the failure of the
authorities to say when or where Dad might finally be

released. In February 1945, Ken Booth of the Royal
Canadian Air Force, stationed in India, was looking forward
to early demob. Two months later he was still in Bombay
waiting for a troopship to England. He reached London
on VE Day.

> The conventional wisdom was that you would be checked
> in, immediately sent on leave and called back within a few
> days to get shipped home. That was the way it had been and
> the way it started for us. But we did not get the call back, so
> we slowly drifted back to find out what was wrong. The POWs
> were being brought back and they had priority once they
> were fit to travel. We could not argue about the justice of
> this, but it was obviously going to delay our own repatriation.
> May dragged on with its inevitable flight parades and other
> square-bashing, but mostly ennui. Rumours began floating
> around that anyone who signed up for service in the Pacific
> would get priority on the ships, but those of us who had been
> there did not want to sign up to serve once again in that
> hellhole. June came and went and our resolve wavered, with
> no hope of seeing a ship to take us home. Finally, about mid-
> July, we said, 'What the hell. OK, I'll sign,' and it was not
> long before we were headed for Liverpool and the *Strathearn*
> for our trip home.[11]

Ken's release had taken all of six months.

Even when Dad was on home ground, his entry into
civvy street could be obstructed beyond reason.

I was working at a shoe factory and every day I went home for lunch. One day a lady who lived a couple of doors away said to me as I passed, 'Your mother has good news for you.' I rushed in and she showed me a telegram from my father which said, 'Arrived safely in Australia and will be home when leave is granted.' I was nearly jumping out of my skin so I went back to work and ran home again when finished. My mother had a note written so I went down to the shops buying all the luxury items we'd now have, ham, cakes etc. At least we were going to give my father a treat. Well, it was six weeks before we saw him . . . Each day I was first out the door of the factory to rush home, there was no stopping me. Well, one day as I rushed out the door there was a soldier standing across the road. I didn't know him so I kept running when one of the girls called out to me. I turned around and walked back slowly towards the soldier. It was my father.[12]

One plucky young New Zealander got so fed up waiting for her husband that she made a pre-emptive strike. Elizabeth Scott packed up her home and sailed for England.

The morning I left I got a cable from my husband telling me not to come. I also got another cable at Panama telling me to turn back. On arrival at Plymouth I had nowhere to live.

There followed a tough few months during which it became clear to Elizabeth that her marriage was unlikely to succeed. Already with one baby, 'I found I was expecting another child. I remember one evening I felt quite ill. I asked Bill to go to the phone box and ring for a doctor. He said he couldn't go because it was raining. I went upstairs to bed and felt worse. It was no good calling my husband as it was still raining. When he did see how bad things were I was dashed off to hospital and lost the baby.'

Elizabeth eventually returned to New Zealand and remarried. She still wonders at the agony she put herself through. 'Was it service life that made my husband the way he was, or was it his nature?'[13]

Soldiers returning home to the Dominions were moving away from the ravages of the war zone and the hardships of reconstruction. Their governments promised a bright future with living standards superior to anything British servicemen could expect for years ahead. Yet the disillusionment felt in Britain was paralleled by a widespread sense of anti-climax experienced throughout the Commonwealth – an indication of how difficult demobilisation was always going to be, even if the social conditions were right. A recurring factor was the pain of readjustment, of losing out on military comradeship and unity of purpose. Civilian life was full of disappointment. Having fought his way through Italy, Valerie Hepburn's father settled back quite comfortably into his old job in Canterbury.

But he did get upset about large blocks of state houses being built for returned servicemen. They were very basic and all the same, and in hindsight he was right – most of them are still ordinary and uninteresting – a shame they weren't built in a scattered fashion so that the impact was not so strong.[14]

It was a mild enough complaint. At least there *was* vacant housing to occupy, which was more than could be said of urban areas of Britain. But knowing that some others were worse off was no consolation.

Extreme sensitivity to real or imagined slights was a common feature of every process of demobilisation, however well organised or generously funded.

The only employment I could find was as a part-time taxi driver and dispatcher. So, I applied for my own taxi licence. I appeared before the police commission, in uniform, wound stripe, ribbons and all. The police chief said he could not recommend my application because he didn't know me. I replied, 'Maybe you haven't noticed, sir. I have been away,' and left.[15]

Servicemen's complaints of indifference to their interests were matched by civilian resentment at having to make way for the victory parade. Had not those on the home front done their bit for the war effort? Was it not about time that they deserved some recognition?

Where job reinstatement was an article of faith, as in Canada, loud complaints were heard from those who felt they had been unfairly displaced. Women who had discovered the joys of economic independence were particulary vociferous.

The before and after war years were equally upsetting, as before the war we walked in the steps of the Great Depression and after the war we had to take a step backwards. The war, which was so unfair to many, gave others, especially women, the opportunity to escape the stereotype existence of going, for many at fifteen, to work at menial, low-paying jobs or marrying while very young. After experiencing four and a half years of the good life while working in a war plant – being royally treated, receiving top pay and benefits – it was devastating to suddenly have it all come to an end.[16]

As ever, there was a minority of determined men who overcame all obstacles to assert their talents. Joyce Batty's husband was the first South Australian to be awarded the Distinguished Conduct Medal. He won it for his part in the assault on Tobruk. The price was a paralysed right arm.

I well recall the major adjustments required by me due to my husband's physical and psychological suffering which eventually, 21 years later, resulted in a major coronary occlusion. During those years I had to adjust to the changes in the stalwart man I'd fallen in love with. He had become unstable emotionally. Frequent hospitalisation made it necessary for me to supplement his meagre pension of 12 shillings and sixpence per week.

Joyce became a journalist, photographer and adventurer, taking part in a world distance gliding record attempt from

Lake Eyre, flying the last leg of the London to Sydney air race and riding motorcycle pillion on a Lake Eyre survey. With her son Christopher she set up what she believes was the first mother and son aerial photographer-pilot team. As she says, 'I've never made much money, but I've had a lot of fun.'[17]

Joyce was a rare free spirit. Other service wives with invalid husbands found it took all their time to restore their families to some semblance of normality. What made it worse was that, as in Britain, while physical disabilities marked out the heroes, psychological illnesses often passed unnoticed by the medical and social services.

> Bill was such a nervous wreck on returning home he wouldn't go outdoors when it was dark, was so frightened he would shake like a leaf. He had malaria a few times after discharge. It took him between 18 months and two years to settle down to life once again on the farm. He was just terrified. I felt sorry for all who took part in the war. They were never the same again.[18]

Who knows how many hardship stories filtered back to the old country? No matter. In austerity Britain, a veritable catalogue of horrors would not have dented the image of the Dominions as lands of prosperity and opportunity. Verses that appeared in the *British Legion Journal* for January 1946 expressed the popular view. The particular reference here was to the United States but Canada, Australia and

New Zealand might just as easily have appeared in the reworking of Kipling.

> If you've got your civvy suit on
> And the world looks good to you;
> If you're full of rum and butter
> And you never have to queue;
>
> If the shops have all you ask for
> And there's service with a smile;
> If your petrol is unrationed
> And you need not walk a mile;
>
> If there's lots of smokes and toffee
> And the beer is flowing free;
> If you've brought a modern villa
> With your war gratuity;
>
> If there's coal inside your cellar
> And your married life's begun
> In a home that's newly furnished
> You're in the USA my son!!

Emigration reached a peak in the late forties but the attraction of the Commonwealth as the provider of a fresh start extended well into the fifties and beyond. For many the impetus came from political disenchantment.

Peter Lord was a flight lieutenant wireless operator; his

wife Ruth, a WAAF, was discharged in February 1944 when she was expecting their first child.

The defeat of Churchill heralded the socialist era. This was in part due to the active communist cells in the POW camps and told to me by a POW. Bomber crews, far from being heroes, were made to feel guilty! Food, fuel, clothes, etc. went on being rationed and while our own workers were on strike the population of Germany were rebuilding their ruins with the only tools they had – their hands. Returned service people found those who had remained at home sat in the best jobs and were resentful of service people as a threat to their security. The unions became very well organised and controlled the *amount* of work done and kept it to a minimum. To live on the weekly pay was to live on the bread line.[19]

An internecine family war spurred Pat Minton to join the exodus.

I was born in Chichester in November 1942. My father went off to India when I was nine months old. For four years all he had of me was a baby picture. I do remember him coming home although I had no idea who he was. I remember asking my mother, 'How long is this man going to stay with us?' 'He's your dad and he lives here now' was the answer. The natural bond was never there. We tolerated each other and as a child I was scared of him. I asked my mother about this years ago and she felt that he was a different man when he came home. I don't think he was brutalised, just a long way from his family. My sister was born in 1947 and all his natural loving poured over her and she has very different memories of him.

My parents didn't have an ideal relationship and I sided with my mother and my sister with Dad. The crunch came when I needed higher education and he didn't want me to do that.[20]

Marriage and Australia beckoned.

Escape from family conflict or an oppressive home environment is frequently mentioned by correspondents as the driving force that took them to a new life, thousands of miles away.

When Roy Smith's dad was posted to the Middle East, he gave his son the parting instruction:

'To look after your mum for me.' This was taken quite seriously as a six-year-old and probably had the effect of teaching me the idea of responsibility at a very young age.

It seemed to me that we coped very well with the situation we found ourselves in. Relatives and friends were always cheerful and quick to offer neighbourly friendship if we needed it.

When I was eight Dad sent home the money to buy my own new bike, which some of my elder cousins taught me to ride. These young men also taught me to fight and how to look out for myself in life.

I seemed to have had most things I wanted, such as toys and books. Someone also encouraged me to join the local library which set me off on a lifetime of reading. I had several good friends and we spent a lot of time playing war or making huts with whatever materials we could find.

Money was short, but Mum did casual work. Sometimes us kids were given a job too and one year I earned enough to buy an overcoat for the winter, as well as pocket money for a holiday at my grandparents. I spent a lot of time at my grandparents during holidays, enjoying a country village type existence . . .

As a growing up 10-year-old, I felt very much in control of my own life. This was to change drastically when Dad came home. We had a telegram letting us know that Dad had arrived back in England and to meet him at the railway station on Saturday morning. We easily picked him out by his bleached, almost white uniform and kit from all the other soldiers in khaki green.

After the normal hugs and kisses I shouldered Dad's kit bag and we made our way out of the station. As usual I made an assessment of the traffic situation and went to cross the road. To my horror, Dad grabbed my hand tight and insisted that I walk with him (like a five-year-old).

My first experience of having a father again!

Unfortunately, this was only the start and I don't think I ever adjusted to his (well-meant) attempts to dominate me – I had tasted independence.

Dad was always generous and kind to me, but I could not

forgive his absence and then overpowering return into our lives, which brought so much upheaval and disruption. He was jealous of the influences of other adults and openly criticised them – perhaps he was right, but it caused a lot of arguments and anger.[21]

Everything centred on Dad. When *he* wanted to move home, Roy lost out on the chance to go to the local grammar school. There were other moves – rows – recriminations – resentments, altogether an unhappy household. When Roy came of age he left for New Zealand. It turned out well, for the rest of the family eventually followed him and, as he says, 'we eventually resolved most of our difficulties'.

The long-term effects of Australian citizenship were less happy for another family under strain. Not wishing to be identified, the Browns, as we may call them, were married just two days before the military intervened. Bill went into the Royal Artillery, Sandra moved in with her in-laws. Occasional leaves produced three children who spent their early years in the cramped surroundings of a bed-sitting room. When Bill came home he went back to his former job with a gas company but soon had to take an inferior job out of London as the only way of moving to the top of a housing list. Bill 'never did get on with the children very well' and was unhappy in his work. An emigrant's passage to Australia offered a way out. But somehow the family was unable to pull itself into reasonable shape. The in-fighting went on and on. After 53 years of unhappy marriage and after seeing the break-up of the marriages of all three children, the Browns separated. Paradoxically, the formal split brought them closer than they had ever been before.

We were both really broken up about our separation. Unbeknown to me, Bill was a nervous wreck, and I know how I felt myself – almost as if I was heading for a nervous breakdown. But because I am a proud person, I put on a brave front and Bill did the same. Finally, in May this year I rang him up and we arranged to meet in town just for a bit of lunch. Nothing was discussed, only that he would be coming into town once a week to the bank and he would meet me for lunch. And that's how it's been ever since.[22]

It was not an ideal situation but then, little to do with demobilisation was ideal. Even after all these years Sandra knows the true cause of her unhappiness: 'I blame THAT WAR!'

CHAPTER TEN

'If It Snaps, There Will Be Chaos . . .'

Ernest Bevin on the demobilisation plan, 1945

This book began as a simple idea. Research has added depth and complexity but not changed the original concept: that the return of four million service men and women after May 1945 must have been a traumatic experience, life-changing, possibly life-destroying, for them and for the wives and children they were returning to after years away. The inspiration came, unwittingly, from a *Sunday Times* colleague in his mid-forties whose elderly mother had just died. How had the funeral gone? he was asked. Not too bad, he replied, but it was worse for my elder brother Jim. He was much closer to her, you see; he was born before the war and had been the man of our house while our father was away.

The thought stuck. There must be millions of Jims, men

and women now in their fifties, who had grown up in what amounted to one-parent families while the war was being won. But how had they coped with the strange and sudden resumption of 'normal' family life when Daddy returned? If it happened today, an army of social workers and therapists would descend on them; stress counsellors would talk them through the experience; documentary-makers with hand-held cameras would plot their every reaction. Clearly that was impossible in 1945; there was neither the time nor the number of 'carers' – nor the inclination – to deal with a social and emotional earthquake of this magnitude. They would just have to get on with it.

Which, of course, they did. But there was a cost in human unhappiness that has been largely unrecognised. In the edition of the *Sunday Times* that marked the fiftieth anniversary of the D-Day landings, we invited readers to send in their reminiscences of the demobilisation that began in the summer of 1945. What happened to you when Daddy came home? we asked. The result was a flood of personal stories – happy, sad, depressing, uplifting, above all bringing alive those strange dog-days of hope and disappointment that marked the end of the first war in modern history that had totally involved entire populations. We put the same request into local newspapers throughout the country and the response was the same. Here was a gold mine of memories that the official histories had missed.

Take one of our most eminent historians, Alan Bullock. His life of Ernest Bevin, who, as Minister of Labour in

Churchill's war-time government, masterminded the demo-bilisation, is not clouded by doubt. He quotes Bevin in a House of Commons debate in November 1944: 'It was quite obvious that we should have to wind this country up to a point at which it had never been wound up before in terms of manpower. The great anxiety which we have had all the time is, having wound it up to such a point, can we unwind it in an orderly way, or will it snap? If it snaps, there will be chaos.'

Bullock commented:

> It did not snap and there was no chaos. Several million men and women moved from the forces and war industry to peace-time occupations without any repetition of the breakdown which followed the 1918 war. Bevin's double achievement, the mobilisation and demobilisation of an entire nation, was complete.[1]

The folk memory differs, as the personal accounts in this book so graphically show. The homecomings were often hard; initial euphoria quickly – the speed is what surprises – turned to disappointment. Fifty years on, the detail, both exquisite and painful, with which those re-unions are recalled indicates how deeply they lodged in minds and memories. These recur: Daddy's moustache is a scratch on the face that still leaves a scar; expulsion from Mummy's bed to make way for 'that strange man' is an innuendo to thrill the sex-crazed psychoanalyst. Did any of us realise before how many children must have spent the war sharing their nights with their mother? The secret is out. But the biggest secret of all is the deep unhappiness that clearly marked the mass return to civilian life. The years have suppressed it until now – which is why the outpourings of our correspondents have a feeling of the confessional about them. Here are demons being exorcised.

That war is disruptive to human lives is a statement of the obvious. Those examining its effects in 1945 have tended to concentrate on the political and economic implications. Where is the great body of research about what happened to *people*? The authors were surprised when they began their inquiries to discover how little, if any, there was. The demobilisation? The men coming home? Interesting, that. On the Blitz, D-Day, life at the front, the libraries were overflowing with information. On the event common to all four million enlisted men and women . . . not a lot. No criticism is intended here; perhaps this book will help them fill the gap. But it is almost as if demobilisation has slipped between two tectonic plates. The historians of the war stop just before it because it is a peace-time event; the historians of the peace pass over it as the final chapter of war-time.

At least that neglect is a fair reflection of the official attitude at the time. Swords were expected to turn into ploughshares, soldiers into civilians, just like that. The politicians and planners had bigger games to play; the people could sort themselves out. Well, some could and some couldn't. Some never did. 'He died a few years ago . . . I never really knew him' – enough of the accounts from our correspondents ended with sad, wistful comments like this for us to realise how long-lasting was the hurt. Relationships were never the same again. Trust, love, respect, mutual understanding, all these were hostages to the fortunes of war.

We cannot avoid the conclusion that the breakdown of the family, such a persistent theme of the 1990s, has its roots here. Divorce and delinquency soared. There were other factors in play, certainly, but the war is, like it or not, the watershed. This is a conclusion that, surprisingly in our blame-obsessed society, others seem to have fought to avoid. Take two works of the new(ish) 'science' of sociology from the bookshelf: *Family and Kinship in East London*[2] and *The Insecure Offenders: Rebellious Youth in the Welfare State*.[3] *Family and Kinship* examined the changes in the early 1950s with the movement from inner-city terraces to out-of-town housing estates. Family life is seen to suffer – but the war is not even considered as a factor. *The Insecure Offenders* at least acknowledges the possibility that the war may have had a lasting effect – 'It has been said that the flare-up of adolescent violence could . . . be traced back to the effects of war-time disruption of family life and the shocks then inflicted on small children' – only to dismiss it – 'the aftermath of the war can be only a very partial explanation of the unrest'. The author prefers to concentrate on 'the affluent society' as the key to rebellious youth.

There is here the same reluctance to accept the basic fact that war has deeply traumatic effects that characterised the demobilisation. It is astonishing that, as we have seen, men coming back were specifically advised *not* to talk about their experiences because that was a barrier to reintegrating into family life. Not talk about events that were the most vivid, the most shattering, the most memorable of their lives? It was silence, separateness, the refusal to share, that built the barriers.

It had to be faced that, for those returning from it, the war had been the biggest thing in their lives. Probably nothing would ever dwarf it as an experience. And yet here they were being asked to forget all about it. Alan Ross, in a book called *The Forties*, published in 1950, gives an all-too-rare insight into how they felt:

For a great many, the end of the war marked the beginning of their decline. The war had been an emotional pinnacle from which, subconsciously, they would have liked to look down for ever. It was a feeling that they would later, except at odd confiding moments, probably deny. But in their bones they knew that they would never feel quite so much, or ask and get so much from life, ever again. Out of the crucible of war, a generation had created certain standards of responsibility, of excitement, of purpose, that no social blueprint could ever live up to. And if indeed those emotional terms of reference were somehow recreated, they too would only be like a debased coinage, a counterfeit cliché of the heart.[4]

Few who heard it will ever forget Enoch Powell's sobs as, in a radio broadcast nearly half a century after the end of the war, he described his guilt that he had survived the war while many of his comrades-in-arms had died. He wished, he said in a hushed voice, he had died with them. The demobilisation programme between 1945 and 1947 failed abysmally to address reactions like this, despite the warnings of Colonel Main, the unsung hero of this book, that here was a psychological minefield that the nation was about to march across. The official help was bureaucratic in the extreme, a warning of what was to come in the new welfare state and the national health service. Caring at a human level was left to voluntary organisations – the Salvation Army, the WVS and so on – despite the Labour government's dismissive attitude to such voluntary bodies. What need was there for them in the new cradle-to-grave Jerusalem?

Anyone who has spent time listening to the reminiscences of war veterans has heard often that these were the best days of their lives. By all accounts, war for the ordinary soldier, seaman and airman was long periods of bull and boredom followed by bursts of intense and terrifying activity. In the memory, though, the mundane is forgotten; the adrenalin is all. The authors recall a friend in his seventies, now sadly dead, proudly declaiming that these had been the greatest times of his life. He did so in the presence of his wife, who had heard it all a thousand times, oblivious to the hurt it caused her as she listened to him place their marriage, their children, their whole life together, on the second rank of things that had meant most to him. Here, nearly 50 years on, was a family for whom the war never really ended.

For millions, the reaction must have been the same. Daddy may have come home, but there was a part of him that would never return.

Postscript

Memories from the German Side

I was just seven and napping in my mother's bed at our home in a village near Frankfurt when something awakened me and I looked straight into a man's stubbled, tired, gaunt but smiling face. I was terrified, and screamed and slapped his face. My mother came in, laughed and said – 'It's your Dad.' This stranger then put his hands into his worn trousers and took out a bag of sweets and gave them to me; the first sweets I had ever seen. Slowly I got used to him being around.

Before the war my father was a teacher and had to join the Party in order to obtain work. Then he had to serve with the army in Finland, Russia, France, eventually with the rank of major, and after being wounded was sent to Corfu for some kind of light duties to recover from his injuries. Before leaving Corfu he was ordered to destroy the harbour but did not obey this command as he realised how essential it was for the local populace. He was sentenced to death for disobeying orders but fortunately was taken prisoner instead. He was captured by the British and flown to Egypt as a POW. I remember my mother being relieved and happy knowing him to be in the hands of the British and therefore safe and well looked after. Little did she know that the POWs were killing each other as the original ones were still fanatical Nazis and the later arrivals knew that the war was lost.

Her brother fell into Russian hands. After five years as a POW in Russia where very few survived the hardship and bitter cold (minus 50°C) he built his own crutches and walked home. Now retired as professor of philology at Münster University, he has compiled a book of the field post letters he had sent to his parents, together with his watercolours of Russia at that time. My children and I have copies of this, for us, very precious book.

My father lived in British POW camps not far from the pyramids for four years before he finally was sent home. All that kept him going were the photographs and letters from home and the thought of his wife and two children, my brother being five years older than me. I still treasure a coloured drawing he did from a photo of me during his captivity.

While my father was a POW, my mother was left alone with two children to look after, had no income whatsoever.

How she managed I do not know but I do remember going into the fields after the farmers had harvested their corn to collect what grain heads had been left on the ground. This my mother took to a mill and received some flour in exchange. I am sure the miller gave her more than he should have.

We also went into the woods to collect fir cones, acorns and broken-off branches for firewood as well as beechnuts for oil. We had strictest instructions not to help ourselves by breaking off branches as this was a punishable offence. We also had to pick Colorado beetles off potato plants in the fields for farmers and had to bring them to a collection point at the local Council yard.

My mother kept chickens, rabbits and geese. I had my clothes trimmed with rabbit fur and mother filled our pillows with goose down. When the tanks rolled down our street all the eggs Mother's goose was sitting on went bad because of the tremors. We had no goslings that year. Once Mother had 'organised' a goat for milk. She kept it in a makeshift pen just for one night. It was stolen. She told me that she had lots of her own milk when I was a baby and not only fed me for nearly two years but a little farmer's boy as well whose mother had dried out. That way she supplemented our diet with gifts from the farmer. Sometimes this farmer gave her some sugar beet and my mother distilled some kind of spirit secretly in the night (this was strictly *verboten* and punished) and sold or exchanged it for food. I still remember the smells.

When my father returned in 1948 he was sent to work in a brick factory and also into the fields and woods to clear them up. After being de-nazified with the help of Jewish friends he was allowed to return to teaching and later became a headmaster.

While my father was away we were overrun by refugees from the East and bombed-out towns. The local Council visited flats and houses in the village and stipulated who had to take refugees and how many. We had a man and his elderly mother put in with us and a grandmother with her daughter and five children fleeing from the Russians put into our loft. The man's mother could not cope and preferred to live in the ruins of her former house in Frankfurt itself, but her son remained with us.

This man never had to go to the front as he was a non-combatant army officer who had 'connections'. Seeing my mother struggle he started to 'organise' for us. He brought white flour, sugar, eggs and even real coffee, a change to the bean/pea-beetle soup. Funny, we ate the beetles in the soup without giving it a thought. Maybe because we did not know otherwise. It was not long before they ended up becoming lovers and this was perhaps quite understandable under the circumstances.

Before Father joined us, my mother asked this man to leave, but Father found out about their relationship, neighbours were keen to tell him about it, and went berserk. From now on our lunches often flew to the ceiling and walls when we had just sat down to enjoy it. Mother jumped out of the ground floor kitchen or bedroom window to save herself from his temper. I can still see red cabbage dripping and hanging off the ceiling. Apparently Father also threatened her with a Finnish dagger he still possessed from his hand-to-hand combat experiences in Finland where the Russians dropped from the trees on to the German troops.

One day, about six months after Father's return, whilst I was playing in the street, my mother brought out her bike, put a little suitcase on its carrier and started to ride off. I asked her, 'Mum, where are you going?' 'That is none of your business,' she replied and rolled off down the village street.

When Father came home that evening from the brick factory he found a note on the kitchen table with the message that Mother had left us. She left me only seven years old behind with a man I scarcely knew.

My father could never forgive her. We were not allowed to mention her name again. When I was ten, he remarried a war widow who not only had lost her husband in Russia but her father, two brothers and a brother-in-law as well, and had a daughter by her. My brother and I were superfluous to his new family and our new stepmother was uncaring and treated us very harshly. My brother went to live with my grandmother when he was sixteen and I ran away just as soon as I could and never returned. My father died last January. He cut us out of his will.

I have lost my mother, my father and my parental home.

There are moments I feel so alone and abandoned. My bilingual children had no German grandparents to go to and to be spoilt by. I have lost my roots but most of the time I am all right.

My loving husband has become mother, father and home for me. I hope I do not ask too much of him. It might be too much for one person to be all for the other.

Life was never the same for me. I am 53 now and still get bouts of unspeakable sadness occasionally and cry into my pillow.

It is said that war is the father of all things but it does leave thousands of broken families in its wake.

Gisela L. Greenaway, East Grinstead

Appendix

Numbers of men and women demobilised month by month:

1945	Month's Total	Cumulative Total
June (18–30)	44,550	44,550
July	103,790	148,340
August	134,820	283,160
September	148,150	431,310
October	280,150	711,460
November	391,080	1,102,540
December	382,260	1,511,800
1946		
January	444,860	1,954,120
February	363,930	2,316,440
March	370,450	2,691,760

April	284,850	2,971,560
May	284,380	3,249,870
June	243,100	3,491,480
July	198,800	3,689,770
August	145,530	3,834,810
September	159,220	3,991,880
October	117,960	4,109,730
November	97,340	4,207,070
December	85,390	4,290,850
1947		
January	48,930	4,337,100

Taken from *Demobilisation in Britain*, Central Office of Information, 1 May 1947.

Notes and References

CHAPTER ONE: 'CALL ME MISTER'

1 Public Record Office, ref: LAB32.32.
2 Dennis Rooke and Alan D'Egville, *Call Me Mister! A Guide to Civilian Life for the Newly Demobilised*, Heinemann, 1946.
3 Maurice Merritt, *Eighth Army Driver*, Midas Books, 1981.
4 Alan Bullock, *The Life and Times of Ernest Bevin*, Vol. 2 1940–45, Heinemann, 1967, p. 273.
5 Winston Churchill, *The Second World War*, Vol. IV, Cassell (1951), p. 861.
6 Memoirs of Brigadier J. V. Faviell, Imperial War Museum.
7 Extract from letter dated 17 May 1945 from Ralph Walton to his bride-to-be, Nancy (Imperial War Museum, ref: 88/21).

8 *Release and Resettlement*, HMSO, 1945.

9 Public Record Office, ref: LAB 18.462.

10 Bullock, op. cit., p. 335.

11 Ibid., p. 363.

12 Peter Hennessy, *Never Again: Britain 1945–51*, Jonathan Cape, 1992.

CHAPTER TWO: 'ANY COLOUR AS LONG AS IT'S BLACK'

1 *Soldier*, 21 July 1945.

2 *The Times*, 12 June 1945.

3 Rt. Hon. Sir James Grigg, War Office, to Rt. Hon. Ernest Bevin, MP, Minister of Labour, 13 March 1945 (Public Record Office, ref: LAB32.2).

4 Rt. Hon. Ernest Bevin, MP, to Rt. Hon. Sir James Grigg, 15 March 1945.

5 *The Times*, 23 July 1945.

6 Ibid., 19 June 1945.

7 Letter from General Sir Ronald Adam, War Office, to H. N. de Villiers, Ministry of Labour, 22 September 1943 (Public Record Office, ref: LAB32.2).

8 The Right to Reinstatement (Public Record Office, ref: LAB32.1).

9 Maurice Merritt, *Eighth Army Driver*, Midas Books, 1981, p. 176.

10 Ibid.

11 Roy Forth, Beverley.

12 Denise Mason, Northampton.

13 Len Goddard, Elizabeth Downs, South Australia.

14 John Row, Ringwood.

15 Iris Stirland, Nottingham.

16 G. Betts, *Autobiography of a Miner's Son*, Imperial War Museum.

17 *The Times*, 22 August 1945.

18 Sergeant J. Shaw, *Something About a Soldier*, Imperial War Museum.

19 Dennis Rooke and Alan D'Egville, *Call Me Mister! A Guide to Civilian Life for the Newly Demobilised*, Heinemann, 1946.

20 Arnold Heaton, Coventry.

21 Edward Smithins, *The Black Economy in England Since 1914*, Gill & Macmillan, 1984, p. 93.

22 Scotland Yard Report, 26 February 1948 (Public Record Office, ref: MEPO2.8793)

23 John Kitch, Penarth.

24 *Soldier*, June 1945.

25 Merritt, op. cit.

26 John Jones, Para Hills, South Australia.

27 Betts, op. cit.

28 Archie Clarke, Wolverhampton.

29 Bert Spencer, Bristol.

30 *Notes on Current Politics. Demobilisation*, Conservative Central Office, December 1945.

31 *The Times*, 23 July 1945.

32 Ibid., 13 August 1945.

33 Ibid., 24 August 1945.

34 Ibid., 4 September 1945.

35 Ibid., 5 September 1945.

36 Ibid., 26 September 1945.

37 *Hansard*, 22 October 1945.

CHAPTER THREE: 'DEPRESSION, JEALOUSY AND RESENTMENT'

1 *War Cry*, 15 September 1945.

2 Ibid., 27 October 1945.

3 T. F. Main, 'Clinical Problems of Repatriates', *Journal of Mental Science*, Vol. XCIII, 1947, pp. 354–63.

4 Trevor Royale, *The Best Years of Their Lives*, Michael Joseph, 1986, p. 21.

5 T. F. Main, *Notes on the Use of Broadcasting in Handling Psychological Problems of the Demobilisation Period*, War Office, March 1944 (BBC Archives).

6 Maurice Merritt, *Eighth Army Driver*, Midas Books, 1981, p. 180.

7 Archie McGowan, Perth.

8 Bernard Maybury, Coventry.

9 Name withheld.

10 Thomas Henley, Paignton.

11 Sydney Hay, Droitwich.

12 Eleanor Meardon, Shrewsbury.

13 Civil Resettlement Units for Army Personnel R1191 (Public Record Office, ref: LAB32.36, Document 14079).

14 Ernest Bevin, 22 August 1944 (Public Record Office, ref: LAB32.32, Document 140790).

15 Public Record Office, ref: LAB32.13, Document 14079.

16 Ibid.

17 Speech to SSAFA Conference, 4 October 1945.

18 Memorandum by Minister of Labour, Lord President's Committee (Public Record Office, ref: LAB32.35, Document 4079).

19 Regional Controllers' Conference, 8 May 1946 (Public Record Office, ref: LAB32.13, Document 14079).

20 Resettlement Advice Service, Discontinuance Circular Minute 131/1949 (Public Record Office, ref: LAB32.13).

21 T. F. Main, op. cit.

22 Merritt, op. cit., p. 178.

23 John Peacock, Crosby.

24 Peter Reese, *Homecoming Heroes*, Leo Cooper, 1992, p. 210.

25 SSAFA Conference Report, 4 October 1945.

26 *British Legion Journal*, March 1946.

27 Ibid., February 1946.

28 Ibid., January 1946.

29 Ibid., October 1947.

30 Ibid.

31 *Daily Mail*, 16 January 1945.

32 SSAFA Report to the Council, 1944.

33 Martin Pugh, *Women and the Women's Movement in Britain 1914–1959*, Macmillan, 1992, p. 268.

34 WVS newsletter, 1943.

35 WVS Report on 25 Years' Work, 1963.

36 WVS bulletin, April 1946.

37 Ibid., December 1945.

38 *The Manchester Regiment Gazette*, April 1946.

39 *On the Way Home*, Salvation Army, 1944.

40 William Booth Memorial Training College Sessional Report, 22 July 1947.

41 *Can I Help You?* John Morgan, BBC, 18 April 1945.

42 Ibid., 8 August 1945.

43 'Civvy Street' by E. Laurie Stone, from *Calling the West Indies*, produced by E. R. Edmett, BBC, 16 March 1946.

CHAPTER FOUR: 'MUMMY, TELL THIS MAN TO PUT ME DOWN'

1　Name withheld.
2　Gwen Price, Reading.
3　George Bennett, Upton.
4　Patricia Trestrow, Liverpool.
5　Helen Clare Kirby, Newcastle.
6　Sandy Gardner, Riding Mill.
7　Margaret Macleod, Milton Keynes.
8　Norman Ball, Victor Harbour, South Australia.
9　Ken Ludkin, Barming.
10　Jane Gladstone, Edenbridge.
11　May Griffiths, Blackpool.
12　Muriel Woodhead, Hexham.
13　Kay Chorley, Shepton Mallet.
14　Anna Farrant, Norwich.
15　As told to E. F. Marsh, Peterborough.
16　J. Gillett, Liverpool.
17　Rosemary Quincey, Barton Seagrave.
18　Sonia Merritt, Chingford.
19　Judy Vaughan, Cheltenham.
20　*Woman's Own*, August 1945.
21　Suzette Cohen, Southport.
22　Celia Butler, Lincoln.
23　Diana Bites, Cowes.
24　Joseph McGhee, Dundee.
25　Mavis Taylor, Darwen.
26　D. B., Dundee.
27　Mena Lewis Jones, Mulhouse.
28　Catherine Sedgebear, Bristol.

29 May Orton, Long Eaton.
30 Sheila Taylor, Tayside.
31 Monica Maher, Southport.
32 Jean Eldred, Luton.
33 Mary Rutter, Westhoughton.
34 Alwyne Fisher, Leeds.
35 Mike Ward, Halifax.
36 Jean Delaney, Wigan.
37 Julie Burville, Dover.
38 Wendy Reeves, Sevenoaks.
39 Jane Gladstone, Edenbridge.
40 Iain Leggatt, Carnoustie.
41 Jill Tyler, Pulham Market.
42 Eileen Dibben, London.
43 Mike Hughes, Newport.
44 John Taylor, Northampton.
45 Rea Lowe, Semley.
46 D. B., Dundee.
47 Brenda Bajak, Dereham.
48 Ian Hoyle-Jackson, Swansea.
49 Margaret Macleod, Milton Keynes.
50 Thomas Lee, Ayr.
51 Janet Worton, Geneva.
52 Tom Robinson, York.
53 Mary Dalton, Kenilworth.
54 Iris Stirland, Nottingham.
55 Bert Spencer, Bristol.
56 Marian Bryan, Formby.
57 Carol Freeman, Sunningdale.
58 Kenneth Russell Jones, Portland.

CHAPTER FIVE: 'DON'T BE JEALOUS . . .'

1 *Back to Civvy Street*, BBC, 4/5 December 1944.
2 *Learning to be a Civilian*, BBC, Janet Dunbar, 13 December 1945.
3 *British Legion Journal*, February 1946.
4 *British Legion Journal*, January 1946.
5 SSAFA Annual Report, December 1946.
6 Martin Pugh, *Women and the Women's Movement in Britain 1914–1959*, Macmillan, 1992, pp. 264–5.
7 Bert Mullen, Weston-super-Mare.
8 George Campbell, Woking.
9 Brenda Lescod, Sunderland.
10 Barbara Cartland, *The Years of Opportunity: 1939–45*, Hutchinson, 1948.
11 John Costello, *Love, Sex and War*, Collins, 1985, p. 23.
12 *Psychological Problems of Troops Overseas*, AMD11, September 1943.
13 J. B. Priestley, *Three Men in New Suits*, Heinemann, 1945, pp. 62–3.
14 Bill Sayles, Sheffield.
15 Lord Hailsham, *A Sparrow's Flight*, Collins, 1990, p. 203.
16 Costello, op. cit., pp. 126–7.
17 Joint Committee on Venereal Disease, 29 September 1943 (Public Record Office, ref: MEPO2.7012).
18 *For Your Guidance*, War Office Revised Edition 1947 (Public Record Office, ref: LAB32.17).
19 Costello, op. cit., p. 277.
20 Costello, op. cit., p. 278.
21 Name withheld.

22 Marilyn Harris, Coventry.

23 John Lathbury, Reading.

24 T. F. Main, *Journal of Mental Science*, Vol. XCIII, 1947, pp. 354–63.

25 Ibid.

26 Ibid.

27 WVS Newsletter, 1945.

28 Name withheld.

29 WVS Newsletter, 1945.

30 *British Legion Journal*, October 1945.

31 'When Peace Broke Out', *Sunday Graphic*, September 1945.

32 Margaret Wilson, Murton.

33 *Living Together Again*, Phoebe and Laurence Bendit, MD, Gramol Publications, 1945.

34 *War Cry*, 22 October 1945.

35 *Memoirs of Mrs Enid Innes Ker*, Imperial War Museum.

36 Ibid.

37 Gladys Constantine, Abingdon.

38 Sybil Hurcomb, Watford.

39 Sheral Towler, Bristol.

40 Alma Morrell, Nottingham.

41 Name withheld.

42 WVS Bulletin, 1943.

43 Ibid.

44 Major R.A.C. Radcliffe, Directorate of Army Welfare Services (Public Record Office, ref: LAB32.32).

45 Ibid.

46 Ann Lavery, Sambourne.

47 Avril Middleton, Leamington Spa.

48 Dorothy Bullock, Liverpool.

49 Derek Bradley, Morley.
50 Betty Colven, Sutton.
51 John Ayres, Farnham.
52 Dorothy Morgan, Jersey.
53 Mabel Harrison, Yeadon.

CHAPTER SIX: 'AN IMMEASURABLE EFFECT ON MARRIED
HAPPINESS'

1 Dorothy Skipp, North Laindon.
2 Final report of the Committee on Procedure in Matrimonial
  Causes, February 1947 (HMSO 7024).
3 SSAFA Report of the Council, 1943.
4 Committee on Procedure in Matrimonial Causes, op.cit.
5 Public Record Office, ref: LCO2.4197.
6 Cabinet Meeting, 20 September 1945 (Public Record Office,
  ref: LCO2.4198).
7 House of Lords, 27 March 1947 (Hansard Vol.146, No.52).
8 House of Lords, 27 March 1947 (Ibid.).
9 Jowitt to Dalton, 2 November 1946 (Public Record Office,
  ref: LCO2.3950).
10 Dalton to Jowitt, 6 November 1946 (Public Record Office,
  ref: LCO2.3950).
11 Committee on Procedure in Matrimonial Causes, op.cit.
12 War Cry, 13 October 1945.
13 WVS bulletin, April 1945.
14 News of the World, 21 October 1945.
15 Ibid., 14 October 1945.
16 Ibid., 11 November 1945.
17 Ibid., 21 October 1945.

18 Ibid., 11 November 1945.

19 Ibid.

20 Ibid., 6 July 1945.

21 Ibid.

22 T. F. Main, 'Clinical Problems of Repatriates', *Journal of Mental Science*, Vol.XCIII, 1947, pp.354–63

23 Name withheld.

24 Richard Davenport-Hines, *Sex, Death and Punishment*, Collins, 1990, p.297.

25 John Costello, *Love, Sex and War*, Collins, 1985, p.162.

26 Davenport-Hines, op.cit., p.297.

27 Sir Robert Bruce Lockhart, *Your England*, Putnam, 1955, p.223.

28 Sheila Lewenhak, *Women and the Trade Unions*, Ernest Benn, 1977, p.246.

29 Henry Yoxall, *Woman's Page*, BBC, 22 September 1944.

30 Metropolitan Police, Criminal Investigation Dept., 28 October 1948 (Public Record Office, ref: 02/8430).

31 H. Silcock, *The Increase in Crimes of Theft*, University Press of Liverpool, 1949, p.15–17.

32 Leslie T. Wilkins, Home Office Research Unit. Quoted in Crowther Report on 15 to 18 Education (HMSO, 1959).

33 Wood Green Y Division Report, 27 October 1948 (Public Record Office, ref: MEPO2/8430).

34 Metropolitan Police, Criminal Investigation Dept., op.cit.

35 *British Legion Journal*, February 1946.

36 Peggy Wolledge, Sudbury.

37 Morag Williams, Neston.

38 Martin Pugh, *Women and the Women's Movement in Britain, 1914–59*, Macmillan 1992, p.291.

39 Germaine Greer, *Daddy We Hardly Knew You*, Hamish Hamilton, 1989, pp.1–14.

CHAPTER SEVEN: 'ARE WE GOING BACK ON THE DOLE AFTERWARDS?'

1 *The British Way and Purpose*, British Directorate of Army Education, 1944, p.14.
2 *The Times*, 18 January 1940.
3 Ibid.
4 Army Education, Development from 1939 to 1943 (Public Record Office, ref: WO32.10462).
5 Army Council Secretariat, 3 October 1942 (Public Record Office, ref: WO32.10454).
6 *The British Way and Purpose*, op.cit., pp. 142–5.
7 *The British Way and Purpose*, op.cit., p.14.
8 War Office memo, 12 August 1943 (Public Record Office, ref: WO32/10462).
9 Executive Committee of the Army Council on Army Education, 3 September 1943 (Public Record Office, ref: WO32/10462).
10 Peter Hennessy, *Never Again: Britain 1945–51*, Cape, 1992, p.73.
11 David Butler, *British General Elections Since 1945*, Basil Blackwell, 1989, p.8.
12 Mass Observation, *The Journey Home*, John Murray, 1943, p.17.
13 Committee on Education in the Demobilisation Period, Report to Secretary of State for War, August 1943 (Public Record Office, ref: WO32/10461).

14 Scope of Education During Demobilisation Period, War Office, July 1943 (Public Record Office, ref: WO32/10456).

15 R. F. Adam, War Office, 2 March 1944 (Public Record Office, ref: WO32/9430).

16 Report on the Educational Preferences of a Sample of the Army, March 1944, War Office (Public Record Office, ref: WO32/9430).

17 Peter Reese, *Homecoming Heroes*, Leo Cooper, 1992, p.195.

18 War Office, 1 June 1945 (Public Record Office, ref: WO32/10982).

19 *The Listener*, 22 March 1945.

20 BBC Education Service, Unit Visit Report, 9 November 1945.

21 Kay Lauder, Rugby.

22 Jeannette Howland, Warrington.

23 Sybil Hurcomb, Watford.

24 Marian Morgan, Aberdare.

25 Standing Consultative Committee for Ex-Service Employment, 5 April 1948.

26 *British Legion Journal*, February 1945.

27 Ibid., November 1945.

28 Regular Forces Employment Association, General Secretary to War Office, 31 January 1945.

29 *British Legion Journal*, January 1946.

30 *Enterprise*, a careers magazine from Lantern Publishing, 1946.

31 Arthur Turner, Blackpool.

32 *British Legion Journal*, January 1947.

33 *The Times*, 27 September 1947.

34 *British Legion Journal*, April 1946.

35 Roy Brewer, Bristol.

36 Margaret Wadsworth, Blackpool.

37 Diane Bites, Cowes.

38 Major R.A.C. Radcliffe, Directorate of Army Welfare Services (Public Record Office, ref: LAB32.32).

39 Millie Kitching, Ockbrook.

40 *British Legion Journal*, April 1946.

41 British Legion Annual Report, 1946–7.

42 Margaret Wadsworth, Blackpool.

43 *British Legion Journal*, June 1946.

44 S. F. Hay, Droitwich.

45 William Smith, Boxworth.

46 Standing Committee for the Co-ordination of Activities of Voluntary Organisations Concerned with Employment of Ex-Service Persons, 27 August 1947.

47 Standing Committee Ex-Services Employment, 5 April 1948.

48 Reese, op.cit., p. 201.

49 *British Legion Journal*, October 1945.

50 Ibid.

51 Ministry of Labour, J. Howie Mitchell memo, 25 May 1946 (Public Record Office, ref: LAB18.462).

52 J. Howie Mitchell, Temporary Assistant Secretary to the Department of Training and Interrupted Apprenticeships, 4 January 1947 (Public Record Office, ref: LAB18/462).

CHAPTER EIGHT: 'TOUGH GOING THESE DAYS'

1 SSAFA Report of 62nd Annual Meeting, 7 October 1948.

2 Peter Hennessy, *Never Again: Britain 1945–51*, Cape, 1992, p. 170.

3   Mrs A. Hurley.
4   Edith Brian, Bungay.
5   SSAFA Report, op.cit.
6   Name withheld.
7   Evelyn Jones, Kettering.
8   George Yorke, Blakeney.
9   John Morgan, *Can I Help You?*, BBC Home Service, 8 August 1945.
10 SSAFA Report, op.cit.
11 Ibid.
12 WVS bulletin, September 1945.
13 Margaret Tamblin, Kelsale, quoted in Jean Turner, *Tin Bath Night*, J. Publishing, 1944, p. 54.
14 H. B. Smith, Acle, quoted in Jean Turner, *A Trip Down the Garden Path*, J. Publishing, 1993, p. 75.
15 British Legion Circular No.2, 1945.
16 *British Legion Journal*, December 1946.
17 SSAFA Annual Conference, 9–10 October 1946.
18 *British Legion Journal*, June 1945.
19 SSAFA Annual Conference, op.cit.

CHAPTER NINE: 'YOU'RE IN THE USA MY SON . . .'

1   Julius Isaacs, *British Post-War Migration*, National Institute of Economic Social Research, Cambridge University Press, 1954.
2   *British Legion Journal*, January 1947.
3   *Soldier*, 4 August 1945.
4   Ibid.
5   Ben Wicks, *Welcome Home*, Bloomsbury, 1991, p. 118.

6 Aline Erickson, Redwood, New Zealand.

7 Helen King, Langford, Australia.

8 Germaine Greer, *Daddy We Hardly Knew You*, Hamish Hamilton, 1989, pp. 1–14.

9 Elizabeth Wright, Mount Claremont, Australia.

10 Joan Benson, Geraldine, New Zealand.

11 Ken Booth.

12 Margaret Kaeding, Adelaide, Australia.

13 Elizabeth Scott, Patea, New Zealand.

14 Valerie Hepburn, Canterbury, New Zealand.

15 Robert Appell, London, Ontario, Canada, quoted in Wicks, op. cit., p. 151.

16 Linda Wigley, Ontario, Canada.

17 Joyce Batty, Seacliff Park, South Australia.

18 Dorothy Marshall, Tasmania.

19 Ruth and Peter Lord, Seaview Downs, South Australia.

20 Pat Minton, Koongamia, Western Australia.

21 Roy Smith, Christchurch, New Zealand.

22 Name withheld.

CHAPTER TEN: 'IF IT SNAPS, THERE WILL BE CHAOS . . .'

1 Alan Bullock, *The Life and Times of Ernest Bevin, Vol. 2 1940–1945*, Heinemann, 1967, p. 336.

2 Michael Young and Peter Willmott, *Family and Kinship in East London*, Routledge & Kegan Paul, 1957.

3 T. R. Fyrel, *The Insecure Offenders: Rebellious Youth in the Welfare State*, Chatto & Windus, 1961.

4 Alan Ross, *The Forties*, Weidenfeld & Nicolson, 1950.

Barry Turner is a writer and historian. His latest books are *Beacon for Change* about the 1951 Festival of Britain and *Outpost of Occupation* on the German occupation of the Channel Islands. He has just completed his seventeenth year as editor of *Statesman's Yearbook*. He lives in London and south-west France.

Tony Rennell was a senior editorial executive on the *Sunday Times* and the *Mail on Sunday* before switching to writing 15 years ago. He is the author and co-author of seven books, of which *When Daddy Came Home* was the first. He writes regularly on a variety of subjects for the *Daily Mail*. He lives in Suffolk. He was born in 1947, the son of a father who came home but never spoke about his war. 'When I told him I was writing this book, he was silent. After he died, I was told that he had read it and, most unusually for him, wept. But, to me, typically, he said not a word.'